Supervision

for

Change

and

Innovation

Adolph Unruh
Saint Louis University

Harold E. Turner
University of Missouri — St. Louis

HOUGHTON MIFFLIN COMPANY • BOSTON

New York   Atlanta   Geneva, Illinois
Dallas   Palo Alto

Editor's Introduction

•

Adolph Unruh and Harold E. Turner are theoreticians and practitioners of the human relations approach to supervision, the most widely accepted viewpoint on supervision in American schools today. Their book, *Supervision for Change and Innovation,* stresses practical applications of current knowledge concerning supervision and realistically emphasizes the daily problems which supervisors encounter in their profession. The insights and experiences of the authors should be particularly helpful to educators who are contemplating entering the field of supervision and to supervisors who wish to examine their own practices and to expand their competencies in their present roles.

The supervisor, whether new or experienced, needs to understand what supervision means in today's society (Chapter One). To be a competent practitioner, he must communicate effectively (Chapter Two), build teacher morale (Chapter Three), and utilize workable human relations approaches (Chapter Four). His work includes developing inservice education programs (Chapter Five), helping to establish a favorable environment for learning (Chapter Six), and changing teacher behavior in the interest of better education (Chapter Seven). The supervisor faces the reality of change in school and society (Chapter Eight); he masters the use of group techniques (Chapter Nine) and plays a major role in controlling and directing curriculum change (Chapter Ten). In his role, he faces difficulties in evaluating both school programs and the work of teachers (Chapter Eleven). As an emerging supervisor in a changing field, he must use his knowledge to come to grips with current problems (Chapter Twelve).

The authors of *Supervision for Change and Innovation* include in their book both thoughtful general discussions of the work of supervisors and abundant demonstrations of the theories they present. They constantly illustrate, not only through the case of Supervisor Garry Bixman, with which they open and close their book, but also through a steady stream of vignettes on practical problems faced by supervisors they have known through their own wide experiences.

Adolph Unruh has been a public school teacher, a high school principal, a school superintendent, a college teacher, and a university administrator. Harold E. Turner has been a supervisor in industry, a public school teacher, a director of elementary education, a principal of a junior-senior high school, an assistant superintendent, and a university teacher. Theirs is no ivory tower approach to supervision. They provide a wide array of suggestions to help the neophyte and the present practitioner to behave effectively in their roles. In the process, they review important ideas underlying the educative process and tell what they think these ideas mean for the better practice of supervision.

William Van Til

Preface

•

Wherever teachers and supervisors gather, the conversation soon
turns to innovations in curriculum and teaching. Such terms as
concepts, processes, curriculum design, and *structure of knowledge*
crop up. There is talk of *heuristic methods, student carrels, teacher
aides,* and *single-concept films.* But not all teachers know of these
new methods and curricula; whether they are recently graduated or
veterans, many need assistance. One of the major concerns of modern supervision is the development of inservice programs to prepare teachers for their changing roles.

Supervision also must change. Supervisors, including special
teachers, department chairmen, principals, central office administrators, and curriculum consultants, must keep themselves current in
relation to curriculum and instruction if they hope to be of any help
to teachers. Considerable momentum has been achieved in curriculum development and in introducing newer teaching methods.
It is largely up to the supervisor to keep the momentum going.

This book is meant for the supervisor or professional educator
who is concerned with innovation and change in his schools. Obviously it will help the graduate student who aspires to be a supervisor and the professional in the field. Here they will find descriptions of concepts, processes, and techniques useful in supervision,
management of people, curriculum work, inservice education, and
individualizing professional assistance. Here may also be found
ways to design, plan, and put in operation programs for supervision
and for faculty development to keep pace with the times. To illustrate points in the discussion and to provide glimpses of actual practices, numerous brief vignettes have been supplied.

The definitions and points of view expressed in these pages can
be utilized in the large city system, the affluent suburban school,
and the smaller, less wealthy school system. Of major concern are
the processes, functions, and purposes of supervision rather than
the position itself, which is not the same in all schools or at all times.
Supervision deals with people, wherever they are, and with ideas,
wherever they are found or may be developed.

Adolph Unruh
Harold E. Turner

Contents

•

Supervision for Change and Innovation

one

•

The Meaning of
Modern Supervision

Supervisor Garry Bixman

Superintendent Robert J. Crosley relaxed in his inner office, sharing a welcome pot of coffee with Mr. Frank Blessing, president of the board of education of the R-4 school district. They had just completed a lengthy and exhausting session of the board, attempting to deal with the multiplicity of never ending problems found in suburban school districts these days. Now, although the hour was late, neither seemed inclined to hurry home. Both men were in a quiet, reflective mood.

"You know, Bob, our new supervisor, Garry Bixman, is all you said he was and more. He certainly made a telling case for his new inservice program tonight. It seems incredible that he could have accomplished so much in such a short time. Let's see, he's been with the district less than a year, hasn't he?"

"That's right, Frank. He started the first of July. What he's been able to do for instruction in our secondary schools makes me want to kick myself for not having moved on this position long ago. I knew we needed a secondary supervisor but I really didn't realize how badly."

The two men thought back on the series of events leading up to tonight's presentation by Supervisor Bixman.

"I recall that you came to the board with a case for a new staff position sometime last winter," said Mr. Blessing. "Some of the board members were considerably impressed with your pitch for an individual who would be concerned especially with the problems of instruction. We recognized that, as the district had been growing

1

so rapidly, neither you nor your assistant superintendent had time to devote to instructional problems. It was all you could do to get enough classrooms and keep teachers in each of them."

"We had been aware of this need for several months," replied the superintendent, "but the teachers really brought it to a head. Their Committee on Professional Problems reminded me that I was expecting a great deal from the teachers in addition to their basic classroom assignment. Yet I wasn't providing them the necessary time or assistance. The department chairmen were willing to help but they didn't have the time nor, too often I'm afraid, the training. Their one period of released time was hardly sufficient to do the departmental chores of ordering supplies and cataloguing materials.

"Our three principals attempted to work together but, with the two junior highs growing so rapidly and the new senior high building under construction, they had little time to devote to instructional problems. In their own way, the administrators also applied some pressure for relief. So altogether, both groups hit me from different directions at the same time I was formulating the secondary supervisory position. Everything seemed to fall into place. I felt I needed someone who could be an innovator, to help us modernize our instructional program, and who could work with our teachers to make a generally good group even better. The administrators recognized their limitations in training, time, and interest. The teachers themselves, very professionally I thought, expressed a desire to do more for their students and to provide the type of quality program of which we could all be proud."

"Tell me, Bob," said the board president, "why did you go to such lengths to decide what the new supervisor should do? I'm quite confident you already knew what most supervisors are supposed to do. I know you involved a lot of people in determining what Bixman's job specifications should be. At the time, I honestly thought you were overdoing it, especially when you solicited input from the board members and PTA Executive Council. It appeared that you would end up with so many different suggestions that no one individual could possibly fill the bill. We certainly wouldn't approach the problem that way in my business."

"Frank, I could have outlined quickly what I wanted this person to do and could have had Personnel looking within twenty-four hours, but I didn't dare. This position is too important to the future of the district for its inception to be handled in so cavalier a manner.

I knew that unless all interested groups had been given an opportunity to think about such a position and what it might mean to their own special interest areas, and furthermore to suggest specific job assignments *before we announced the job specifications,* the person eventually occupying that spot would have many unnecessary problems. In other words, not only must the supervisor have a clear perception of the job, with its many ramifications, but those with whom he comes in direct contact must also have a compatible perception if he is to be successful in his endeavors. Even then, he is bound to have lots of problems, frustrations, and hangups as he deals with a fluid, tenuous, sometimes highly volatile operation. It was my intent to pave the way and make the new man more acceptable to those with whom he would work. I believe you can see already some fruits of this in the way Garry has been able to move this winter. He certainly is still in the 'honeymoon' period, but also he is making the most of his opportunity to get an acceptable, positive momentum developed that will touch many people in the secondary schools."

"I believe I can see what you were doing. Let everyone have the chance 'to get into the act.' Not only can you build a stronger overall plan this way, but you can get the interest and attention of many different individuals who are able to relate better with the activities of the supervisor as he develops the job. Bob, I like the idea and, more importantly, I like the results you're getting. You know, we were very fortunate to have been able to attract Garry Bixman. He could have picked any number of jobs, some of which would have paid more than we offered."

"That's true, Frank. I was banking on this very thing happening, although at that time, of course, I had not met our man Garry. We advertised outside the district. There were several interested individuals from the high school staff, but in each instance they proved not to fit our requirements or decided they would not or could not handle the job. We screened many from around the country before narrowing the candidate list to the three we actually invited here for a personal interview. When we talked to Garry and listened to his ideas, we all knew our search was over.

"We had agreed to ask each candidate to present his long-range and short-term plans in order to find the depth of thinking and level of expertise he might possess. We also wanted to see how each would react under tension and pressure, since we know the supervisor will often find himself in such a situation. I saved the tape Garry made during his interview and have replayed it once or twice, mostly for my own satisfaction as I have observed his plans developing during the year."

Superintendent Crosley paused briefly to refill his cup, lit his pipe, and continued his account of Garry Bixman's interview.

"As I remember Garry's approach to the problem we presented him, he gave every assurance of a man knowing what he was doing and where he was going. He fairly radiated self-confidence and enthusiasm. He probably said less about educational leadership but demonstrated a more dynamic type of leadership through his approach to the interview itself than many others might have done.

"Garry started by explaining his firm belief in a strong, well-coordinated inservice program. He built the case step by step — the need to help new teachers become well adjusted in their classes, the need to help experienced teachers try more things and continue to improve their techniques, and the need to work in a somewhat different manner with the old-timers in the schools. He explained that he could make good use of the talent and expertise available within the teaching staff as he developed the overall inservice program. It certainly made sense at the time. More importantly, our teachers have become enthusiastic over this new emphasis and have supported his initial efforts quite eagerly. I believe that they, too, recognize the logic and consistency of his inservice plan.

"Garry quickly interested me when he started discussing curriculum development and when he emphasized its importance to the supervisor. Just as the inservice program represents the warp of instruction, so to speak, the curriculum represents the woof. He indicated interest in a steady, well planned curriculum development program involving as large a portion of the entire staff as possible. He even gave an example or two of how he might develop a curriculum innovation, which I can tell you really sold me on his ability and sound judgment. He repeatedly pointed out how his goals and objectives must be tempered and meshed with those of the community and the professional staff and said he felt sure he could provide leadership toward some stated goal, but within a context of overall consensus. He gave the impression of a 'solid citizen.'

"There were other things he included, all important in their own way. He felt a strong commitment to the establishment of clear, two-way communications and indicated he would strive to maintain open channels. His plans called for setting up specific, clearly identified activities almost immediately. I knew this would be construed by the teachers as a move in the right direction; it represented a start in developing and improving morale throughout the secondary schools. He went into detail concerning his philosophy of strong, positive human relations and the importance to morale. He also outlined some other plans, but I believe in some manner they could be related to the broad items I've already mentioned.

"To me, his summary was a classic. He explained the significance of role perception to effective supervision. Garry must have a clear picture of what he is attempting, of his specific job description, and of what tasks, no matter how enjoyable or interesting, are beyond his province. The rest of us — you on the board, the administrators, and the teachers — must have a compatible perception of Garry's assignment so that we can all work together and not in opposition to one another. I recognize, as does Garry, that too many superintendents assign someone to be a supervisor with no understanding of the role and consequently have the person expending his resources and energy in unrelated activities. The obvious result is ineffective supervision, and everyone eventually reaches that conclusion and wonders what was wrong with the poor fellow hired as the supervisor. In many instances nothing was wrong with him; the fault was in the original assignment or lack of job description.

"Garry went on to explain supervision in terms of processes. I believe he stated that a simple definition of supervision was impossible because of its tremendous complexity. Anyway, he indicated that the concept of supervision became easier for him to comprehend if he thought of it as three processes: social, psychological, and educational. The supervisor, he said, almost always operates in a social context; he works with, for, and through a wide variety of people as he attempts to achieve his overall goals. He must be conscious of the psychological implications as he deals with these individuals, with their emotions, sensitivities, ambitions, and fears, especially as he follows the method of problem solving. Then he is concerned with the educational process; he works not only with the instructional program of the district, which represents his primary target, but also with the educational program of the professional staff. There will always be diverse needs: to provide educational experiences for both administrators and teachers, to remedy any lacks, to strengthen and reinforce existing techniques, and to question or revise poor or out-of-date procedures, for example.

"Finally, Garry explained how he would go about the job of supervision through what he termed *functions.* By this he meant educational leadership, democratically oriented, through which he expected to be able to move his program. He intended to develop a clear approach to teacher role definition as well as supervisory role definition to establish improved cooperation. He planned to aid, support, and stimulate teachers so that they might become better teachers, at whatever stage of development they might be. He closed with a strong statement to the effect that all he had described or implied was for one purpose — to help each student learn to the extent that he could or would. For those of us who conducted the interview it was truly an educational experience."

"Well, Bob, I've certainly enjoyed this opportunity to hear the entire story. I've known parts and pieces of how we came to have Garry Bixman on our staff, but this is the first time I've been able to get it all straight. I know the board is pleased with him, and we certainly hope we'll be able to keep him in the district for a long time. Now I think we'd both better head for home. It's been a long day, and tomorrow will be another."

The two men picked up their coats and papers and quietly left the office for their homes and a short night's rest.

The preceding mythical episode might take place in many school districts next year. If it did, the prospects for a successful experience for the new supervisor would be good. More probably, however, the supervisor will succeed to the position from a quite different assignment within his district. He will perhaps have had little actual training for the position and he may have received only vague, uncertain directions from his superior. Under such circumstances his potential effectiveness will have been eroded, thereby causing many unnecessary pitfalls for the neophyte.

Who Is the Supervisor?

What is supervision? Who is the supervisor? What does he do? The profession has long been plagued by questions such as these. As elsewhere in our society, changes are rapidly occurring in supervision. The role the supervisor will be expected to play tomorrow promises to be quite different from the one he occupied yesterday. In modern school systems various persons provide some supervisory services.[1] Supervision and its attending responsibilities are not organized in the same way and do not have the same impact and importance in all school systems. Too often the kinds of services offered depend upon the individual — his personality, his training, his understanding of the tasks to be performed.

The supervisor has usually been a general supervisor, sometimes called curriculum director or curriculum supervisor, with a general knowledge of subject matter areas and a concern for all subjects and usually at all levels. He has placed more emphasis upon broad problems of instruction than upon the technicalities of a specific discipline. He has been the individual in the school system most concerned with instruction in its entirety, including especially inter-relationships of content from the various disciplines.

The practice of employing subject matter supervisors is fairly common. The mathematics or science supervisor or the English program specialist is recognized as an expert in his field. In addition, he understands the problems involved in working with adults and in dealing with students in the teaching-learning process. Normally he functions in a staff capacity and concentrates primarily on the instructional aspects of his specialty.

The two types of supervisors differ mainly in degree of expertise — a single discipline on the part of the subject supervisor as contrasted with a general knowledge in all or most disciplines on the part of the general supervisor. They also differ in that the generalist exercises limited line authority.

A limited version of the subject supervisor is the coordinator. Recognized first and foremost as a master teacher, he is readily accepted by all as a helper of teachers for he represents no threat to the person with an instructional problem. He usually works in a single building or a few buildings, on call from the administrators or the teachers themselves. He serves as a troubleshooter, showing teachers how to handle teaching problems. The coordinator seldom if ever is expected to provide educational leadership for program development. His assignment may be for a limited period of time,

---

[1] Robert C. McKean and H. H. Mills, *The Supervisor* (New York: Center for Applied Research in Education, 1964), pp. 14–24.

usually one to three years, after which he is to return to his original classroom.

One of the innovations in supervision has been the development of the position, similar to that of the coordinator, of helping teacher, facilitating teacher, or resource teacher. It carries no authority and does not create a threatening situation to teachers being helped. Such a person brings no pressure on the teacher except (1) by the use of reason, (2) from his greater depth of knowledge, and (3) from the breadth of his practical intelligence. The position requires a high level of competence and leadership skills. In this instance as in others, how it is filled depends on perceptions and expectations.

The Denver public schools have provided professional help for their elementary teachers through what is called the Elementary Coordinator Program.[2] The work of the coordinator is centered on helping teachers, but the role is more complicated than the term implies. For example, the coordinator provides a distribution service, making available instructional aids, guides, outlines, materials, etc.; he may act as a consultant, providing technical and professional help wherever and whenever needed; he is also a teacher of teachers.

In many school systems, various part- and full-time administrators perform the role of supervisor. Small districts often have so abbreviated an administrative staff that the superintendent is forced to undertake the supervisory function.[3] Inasmuch as he is preoccupied with serving as the chief school officer, the superintendent usually finds little time to act as instructional supervisor. Frequently he is poorly prepared and actually incompetent to supervise instruction.

Normally the full-time supervisor operates from the central office and reports directly to the superintendent. In many such instances the line authority, either real or implied, tends to blunt the total effectiveness of the position. To the extent that teachers feel threatened in their relationship with the supervisor, good supervision becomes difficult to achieve.

Probably a better situation exists when the supervisor reports to

[2] Elementary Coordinator Program, *Professional Help for the Classroom Teacher* (monograph) (Denver, Colo.: Denver Public Schools, 1961).
[3] Ross L. Neagley and N. Dean Evans, *Handbook for Effective Supervision of Instruction* (Englewood Cliffs, N.J.: Prentice-Hall, 1964), pp. 10–11.

someone other than the superintendent — the director of instruction, or the deputy or assistant superintendent for instruction. In
this case the supervisor may be identified more readily as staff, and
a rapport with classroom teachers is more easily established.

Line and Staff Relationship

Superintendent

Assistant Superintendent for Instruction

Supervisors

Building Principals

Department Chairmen

Teachers

_ _ _ _ _ staff relationship

——— line authority

The principal is traditionally recognized as the instructional
leader of his building. As such, he is expected to spend considerable
time away from his desk and out in the classrooms assisting teachers
with instructional problems. A great number of administrators find
this responsibility difficult to meet. True, more administrators today
are better educated in some subject area than in the past and better
prepared to operate as instructional supervisors, in addition to their
usual administrative role. However, the magnitude of their job prevents many principals from giving adequate attention to instruction.
Rapid changes taking place within the various disciplines require
increasingly large amounts of time to keep abreast of each discipline; it is unreasonable to expect a principal to remain current in
all of these areas and in administration too. Mounting problems involved with general school management take more and more of the
principal's time. As a result, building administrators are being
forced to turn to others for assistance, namely, to instructional
supervisors equipped with the necessary expertise for the instructional program.

    Larger high schools tend to delegate to an assistant principal the
responsibility for dealing with curricular problems and helping
teachers improve their performance. He is often at a disadvantage,

however, in his supervisory relationships with teachers because he functions in a line position and is capable of jeopardizing the professional future of the teacher.

When supervisors are not available, principals often depend upon departmental leaders to provide stimulation and direction for the faculty. In most senior high schools having several teachers in the same subject area, one is usually designated as department chairman. Often some salary differential is tied to the title and a small amount of released time is allowed. In addition to caring for routine departmental business and supplying leadership for the instructional program, the chairman is expected to undertake some classroom supervision. Unfortunately, most department chairmen are not adequately prepared to assume supervisory leadership and are not given the time necessary to accomplish more than a rudimentary program. Junior high schools seldom can boast the luxury of a department chairman. At best, a head teacher functions within the department with little or no released time at his disposal.

Hipps contends that the weakest link in the line and staff organization is the department head.[4] There is little agreement within the profession on the administrative and supervisory duties of the chairman. These responsibilities should be carefully described and the expectations clearly stated. Any accountability attached to the supervisory function must be matched with appropriate preparation, competence, and administrative support. In many schools the functions of chairmen are mainly administrative and clerical.

There are both advantages and disadvantages to a department chairman's functioning as a supervisor.[5]

Advantages	*Disadvantages*
1. Better internal communications	1. Poor preparation for position
2. More inspired teaching	2. Poor selection (may be selected because of seniority)
3. Higher morale	3. Possible nonacceptance by faculty
4. More effective planning and coordination	4. Intradepartmental competition

---

[4] Melvin Hipps, "Supervision: A Basic Responsibility of the Department Head," *Clearing House*, 40:487–491 (Apr., 1965).
[5] Claude Stephenson, "Departmental Organization for Better Instruction," *Bulletin of the National Association of Secondary School Principals*, 45:9–14 (Dec., 1961). Paul B. High, "The Supervisory Role of the Department Head," *Clearing House*, 40:213–215 (Dec., 1965).

Advantages	*Disadvantages*
5. More teacher cooperation	5. No consideration in terms of salary or time to do the work
6. Accessibility of leader	6. Lack of knowledge of how to supervise
7. Chairman a teacher	
8. Chairman usually well prepared	7. Inability to keep up with trends in the discipline
9. Chairman acting as specialist (can keep content in line with modern trends)	8. Position not clearly defined
	9. Inadequate support from administration
10. Status less threatening to teachers who respond to chairman's leadership	10. Need for much inservice training to be effective as a leader
	11. Functions too narrowly perceived

Sometimes the team leader of a team teaching program spends part of his time in the role of a subject matter supervisor, and his influence in such a situation can be very great. While the number of team programs throughout the country is growing, they are still used in relatively few secondary schools.

Thus, individuals who perform supervisory functions have widely divergent interests and professional preparation. Some dilute their effectiveness by adding to their supervisory responsibilities still other assignments. Some bring to their task special biases toward supervision. Throughout this book the term *supervisor*, unless otherwise stated, refers to the full-time secondary supervisor, either general or special subject area, who is concerned with exercising educational leadership and with keeping the total instructional picture in proper focus.

The Supervisory Role

The role of supervision must be clarified within both education and society. Such a conceptualization must provide the framework in which supervision is integrated into the total program of instruction, specialized services, and administration. It must take cognizance of the new forces and agents for planning, organizing, and coordinating programs and services to achieve accepted educational objectives. This understanding should lead to both better theories and improved practice in supervision.

A New Chairman

Miss Jones has been promoted to the chairmanship of the Business Education Department. The principal spent considerable time with her when he offered her the position. He wanted to make sure that she thoroughly understood what was expected of the chairman as well as what was not desired. He went through the various duties — preparation of department budget, responsibility for supplies, equipment maintenance, etc. — and in particular the relationship of the chairman to other members of the department. The principal insisted that Miss Jones was to provide instructional leadership to the department. He also explained at length how important it was for Miss Jones to work at establishing a good, professional rapport with members of her department and not try to push them around.

Before the term started, Miss Jones knew exactly what the limits of her responsibilities were and what was expected of her and she was hard at work on the new assignment, comfortable in the knowledge that she had specific directions to follow.

Is it better to provide a chairman with specific guidelines as this principal did, or to allow considerable flexibility?

Many positions within the school system carry some responsibility for instructional supervision, and the individuals occupying these positions view their assignments differently. Lack of clearly defined procedures has led to so much overlapping of responsibility in some instances and unnecessary confusion in others that the effectiveness of instructional supervision has been impaired. Obviously, identification and definition of role is called for.

A Definition of Role

Heyns stated that social behaviorists found it useful to analyze the complex organization of society through the positions occupied by the people within it.[6] The elements of the positions, or roles, are the behaviors, attitudes, and expectations attached to them. This is the case also for the supervisory role.[7] It too is composed of all the

---

[6] Roger W. Heyns, *The Psychology of Personal Adjustment* (New York: Dryden Press, 1958), p. 273.

[7] Association for Supervision and Curriculum Development, "Theme B. Coping with Role Realities," *The Supervisor: New Demands; New Dimensions* (Washington: The Association, 1969), pp. 19–70.

behavior patterns related to it or associated with it. Attitudes, values, and expectations are important ingredients.[8]

Rapid changes in education and in society as a whole have forced major shifts in the supervisory role, primarily the emergence of the supervisor as a staff rather than a line officer. His basic and most compelling interest is in the instructional program. His goal is to provide the most meaningful education for every student. To this end, his time and energy are devoted to the solving of curriculum problems, to the development of new programs, and to the modification or strengthening of old ones. He is less interested in enforcing teacher compliance with the district curriculum guides; he is more concerned with assisting teachers to become more effective and to maintain a high level of expertise as innovative programs are instituted.

The supervisory role promises to increase in complexity and importance. Hence the growing need for competent, well-trained supervisors.[9] As educational technology develops and is augmented by rapid advances in the electronics and communications fields, the supervisor must revamp his operation to keep pace. As the shifting power struggle within the educational profession continues, new groups, forces, and factors come increasingly into play, modifying and revising the emphasis and even the basic tasks of the supervisor. Those supervisors who can adapt will survive and become even more influential and important to teachers; those who cannot accept the new look in staff relationships will quickly fade from the scene.

Supervisors' Perceptions of Themselves

The expectations held by others (teachers, principals, superintendents, and other professional personnel) are crucial forces shaping the behavior of the supervisor. The latter's own understanding and expectation of himself and his role are also powerful conditioning factors. If the supervisor sees himself as impotent because he is a staff rather than line officer, and if he believes that staff officers have no authority, he may be extremely ineffective.

---

[8] Ben M. Harris and Wailand Bessent, *In-Service Education: A Guide to Better Practice* (Englewood Cliffs, N.J.: Prentice-Hall, 1969), pp. 261–262.
[9] Rowannetta S. Allen, "Role and Function of Supervisors and Curriculum Workers," *Educational Leadership,* 23:330–333 (Jan., 1966). Gordon N. Mackenzie, "Role of the Supervisor," *Educational Leadership,* 19:86–90 (Nov., 1961).

Some supervisors perceive themselves to be successful when they can count the number of hours daily on the job, the number of people they have seen, the number of bulletins they have written, the amount of materials they have ordered, or the number of books in the professional library. Other supervisors think of success in terms of improvement of units of subject matter for teaching purposes, higher achievement test scores of the students, increased number of higher degrees earned by the staff, or the number of experiments going on throughout the system. Basically they tend to evaluate their work quantitatively.

The traditional perception of supervision and the need for changing it are described by Harvey and by McMaster. Harvey emphasized that if the supervisor is successful in breaking down his staff's perception of him as "boss," his plans for producing change may then become effective. Unless teachers realize that the supervisor is working for them and with them to improve instruction, they may resist his suggestions and evade his planned activities.[10] McMaster listed six factors as basic to effective supervision: the supervisor himself, the team approach, support by the administration, sensitivity and patience, seeing worth in others, and recognizing the self-other relationship.[11]

The Supervisor's Role

In the fall of 1968, two new supervisors, Herbert Powell and Warren Klein, came to the school district of University Heights. They disagreed as to the role they should play. Powell perceived of himself as the leader who made decisions in most cases, because someone had to, and approved or disapproved classroom innovative practices. His goal was to run a tight ship and to avoid dissension. But he found himself under constant tension because teachers were prone to act without clearing with him first.

Klein's pattern of behavior included consulting with teachers, offering his professional advice, coordinating numerous related activities, and attempting to stimulate and certainly support creativity. He felt a sense of satisfaction because he saw teachers assuming more initiative, requesting time to discuss ideas, and experimenting

---

[10] Virginia Harvey, "The Change That Counts," *Educational Leadership,* 21:292–296 (Feb., 1964).
[11] Alice McMaster, "Supervision: Loneliness and Rewards," *Educational Leadership,* 23:626–629 (May, 1966).

with methods. Powell chided Klein about his "permissiveness," sugesting there would be little progress.

The question is: Could both men be right in their own situations?

The Perception of Supervisors by Others

The supervisor must be aware of the fact that the teachers' perception of him and his role in the school district determines how they will receive his attention and suggestions. This perception is the result of the teachers' direct and indirect experiences, the gossip they have heard about some supervisors, what they have read about supervisors, even imaginary actions or intentions of supervisors. If teachers see the supervisor as being supportive and sympathetic, they will feel kindly disposed to his suggestions. If they see him in an autocratic role, or as a representative of the administration in the central office, they may react unfavorably to anything he offers.

If there is a wide divergence between how the supervisor perceives his role and how the teachers perceive it, problems will immediately arise. Lack of understanding and communication in such a situation will severely limit supervisory effectiveness or will cause the entire operation to abort, doing much damage to staff morale and to overall instructional efforts. If the administrators have a still different view of the supervisory role, complete chaos may develop. Staff members' perceptions of their own or others' roles are significant for the success of any organization.[12] Therefore, if supervisors are skillful and perceptive leaders, they will be sensitive to the perceptions and expectations of the faculty, individually and in groups. And if they consider their roles desirable and appropriate in the social context, they will be less subject to personal and professional frustrations and problems which adversely affect their performance.

In an attempt to identify the problems of perception, one of the writers of this book asked one hundred teachers and principals to describe the role of a supervisor as they had observed it. The result was a list of ninety-two different roles although, of course, many were similar. The frequency with which they were mentioned

---

[12] Association for Supervision and Curriculum Development, *Leadership for Improving Instruction,* 1960 Yearbook (Washington: The Association, 1960), p. 85.

ranged from one to one hundred. The twelve most frequently mentioned roles were as follows:

Order	Role	Order	Role
1.	Planner	7.	Guider
2.	Student of pupils	8.	Critic
3.	Participator	9.	Creator
4.	Goal setter	10.	Selector
5.	Evaluator	11.	Supplementor
6.	Cooperator	12.	Committeeman

Ten unusual roles ascribed to the supervisor are also revealing of expectations of teachers. These roles were seldom listed:

1. Pressure evener		6. Forecaster
2. Personality builder		7. Motivator
3. Specialist in his own field		8. Workshopper
4. Ego builder		9. Timer
5. Blocker		10. Technician

These twenty-two roles taken from both ends of the frequency order illustrate the wide range of perceptions of teachers. If they are sharply different from the supervisor's self-perception, the discrepancies must be eliminated if possible. A wide gap between the two will seriously hinder the effectiveness of supervision.

Who Should Get the Credit?

Supervisor Giesecke was a new addition to the staff of the R-1 school district. He had been hired with much fanfare and extensive news coverage as the curriculum innovator who was going to help the R-1 staff completely revamp the secondary curriculum. Because Mr. Giesecke had the personality to "make news," he was often sought by the local press and other news media. His name appeared as the originator of the new mathematics program, of the use of modular scheduling in the high school, and of team teaching in all the secondary schools. The general public began to relate the name Giesecke to educational innovation and developed a great respect for him and his abilities.

Not generally known in the community, however, was the fact that each of the three innovations had been in the planning stage for at least a year prior to the arrival of Supervisor Giesecke. The teachers in the R-1 secondary schools were aware of it, especially those who had fought for these changes at the very beginning and who had expended much personal time and effort to put them into effect. Many teachers were greatly disturbed because they felt the new supervisor was accepting public credit for things which he had not done and was deliberately ignoring those who had actually been responsible for the innovations.

Do you think Mr. Giesecke will receive much cooperation from these teachers in the future?

The Nature of Supervision

We have identified those who perform supervisory tasks and have examined the supervisory role. Supervision can be described additionally in terms of process, of function, and of educational leadership.

Supervision as Process

Social, psychological, and educational processes are involved in supervision.

The Social Process. Supervision as a social process is a means of stimulating, nurturing, and appraising the professional growth of teachers. It takes place in a social context in which people are working and in which some are giving leadership. Therefore, people become the central element. Their relationships with each other, their roles in society, and their positions within the bureaucracy all have a bearing on what supervision is and does.

At one time supervision represented what was done *to* teachers. It was largely a controlling function. Teachers were required to follow outlines, courses of study, or textbooks, and often specific methods were prescribed. Most educators now consider this approach autocratic, dogmatic, and unrealistic. The modern approach to solving educational problems is more democratic, more human relations oriented, more innovative. Supervision depends upon cooperation and teamwork. It recognizes that only individuals themselves can change their behavior. Hence, methods for stimulating behavioral changes, such as the involvement of teachers in the social process, become more critical.

An important element in the social process is interaction. It provides not only the basis for relationships among people but also a method for discovering and developing ideas. In addition, it is the foundation for cooperation and for the continued professional growth of teachers and other school personnel, which is essential in curriculum development. When two or more departments are engaged in an interdisciplinary approach to learning, the cooperation of teachers and supervisors in planning the curriculum, developing the materials and methods, and evaluating the product becomes crucial.

The supervisor should be cognizant of the different forms of social adjustment which may result from interaction. He cannot always anticipate the outcome. Problems may arise, for example, in the area of accommodation. In the case of Mr. Jantz, a history teacher, and Miss Raheem, an English teacher, jointly developing a unit in American history and literature, Mr. Jantz is more aggressive in presenting his point of view, and the forthcoming unit of correlated learning experiences is heavily loaded with history. The resultant teaching may reflect this bias. Here Miss Raheem has accommodated herself to the style and personality of her partner. If Miss Raheem had been equally aggressive, Mr. Jantz might have found it necessary to give ground on some points in order to obtain others. Thus interaction can result in compromise. If these confrontations take place in the presence of the supervisor, each teacher may appeal to him for support on certain points. The supervisor is then required to use considerable tact and judgment. When an impasse is reached, there is always the temptation to render an arbitrary decision. A more profitable approach might be to redirect the discussion, raising additional questions regarding the relative merits of each position and striving for a middle ground acceptable to both teachers, rather than to interject a third bias into the proceedings.

Another element in the social process is participation. The individual who is not permitted to participate in his culture, or is denied access to institutions and sources of information and hence social and intellectual intercourse, will be unable to function as a citizen in a democracy should. Similarly, a teacher who has no opportunity to take part in the important discussions and decision making related to his work can be expected to develop a poor professional attitude.

Still another element is communication, the *modus operandi* through which most education takes place. It is the process through which a community of ideas is generated, common needs and aspirations are recognized, and human behavior is shaped and controlled. Much attention should be given to communication in all aspects of supervisory behavior, especially in a supervisor-teacher conference.

If either party fails to communicate the problem clearly and accurately, its possible solutions, or the actions which either or both are to take, the conference may well prove to be fruitless.

Social process forms the foundation for good human relations. It takes into consideration teachers' status feelings, group membership, likes and dislikes, and needs and attitudes, and it fosters interaction skills.

The Psychological Process. There is much in supervision that comes under the category of psychological process — problem solving, the feelings and emotions of teachers, and the various kinds of psychological mechanisms teachers and school personnel employ in their relations with others, for instance.

Problem solving begins with the identification of a problem, then moves to the formulation of one or more hypotheses as guidelines for action, to the collection of data, to the evaluation of these data, and eventually to the interpretation of findings. Such a procedure may be applied to learning problems and professional problems as well as personal relations.

One can develop a more sophisticated approach to problem solving through use of either action or theoretical research. Increasingly school systems are utilizing action research. This type of problem solving has become more common with the burgeoning of federal projects, university research and development centers, regional educational laboratories, and with the growing sophistication of school personnel themselves.

Unless the supervisor can clearly demonstrate that there have been changes in teacher and student behavior, he will soon be in difficulty. The changing of behavior is dependent upon the learning process, another aspect of psychology. If a teacher is to discard the use of lecturing and the direct assignment method in favor of the skillful use of inquiry, a multimedia approach, independent study, and Individualized Prescribed Instruction (IPI), he must not only learn these techniques but see how they relate to the learning process. The college graduate, having been a student for so many years, must learn how to devise stimulating learning situations for students. The supervisor attempts to provide a similar service for teachers. Successful supervisors know how to assist teachers to eliminate undesirable behavior patterns and to learn more appropriate teaching techniques based on a sound learning process. Everything possible should be done by the supervisor to reward and reinforce these changed learnings as they gradually emerge. Some types of rewards are listed in Chapter Twelve.

The Educational Process. Every good supervisory program provides for the continuing education of teachers, utilizing workshops, institutes, consultants, independent studies, conventions, and school visits. Teacher education begins in colleges and universities, but most professionals would agree that four years of education, or even five, do not necessarily guarantee a professional performance in the classroom or in the community.

School systems have instituted their own continuing inservice education. Small districts have two handicaps: limited educational leadership and inadequate funds. However, as reorganization of school districts moves ahead, more wealth becomes available and dynamic programs should emerge. The day is not far distant when inservice education will become a universal requirement. As the caliber of preservice education improves, so will the quality of the district inservice program. In a few instances school systems and divisions of teacher education are "adopting" each other and cooperatively planning preservice and inservice programs as well as exchanging faculty.

More needs to be known about how to improve teaching methods, how to devise challenging learning situations, and how to use multi-media and learning resource centers. Teaching is a learning process for the professional person when he searches for better instructional methods and materials. Supervisors and teachers must constantly seek ways to make the curriculum more relevant for students and at the same time provide greater depth and understanding. They must find better testing techniques and interpretations of test data. They must be concerned with student motivation, student abilities, aptitudes, and achievement.

Supervision as Functions

Many writers have tried to define supervision in terms of functions. Wiles noted that supervision is a service to teachers to help them do a better job.[13] Over the past decade it has been generally agreed that supervision should provide a technical service related to learning and pupil growth. Its purpose is to improve the learning

---

[13] Kimball Wiles, *Supervision for Better Schools,* 3rd ed. (New York: Prentice-Hall, 1967), p. 5.

situation, and this is accomplished indirectly by working with the teacher.

Some writers think of supervision as helping teachers grow professionally while on the job. For others it means developing materials for instruction and learning, improving the curriculum, and initiating inservice education. Inservice education is undergoing change also as the staff becomes diversified and teacher aides and other paraprofessionals come into the picture. In some schools inservice programs are developed for all faculty and staff, instructional and noninstructional. Harris and Bessent draw a distinction between supervision and inservice education, the latter being a more limited concept.[14] For Curtin[15] and Gwynn[16] the concept of supervision includes giving teachers any kind of assistance needed, coordinating system-wide instructional services, and upgrading evaluation. Other important functions of supervision are to help teachers define their roles and the roles of others in the social context of the school and to facilitate cooperation and interaction among faculty and staff.

It is equally important for the supervisor to provide a vision for the staff and faculty. Teachers, especially, need to conceptualize teaching in a way that places all components in a proper and workable relationship with one another. The teacher must view instruction in reference to the whole picture: community support, administration (with its concern for finances), personnel, public relations, curriculum development, faculty improvement, auxiliary services, and extracurricular activities.

Supervision as Educational Leadership

The most significant of all supervisory components is educational leadership. The supervisor who chooses not to lead or who cannot lead in a democratic fashion will not long survive. Supervision *is* leadership.[17] This position has been the subject of much specula-

---

[14] Harris and Bessent, *op. cit.*, pp. 1–4.

[15] James Curtin, *Supervision in Today's Elementary Schools* (New York: The Macmillan Company, 1964), pp. 10–11.

[16] J. Minor Gwynn, *Theory and Practice of Supervision* (New York: Dodd, Mead and Co., 1961), pp. 27–31.

[17] Jane Franseth, *Supervision as Leadership* (Evanston, Ill.: Row, Peterson and Co., 1961), p. 1. Mildred E. Swearington, *Supervision of Instruction: Foundations and Dimensions* (Boston: Allyn & Bacon, 1962), p. 53.

tion and some research. Inspection, once so prominent, is no longer a part of supervision. The practice of quality control has been considerably modified. Standards cannot be enforced by means of outlines, courses of study, adopted texts and inspection; they are promoted, rather, through freedom to teach and to learn, to experiment and to innovate. Leadership plays an important role in providing opportunities for and in stimulating such teacher activities.

Leadership Traits. Studies of leadership in the armed forces found that servicemen preferred officers who (1) showed an interest in their welfare, (2) made prompt decisions, (3) demonstrated good judgment, (4) were good teachers, (5) showed appreciation for good work, (6) avoided bossing men around, and (7) gave orders in clear and precise language.[18] Persons who could meet these qualifications were found to come from backgrounds which had given them greater socioeconomic advantages. In general, they were superior in such characteristics as intelligence, scholarship, knowledge, vitality, self-confidence and social adaptability.

Recent studies of leadership have added some traits which appear to be important and have increased our insight into this very complex phenomenon.[19] Leaders, it seems, have the ability to predict group needs and are sensitive to individual needs; they are capable of responding to such needs in acceptable ways. Leaders are supportive and facilitate both group work and individual tasks. Leader behavior is goal oriented, and leaders are usually above average in communication and interaction skills.[20]

Leadership Skills. If leadership were a natural phenomenon, there would be no need for training programs and the leadership courses mounted by business and industry would be useless. However, since such is far from the case, programs to develop leadership skills are constantly being presented.

People generally undertake tasks in random fashion. Some tasks will be completed while others remain on the drawing boards for varying periods of time and a few are forgotten. *Planning* demands

---

18 Walter S. Monroe, ed., *Encyclopedia of Educational Research*, 2nd ed. (New York: The Macmillan Company, 1950), pp. 662–663.
19 Wiles, *op. cit.*, pp. 32–36.
20 Robert L. Ebel, Victor H. Noll, and Roger M. Bauer, eds., *Encyclopedia of Educational Research*, 4th ed. (New York: The Macmillan Company, 1969), pp. 700–701. See also the third edition, 1960, p. 607.

that decisions be made in advance relative to what is necessary for future purposeful activity. As an intellectual process, planning involves manipulating ideas, relationships, concepts, and models of concepts and making decisions about them. Planning takes into account goals and the steps necessary to achieve them; it identifies and assigns responsibilities. One result of planning is the reduction of waste in time, energy, and money. Planning provides for the anticipation of consequences and for review and evaluation procedures.

Organizing refers to the orderly arrangement of events, items, or actions. It is the process of allocating and assigning specific duties to given individuals. Organizing is concerned with priorities and with establishing relationships among people and events. It applies to personnel (teachers, teacher aides, principals, consultants, and others), to materials (outlines, books and pamphlets, periodicals, etc.), and to time (duration of a unit, sequences, articulation of services and elements of a strategy).

The operation of an assembly line in a modern automobile factory and the production of a space vehicle through elaborate systems planning are examples of *coordination*. Many different parts, carefully and scientifically prepared and finished, are brought together at a given place and at a predetermined time so the vehicles may be properly manufactured. Similarly, in supervision one task is to bring to bear, at the appointed times, the special service personnel and the various auxiliary services so that instruction and learning continue without interruption. Clerical assistance, building maintenance, library services, the requisitioning and ordering of supplies, and preparation of audio-visual materials are only a few of the components of the support system. When these services become misaligned or dysfunctional, someone, usually the supervisor, sees that corrections are made.

Language is the basis of *communication,* and communication is the process of exchanging meaning. Communication makes it possible to discuss ideas or problems and to become aware of the needs of teachers, to share goals, influence actions, and achieve group consensus. Communication is also nonverbal, and it is necessary to see that nonverbal cues are consistent with verbal communication. If the two kinds of communication are contradictory, the true meaning of any message will be lost. The flow of communications among personnel and between school and community must be free and easy. All normal channels must be open, and messages must be transmitted as originated lest rumor and gossip impede the work of supervision.

Delegating includes the distribution of the necessary labor between or among the chief actors in a project on a basis that is mutually acceptable. Delegating comes naturally for the supervisor because he visualizes his task as more than something which can be accomplished by one person. He analyzes the work flow, prepares job analyses, and helps teachers perceive the sequence of steps that must be pursued. If the suggestions incorporate specified methods of accomplishing a task, then delegation can be instrumental in setting standards. It is not a simple procedure, however. Each of the parties has to agree to accept certain specific responsibilities and to refrain from interfering with those of the other. This is an informal contract in which each has accorded the other the authority to carry out his share of the project. It involves mutual expectations of high-quality performance. Should one or the other fail in his responsibility, an evaluation of the causes of failure is in order. Delegation, like communication, is a two-way affair.

Evaluation is a process of applying standards or criteria and making judgments. It is basic to the determination of success, or quality of performance, or measurement of progress. Leadership is heavily dependent on proper evaluation, which includes interpretation, elaboration, and projection and extends far beyond mere data gathering. Evaluation requires intellectual honesty, objectivity, and careful consideration of all the facts regardless of time and source. Trends in modern evaluation are toward more open-ended procedures, greater involvement of teachers, and more reliance on consent and consensus.

Leadership Skills

Mr. Frederick is the newly appointed supervisor for his district, having been promoted last spring from the classroom. He came to the job in the fall untested and unsure of himself in this capacity. In a supervision course taken at the local university this summer, Mr. Frederick learned that one of the important aspects of his role was to recognize and to develop certain leadership skills. He carefully began to *plan* in advance and in detail. He *organized* his time methodically. He immediately attempted to establish a scheme of *evaluation* of his operation. As a beginner he felt that these activities were priorities and he could move into other important areas such as curriculum analysis when he became secure in his new position. He was off to a good start in his first year.

Was his set of priorities a good one? What other leadership skills will he need to master?

Operational Strategy of Leadership. The first task of supervisory leadership is the identification of the uniqueness of each individual teacher. The supervisor discovers the abilities, capacities, and interests of the teacher and explores them for their dimensions. It is unlikely that these will be discovered in casual meetings in the corridor, or on an occasional visit to the classroom. They must be the object of a continuous search by the supervisor.

The second task consists in providing for the development of the abilities, capacities, and interests of teachers. Miss Hudson, who would like to teach American history from a series of paperbacks, may welcome a period or two in the school day freed from classroom chores and clerical or disciplinary duties while she plans the course. This arrangement might be more rewarding than several hundred dollars in salary increments. Concern for professional growth is a prime purpose of supervision. In some institutions it is known as faculty development and in some as inservice education.

The third task in the operational strategy is intelligent direction and coordination of teachers' activities. Highly motivated, able teachers working independently of one another will soon find themselves beset by staff problems and frustrations. The more intelligent and competent they are, the more likely they are to object to restrictions, lack of materials and equipment, and bureaucratic rigidity. Unless their several efforts are coordinated within some identifiable design, they will eventually be working at cross-purposes and personal conflicts may arise. Their energies and competences must be harnessed to the total educational program. Proper direction and coordination will develop a productive team approach.

Through operational strategy, supervision has the difficult job of finding and releasing the creative energies of teachers — and indirectly of pupils — for educational purposes. This requires bringing people into the proper relationship with each other in the educational program if their potentialities are to be realized. The supervisor is the diagnostician. He works out the problem carefully, with the assistance of the personnel involved, and together they lay the foundation for future action.

In addition, leadership embodies that intangible quality of empathy for fellow professionals which can evoke the best individual effort. It includes sound, logically consistent judgment radiating from a firmly implanted educational philosophy. It assumes a basic competence in dealing with educational issues, both theoretical and pragmatic. It thrives in an atmosphere of involvement and honest interaction. Above all else, it stimulates others to strive for new levels of performance. The democratic supervisor must use the mastic of educational leadership as he cements together the components of supervisory role, process, and function.

Summary

Chapter One opened with the story of how one school district prepared for the employment of a supervisor. The position was defined as staff, and all school personnel had the opportunity to discuss it fully. Garry Bixman had the appropriate training, philosophy, and ability to work with the staff. Garry would have considerable help because in modern education a variety of people — principals, veteran teachers, special teachers, department chairmen, central office personnel — get into the act. However, in the authors' opinion the supervisor should report to someone other than the superintendent.

A supervisory role results from the expectations and perceptions of both personnel and the supervisor. The best possible working relationships require that these expectations and perceptions be very similar or congruent. Next, supervision was defined as processes (social, psychological, and educational), as functions, and as leadership. Some leadership skills can be learned: planning, organizing, coordinating, communicating, delegating, and evaluating. Operational strategy calls for identifying interests, talents, capacities, and skills of teachers, organizing the personnel in ways to maximize these traits, and mobilizing the resultant power for the improvement of instruction and learning.

Problems for Group Discussion

Analyze the following situations. In each, identify supervisory principles representing sound theory, if any are included. What are the basic elements which made a difference? How would you have approached the situation?

1. Principal Skinker has been in the business for a long time. The superintendent refers to him as a "salty old administrator." Recently Mr. Skinker has been thinking about the need to supervise his teachers. Since his is a "pretty tight ship," he feels he should tell his teachers of new ideas he wants them to put into effect. Accordingly, he has set his schedule to permit him to visit his teachers two days per week for the next three or four weeks. How does Skinker define supervision? How does his view compare with the definition in this chapter?

2. Mr. O'Malley has just been appointed department chairman. He will be the first the school has had, so he is rather uncertain about what he should do. The principal has told him he will have two free periods for departmental business and supervision. He is somewhat apprehensive as to how other teachers are going to react when he starts telling them what and how they should teach. If Mr. O'Malley had read the foregoing chapter, how might he change his approach?

3. Supervisor Burstein has held his position for the past five years. He is quite satisfied with the post. It was a little rough at first, but after he convinced several teachers that they really didn't fit in his district the rest fell into line rather well and now things are progressing pretty much the way he wants them to go. How else might Burstein get the group started? How durable do you think such changes will be?

Selected Readings

Allen, Rowannetta S. "Role and Function of Supervisors and Curriculum Workers," *Educational Leadership,* 23:330–333 (Jan., 1966).

Association for Supervision and Curriculum Development. *Leadership for Improving Instruction.* 1960 Yearbook. Washington: The Association, 1960.

Association for Supervision and Curriculum Development. *Supervision: Perspectives and Propositions.* Washington: The Association, Department of Superintendence, 1930.

Association for Supervision and Curriculum Development. "Theme B. Coping with Role Realities," *The Supervisor: New Demand; New Dimensions.* Washington: The Association, 1969.

Curtin, James. *Supervision in Today's Elementary Schools.* New York: The Macmillan Company, 1964.

Ebel, Robert L., Victor H. Noll, and Roger M. Bauer, eds. *Encyclopedia of Educational Research,* 4th ed. New York: The Macmillan Company, 1969.

Elementary Coordinator Program. *Professional Help for the Classroom Teacher.* Monograph. Denver, Colo.: Denver Public Schools, 1961.

Franseth, Jane. *Supervision as Leadership*. Evanston, Ill.: Row, Peterson and Co., 1961.

Gwynn, J. Minor. *Theory and Practice of Supervision*. New York: Dodd, Mead and Co., 1961.

Harris, Ben M., and Wailand Bessent. *In-Service Education: A Guide to Better Practice*. Englewood Cliffs, N.J.: Prentice-Hall, 1969.

Harris, Chester W., ed. *Encyclopedia of Educational Research*, 3rd ed. New York: The Macmillan Company, 1960.

Harvey, Virginia. "The Change That Counts," *Educational Leadership*, 21:292–296 (Feb., 1964).

Heyns, Roger W. *The Psychology of Personal Adjustment*. New York: Dryden Press, 1958.

High, Paul B. "The Supervisory Role of the Department Head," *Clearing House*, 40:213–215 (Dec., 1965).

Hipps, Melvin. "Supervision: A Basic Responsibility of the Department Head," *Clearing House*, 40:487–491 (Apr., 1965).

Mackenzie, Gordon N. "Role of the Supervisor," *Educational Leadership*, 19:86–90 (Nov., 1961).

McKean, Robert C., and H. H. Mills. *The Supervisor*. New York: Center for Applied Research in Education, 1964.

McMaster, Alice. "Supervision: Loneliness and Rewards," *Educational Leadership*, 23:626–629 (May, 1966).

Monroe, Walter S., ed. *Encyclopedia of Educational Research*, 2nd ed. New York: The Macmillan Company, 1950.

Neagley, Ross L., and N. Dean Evans. *Handbook for Effective Supervision of Instruction*. Englewood Cliffs, N.J.: Prentice-Hall, 1964.

Stephenson, Claude. "Departmental Organization for Better Instruction," *Bulletin of the National Association of Secondary School Principals*, 45:9–14 (Dec., 1961).

Swearington, Mildred E. *Supervision of Instruction: Foundations and Dimensions*. Boston: Allyn & Bacon, 1962.

Wiles, Kimball. *Supervision for Better Schools*, 3rd ed. New York: Prentice-Hall, 1967.

two

•

Communication and the
Effectiveness of Supervision

Communication is fundamental to every human enterprise. Since supervision is so deeply concerned with teachers and their behavior, communication becomes a central process in developing optimum conditions for learning for both pupil and teacher. It provides a method of sharing expectations and perceptions and can be used to build unity or discord. It is a means by which an individual can influence a group or a group can control one of its members.

Within groups one finds formal communication channels usually used by officers, their staffs, and sometimes their supporters. Every human group also has an informal communication system through which information is disseminated to the membership. Supervisors utilize both formal structures and informal networks to reach persons and to involve them in the total effort, whether it be curriculum innovation or faculty improvement. An understanding of the communication process will help the supervisor improve his communication skills and more effectively implement his strategy for change.

The Process of Communication

The accepted universe of discourse includes words, special vocabularies, symbols, structures, attitudes, and nonverbal cues, and how well one supervises may depend on how well he uses these elements. Communication is, indeed, the mortar which holds together the organization for supervision and inservice education. Lack of it causes faculties to break up into splinter groups.

Bristow described the problems involved in communication: ineffective use of mass media, ineffective directions, badly timed messages, lack of research in methods of communicating.[1] Analysis of these problems suggests ways of improving techniques. First, words which have meaning for the hearer must be chosen. Second, a multimedia approach, since it utilizes sight and sound, is often of value. Third, communication should be provided when the recipient needs it. Communication should flow easily in any direction, up or down, or back and forth, in and out, or laterally. And finally, continued study in the field of communication theory and techniques will provide new insights for the supervisor.

Some of the problems in communication result from misperception, lack of attention, and failure on the part of the supervisor to provide a good situation for the exchange of meaning. If, for example, nonverbal cues contradict the words used, confusion arises in the minds of the receivers. Mr. Porter, director of instruction in the Washington Heights public schools, announced a meeting of the faculty on Tuesday at 3:30 P.M. in Room 153 to discuss whether the school should change its methods of reading instruction and whether the use of i/t/a/ (Initial Teaching Alphabet) should be introduced. Arriving in Room 153, the faculty discovered a lectern on the teacher's desk, which did not seem exactly right if discussion was anticipated. The chairs were arranged in straight rows, and it even seemed improbable that the meeting would be opened by a panel, or by the presentation of pros and cons, because there was only one chair behind the desk. Friendly countenances turned sober, and pleasant conversation faded. "What's bugging Porter?" and "A lecture is just what we need after a hard day's work" were heard. Hostility for Mr. Porter lay near the surface. Regardless of what he had planned to do that afternoon, his nonverbal communication was about to arouse opposition to anything he might suggest.

A Definition of Communication

Communication is the giving and receiving of meaning. This process is fundamental to living in a community and to progress. Meaning is influenced by group membership, the environment and background of people, positional relationships in the institutional

---

[1] William H. Bristow, "Communication in Curriculum," *Educational Leadership,* 23:143–151 (Nov., 1965).

structure, and the type and amount of education participants have. The more education one has, the more critical he is of meanings. Thus the communicator must be acutely aware of the many possible meanings from which the receiver will select precisely those he thinks were intended.

The basic ingredients of a culture are ideas, ideals, feelings, perceptions, expectations, codes controlling behavior, symbols, techniques, and taboos. These elements exist also in a profession and they are transmitted by what is known as jargon. Such language presumably facilitates understanding. The meanings of words have been fairly well standardized, reducing speculation over intended meanings and inferences. An appropriate selection of symbols from a given community of discourse improves the chances of transmitting and exchanging precise meanings.

Merrihue defined communication as a mutual exchange of thoughts, facts, opinions, or emotions. This process of presentation and reception should result in understanding but it does not necessarily result in agreement.[2] Kelley and Rasey defined communication as a process permitting one person to know what another person thinks and feels and providing an assessment of his beliefs.[3] One of life's problems is communication between people, between nations, and between cultures. Communication has three very important functions: satisfying an individual's need for others, social and psychological growth, and development of human relatedness.

Communication is, then, not a simple thing. Rarely will two persons receive exactly the same impressions from a given verbal stimulus or perceive it in precisely the same way. The greater the number of people involved, and the more complex the situation becomes under which communication is attempted, the more difficult it is to convey identical and exact meanings to all.

Activities Inherent in Communication

The activities of communication may be divided into four categories for more intensive study. The first category consists in giving directions, either to individuals or to groups: supplying information,

---

[2] Willard V. Merrihue, *Managing by Communication* (New York: McGraw-Hill Book Company, 1960), p. 15.
[3] E. C. Kelley and M. I. Rasey, *Education and the Nature of Man* (New York: Harper & Brothers, 1952), p. 78.

interpreting, instructing, making assignments, advising, correcting, and persuading. These activities may take the form of conferences, lectures, bulletins, memos, letters, and posters.

Supervisors who like working with people find individual contacts to give directions appealing. There is more opportunity to receive immediate feedback, so the supervisor is more assured of an open communication line.

An instructional supervisor must be cognizant of the necessity for, as well as the inherent problems associated with, the use of various methods of communication. Each person will find a pattern best suited to his purposes which will vary somewhat from others. No supervisor can expect to succeed for long without at least a minimum level of organized communication.

If the ratio of teachers to supervisor is too large to permit personal contacts, or the problems are so numerous and varied that specialized attention is required, supervisors, directors of instruction, and supervising principals tend to resort to memos, bulletins, and the distribution of prepared materials. Often there is an overemphasis on this type of communication. It is about as ineffective today as it was a generation ago.

The second category of communication consists in obtaining information. Supervisors should be concerned with follow-up studies, surveys, interviews, observations, and listening to discussions. More important, they must help teachers develop objective ways of looking at the instructional program, to see to what extent it has been successful and appropriate. The techniques of self-evaluation are not easily learned because teachers have a conflict of interest. Since they have invested great amounts of time and energy, and of themselves, they are identified with the product and therefore are usually not objective about their handiwork. They tend to evaluate it in terms of intent rather than achievement.

More and more districts are gaining access to computers. The type of minute instructional data which can be placed in computer storage banks can prove invaluable to the supervisor. Now, for the first time, he is able to examine in depth various aspects of the instructional program in a manner impossible before the computers. Such information can provide the district with a new dimension of communication vital to the whole instructional program.

The third category of activities consists in cooperation, collaboration, and interaction. Communication is definitely a two-way process involving the exchange of meaning and the achievement of agreements and understandings. Some of the techniques used are discussions, conferences, and negotiations. Such exchanges serve as important feedback devices for the supervisor. The firsthand data from groups actively attacking problems can help him determine future directions, assign priorities, and recognize possible trouble spots.

The fourth category consists of those activities which build and maintain the structures through which communication, formal and informal, takes place. Committees are set up, individual contributions solicited, and conferences arranged. The informal networks in particular must receive a constant input of information and specially designed content. The supervisor often is the person who must take the initiative in establishing agreed-upon projects. He also can encourage the line administrators to provide the necessary communications structure to reinforce such activities and opportunities for stimulating interaction.

This category rests largely on the educational leadership supplied by the supervisor. It represents the positive momentum of the district in the constant attempt to improve instruction. It includes the facilitating aspect of the supervisor's job as he makes possible confrontations, encounters, and forums for ideas and opinions which foster instructional planning.

Factors that may slow down, inhibit, or even prohibit communication must be taken into account. For example, if a communicator is too aggressive he may be overstating his case, giving the listener a hard sell, and hence communicating more of himself and less of his message. If the image the listener has of the speaker is incongruent with the image the speaker has of himself and his mission, there will be misunderstanding. The misuse of group meetings or of a vehicle of communication presents a barrier through which meaning is not likely to penetrate.

Newsletter Reveals Bias

Harry Mays, the science supervisor, is attempting to keep all science teachers in his district aware of the latest activities in the field by means of regularly scheduled science newsletters which he writes and sends them. In the newsletters he reviews promising innovations in science.

He is not aware that his own bias toward one program in particular has been so obvious that the science teachers are being divided into two groups, those who go along with his interest and those who are reacting negatively — more, actually, to the supervisor than to his pet program. Unless Mr. Mays improves his communications rapidly, he runs the risk of producing a major schism which will seriously hinder the science program of the district. How can a supervisor guard against making such mistakes?

Basic Elements of Communication

Dr. Haller, the new supervisor of instruction at Eureka, has taught courses in the improvement of instruction at the local state university. He used a physical model of communication to illustrate the elements and their relationships to each other:

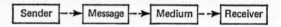

The sender is sometimes called the communicator or the encoder. His personality, his position in the hierarchy, his status in the profession and in the community may become attached to his communication as riders. His habits, idiosyncrasies, likes and dislikes, manners, style of operating, may also come through. Therefore who the sender *is* may communicate more than what he is saying. Mr. Saud, a student in Dr. Haller's class, said one day that he could not remember what Dr. Haller had said but knew he disliked him. This reaction was due to an unconscious transmission of personal characteristics of communication. But Dr. Haller could also have sent out selected cues with his message and thus deliberately slanted it.

The second important element in communication is the message itself. Whatever the content of the message, it is greatly affected by a number of factors such as the tone of voice of the sender, or, in written communication, the choice of words.[4] Any words that have emotional overtones, such as *integration* or *segregation, communism* or *propaganda,* will arouse responses which may not have been intended by the sender. In supervisory messages many words may arouse the emotions and obscure the meaning of the message: *Merit, evaluation, objective tests* — the word *supervision* itself — arouse

---

[4] Marshall McLuhan, "The Medium Is the Message," *N.E.A. Journal,* 56:24–27 (Oct., 1967).

so many and such confusing stimuli within the receiver that anything said or written is easily misunderstood.

Stageberg pointed out that both intentional and unintentional distortions of statements are almost inevitable in group conferences.[5] Single words often present almost insurmountable barriers to the progress of the discussion. Some words may be interpreted in several ways and will be, depending upon a person's background and experience. Other words seem vague and the meaning changes. Words may be used to obscure meaning or to arouse emotions or they may be very narrow in meaning and discriminative. People often reveal their prejudices with the injection of a single word; note the difference between "a third-grade teacher" and "a gossipy third-grade teacher." Generalizations do not communicate well and may leave an unsavory residue. For instance, the statement "Teachers need supervision" is so general and in need of refinement that it is not likely to create a response in the reader or receiver.

If the supervisor is alert to words and their meanings, his communications will be more effective since he is less likely to suggest unwanted meanings and arouse emotions. His purpose will be better served by carefully planned messages properly worded.[6]

The third element is the method or medium of communication. The method may be formal or informal, whether the communication takes place in conference or in written form. Keeping all the possible factors in mind, the sender must decide whether to telephone, write the message formally or informally, seek a face-to-face situation, transmit the message through another human being, or use some other method. He must always remember that he is also communicating by means of his facial expressions, his gestures, the flourishes on his signature, or the inflection of his voice. Some supervisors use these telltale devices purposely, deliberately assuming an attitude or posture to obtain a desired effect. In any event, personality is a medium of communication.

The fourth component in communication is the receiver. If the supervisor has an expert knowledge of the individual differences of teachers with whom he works — their prejudices, their frustrations,

---

[5] Norman C. Stageberg, "Obstacle Words in Group Conference," *Journal of Communication*, 2:82–87 (May, 1952).
[6] See also Lawrence Borosage, Model of Communication, Fig. 3 in "A Basis for Viewing Communication," *National Elementary Principal*, 7:11 (May, 1962).

their aspirations and expectations — he can do a better job of composing his message. The receiver brings everything he knows to bear upon the message, but *only* what he knows, not what he may be expected to know. His entire past — training, education, experience, intelligence, social and cultural conditioning, problems — influences his interpretation of the message. He will receive some meanings and stimuli and not others. The message may arouse his prejudices, his fears, or perhaps his hopes, and its deeper content may be lost on him.

The Too-Busy Supervisor

Supervisor Levy is a very busy man. In fact, with the new programs recently started in the district, there is just too much to do. He has attempted to delegate work whenever possible and to use his time to the best advantage. One means of delegating work has been in the writing of memos. Mr. Levy has developed the habit of verbally describing to his secretary what he wants conveyed and permitting her to prepare and send the actual memo. Words do not fall into place easily for him and this saves much time.

Miss Carmichael, being a good secretary, conveys his wishes in words which clearly indicate to the reader what he is to do. In her zeal, however, she put more of a commanding tone in the communications than Mr. Levy intended. He knows how sensitive some of the teachers can be and is usually very circumspect in the way he presents a suggestion. But now he is too busy to take time. Is he really saving time in the long run? What surprises await him?

Communication Channels

The channels of information may be categorized roughly as formal and informal. The formal are probably the best known to teachers and involve the direct line of authority running from the board to the superintendent, to the assistant superintendent, to the principal, to the supervisor, and finally to the teacher. In any organization there is generally a top (the officers) and a bottom (the membership). In highly organized institutions one observes what is known as protocol: Messages go through all the offices on the way up. However, a communication may be blocked anywhere along the line. At times messages transmitted from one level to another are changed, being either reduced or elaborated in wording and hence in meaning. Such modification may occur through deliberate intent of the transmitter. He may feel that the sender's original message is too harsh, or is somewhat inaccurate, or will be received unfavorably by his superior. Or he may in good faith attempt to improve on the wording to make the message more understandable, more inclusive, or more concise. In any event, the particular administrator may feel perfectly justified in taking action which results in a modification of the communication in transmission. The original sender may not be at all pleased with the outcome.

Often internal pressure for better communication may be observed within a school and within a school system. If the formal routes are blocked, or inoperative, the need for better communication will bring other channels into existence. One such is the informal group and the informal network of communication. The small informal group may be needed for personal satisfaction and may be used for personal aims. When it becomes more compacted, perhaps because its members feel threatened, the splinter group or the clique develops. Some schools have a large number of small informal groups or cliques. A study of ten schools showed that not one was free of this phenomenon; all had both small and large informal groups. Information traveled very rapidly through them. Cliques may be used by the skillful supervisor to disseminate information and to provide a nucleus for a curriculum or instructional project.

Knowledge of the existence of informal groups should be a prerequisite for the supervisor contemplating any kind of instructional improvement project. They can provide both input and feedback if he is willing to utilize such information. Many supervisors hesitate to rely too heavily on this kind of group for fear that the reasons for its original development might produce an unwelcome bias in response to their efforts. As a result of this often unnecessary caution, valuable assistance is lost — frequently at a time when it is needed most.

If communication lines are blocked so that no messages are being transmitted up and down or back and forth, groups may manufacture information in their own way. From incomplete observations, from fleeting glimpses of behavior, from rumors and bits of conversations here and there, false meanings are read into the actions of others. Then comments, remarks, and suggestions are offered to the group in lieu of valid information and may be passed on until they assume the status of facts. Such "facts" have been known to affect teaching for considerable periods of time, and clearly out of proportion to any original value they may have had. Supervisors who create permissive climates and stress communication have a minimum of irritation from problems of this type.

Competent, professional supervisors should constantly search for new means of exchanging ideas. Industry takes interesting approaches: rumor clinics (analysis of rumors, their source, and comparisons with the truth); the "Squawk Box" used by the Coleman Company;[7] house organs, bulletins, and memos.[8] Surveys of attitudes and opinions and activation of grievance machinery represent additional channels. Exit interviews, professionally conducted, often provide information which can be used to establish rapport among groups, or to suggest how rapport may be improved. Information must be allowed to travel freely within the structure and if this is not occurring, it should be actively encouraged. Teacher publications, written by teachers for teachers and managed by teachers, are excellent channels. The supervisor himself is a channel of communication. In one sense, liaison is an important ongoing component of his job. He should play the liaison role judiciously lest it supplant other equally important functions and lest he infringe upon the rights and roles of the teacher. He should be prepared, however, to provide the impetus necessary to support the liaison function when needed.

McGrew has noted that traditionally communication has been a major problem in educational administration.[9] The cry of "too many meetings" has finally placed faculty meetings among the negotiable items because the warning signals did not get through. Staff newsletters, daily bulletins, department meetings, items posted in the faculty lounge or inserted in the school newspaper — these are means of circulating pertinent information to staff members instead of too many meetings of the entire staff. But people read selectively. No two people will be reached in the same way by any given medium, nor will any person always receive news in the same way. Selective perception controls what teachers see, read, and hear.

Communication is a basic process in the development of the individual and in integrating him into the group. His personality is

---

[7] National Association of Manufacturers, *Case Book of Employee Communications in Action* (New York: Industrial Relations Division, NAM, 1952).
[8] *Ibid.*
[9] John McGrew, "Improving Staff Communications," *Clearing House* 40:475–477 (Apr., 1966).

shaped by the communities in which he lives, and communication is the main tool used to reward, punish, and control behavior. If a person is to make common cause with others (in a profession, for example), then communication is the key.

Using Informal Channels

Mr. Art Allen, the secondary supervisor for the district, knows the value of good communication. He also recognizes the weakness of the printed word.

In an endeavor to keep communication channels free, Mr. Allen has identified several individuals, both teachers and department chairmen, who are greatly respected by their peers. He knows that these people are directly involved in the informal power structure of the district. Whenever an item of a complicated or controversial nature is being dealt with, Mr. Allen makes sure that these key individuals are briefed on the problem and its implications. He knows that such basic understanding can help avert misconceptions and alleviate potential unrest throughout the district much better than he alone could. Are there any disadvantages in Mr. Allen's procedure?

Communications and the Supervisory Load

The question often arises, "How many teachers can one individual supervise?" Several considerations are important in this connection. One is the level of education possessed by the faculty. It may be assumed that a well-educated, professional faculty becomes more and more self-reliant and self-sufficient and requires less direct assistance. In such a case a supervisor could serve a larger number of persons than he could if the faculty were poorly educated.

A second consideration is the kind of communication to be utilized. If a primary face-to-face condition with faculty members is required for a sustained period, the supervisor's load must be drastically reduced. Down through the years a give-and-take atmosphere of supervisors with faculty members has been considered one of the key strengths of a good supervisory program. Mutually satisfying two-way communication was regularly and adequately maintained in good programs. Both supervisor and teachers understood each other's position and easily related to each other. The recent increased ratio of teachers to supervisory personnel has been a cause of much difficulty. Obviously, the greater the number of teachers per supervisor, the less face-to-face procedures can be utilized. Also, a faculty with a large proportion of new members, or beginners, requires much supervisory time. Even an experienced faculty deeply involved in curriculum development calls for a lot of supervisory help.

A third consideration is the number of teachers an individual can supervise when the district is involved in change. The introduction of a system-wide change in services, methods, or curriculum requires much professional assistance. Examples of changes include the introduction of psychological services, the provision of clerical help for all teachers, the grouping of pupils (with the attendant problem of modifying the instructional methods), and the establishment and use of a new instructional materials center. The supervisor will have to work especially hard on effective communications when any change of this magnitude occurs. He knows that good communications make the difference between success and failure. If the supervisory contact is limited to an audience situation in which he addresses the faculty and staff over a public-address system, the number that can be reached is large. Similarly, if the supervisory staff relies on the use of bulletins, memoranda, and other written materials, the number that can be addressed is substantial.[10] But mass media should be used only by design and for specific purposes. Their overuse may mean a reduction in the effectiveness of communication.

Vertical and Horizontal Communication

Supervisors and school leaders have numerous ways of communicating with their constituents. Some are designed for vertical transmission, usually from top to bottom. Some are designed to communicate across a section of the personnel, or in a horizontal direction.

A variety of techniques may be utilized for vertical communication. (1) It is relatively easy to distribute materials, memos, bulletins, and announcements from the supervisor, curriculum coordinator, or special services director to staff members, department chairmen, principals, and their assistants. (2) The distribution of resources guides to department heads and teachers from kindergarten through Grade 12 presents no problem. (3) Meetings may be scheduled for teachers from kindergarten through Grade 6 to

---

[10] John A. Bartky, *Supervision as Human Relations* (Boston: D. C. Heath & Company, 1953), pp. 272–273.

work on reading instruction, mathematical sequences, the scope and materials of the social sciences, and so on. (4) Leadership meetings involving the superintendent, his assistants and staff, or building administrators are other examples of vertical communication. (5) Meetings of all teachers in a given subject, kindergarten through Grade 12, to discuss current materials or new sources, or to work with consultants, are additional illustrations.

A number of techniques for communicating laterally have been used for various purposes. (a) The most common scheme is a grade-level conference in which, for example, all eighth-grade teachers are called together. Or all high school science teachers meet to discuss a new science curriculum. (b) Some large districts use departmental councils, in which all heads of departments of the high schools meet with supervisors and consultants. (c) The supervisor might hold a conference for all secondary principals, or (d) organize a demonstration for all remedial reading teachers.

Certain methods of communicating combine vertical and horizontal structures. (1) The all-faculty meeting cuts across subject and grade lines. (2) The resource guide, or curriculum guide, may have both vertical and horizontal dimensions; it could, for example, be the basis for a discussion aimed at improving correlation of two or more subjects in several grades. (3) Educational clinics considering problem cases, or symposia on delinquency, homework, discipline, or dropouts might require the participation of personnel from all levels and academic areas.

Creative supervisors are constantly inventing new communication projects, and modifying old ones. A good communication program is one which uses all available channels, formal and informal.

Supervisors' Guidelines

As the supervisor attempts to fashion an operational pattern for himself and takes up the various problems of communication, he should check his activities from time to time to ascertain whether he is improving his communication effectiveness. The following suggestions are representative and not intended to be all-inclusive.

1. A set of clearly stated objectives should be developed which will serve as guidelines for improving communication activities in the supervisory program.

2. The supervisor should identify and analyze the receiver, or the audience. Either an underestimation or an overestimation of the education, ability, or professional training of the receiver may nullify the intended meaning of the message.

3. He should plan and design the message carefully, giving much attention to the selection and use of words so as to be assured of an appropriate response.

4. He should strive to develop the personal needs aspect of communication so that the receiver will identify with the objectives and intent of the communication. Thus mutual interest and involvement are fostered and the motive for action is provided.

5. The stimulus (message) should be timed so as to make the best possible use of the psychology of personal needs and to utilize reinforcement and personal commitment.

6. A variety of approaches, media, and messages should be utilized in order to appeal to different individuals. One medium is teacher participation in all phases of the supervisory program from planning to evaluation.

7. Face-to-face conversations are the best means of exchanging meanings and developing mutual understanding. When direct techniques are not feasible, only those indirect methods should be selected which will be most likely to produce the desired result. Provision should be made for feedback whenever possible.

8. The supervisor, in cooperation with others, should develop criteria and instruments for evaluating the effectiveness of communication. Then he should move quickly to implement the results of the evaluation.

9. He should be aware of the communicative potential of behavior, of the muted cues, and he should realize that they may contaminate the intended message.

10. Finally, he should strive constantly to improve his own communicative skills.

Summary

Communication is the giving and receiving of meaning. Inherent in this process are giving directions, obtaining information, collaboration, and maintaining structures. Its basic elements are the sender, the message, the medium, and the receiver. The direction of communication varies.

Channels must be kept open if supervision is to be successful. The level of education possessed by teachers, the nature of the communication (message, medium) selected for use, and the amount of change taking place within the district affect the load a supervisor can carry. Vertical and horizontal structures utilized in communication affect both the classification of faculty involved (levels or subject matter) and the substance of communication. Finally, the supervisor should develop his own set of working guidelines for improving his communications.

Problems for Group Discussion

Analyze the following situations. In each, identify supervisory principles representing sound theory, if any are included. What are the basic elements which made a difference? How would you have approached the situation?

1. The supervisor sent a memo to all teachers he worked with at the start of school in the fall asking them to start thinking about possible agenda items for a workshop to be held in November. The teachers heard nothing more until a meeting on Friday afternoon preceding the workshop date. The supervisor was disturbed because few suggestions had been presented. At the workshop the supervisor explained that since the few teacher suggestions had been inappropriate he had prepared the agenda himself. At this point the teachers also became disturbed. What are the basic problems in this situation?

2. The supervisor recognizes the value of feedback from the field. He regularly checks with some of the teachers to see how his various programs are being received. This practice has been carried out for the past five years and the supervisor has gradually identified about a dozen teachers, in various parts of the district, who can be counted on to respond when he needs feedback. He always calls on them. Why? How can he bring the rest of the faculty into the inner circle? What would you do about the few who are always "different"?

Selected Readings

Barlund, Dean C. *Interpersonal Communication: Survey And Studies*. Boston: Houghton Mifflin Company, 1968.

Bartky, John A. *Supervision as Human Relations.* Boston: D. C. Heath & Company, 1953, pp. 272–273.

Borosage, Lawrence. Model of Communication, Fig. 3 in "A Basis for Viewing Communication," *National Elementary Principal,* 7:11 (May, 1962).

Bristow, William H. "Communication in Curriculum," *Educational Leadership,* 23:143–151 (Nov., 1965).

Chase, Stuart. *Power of Words.* New York: Harcourt, Brace & World, 1954.

Kelley, E. C., and M. I. Rasey. *Education and the Nature of Man.* New York: Harper & Brothers, 1952.

McGrew, John. "Improving Staff Communications," *Clearing House.* 40:475–477 (Apr., 1966).

McLuhan, Marshall. "The Medium Is the Message," *NEA Journal,* 56:24–27 (Oct., 1967).

Merrihue, Willard V. *Managing by Communication.* New York: Mc-Graw-Hill Book Company, 1960.

Merrill, Edward C., Jr. "How the Word Gets Around," *American School Board Journal* 130:29–30 (Feb., 1955).

National Association of Manufacturers. *Case Book of Employee Communications in Action.* New York: Industrial Relations Division, NAM, 1952.

National Education Association. *Mass Communication and Education.* Washington: Educational Policies Commission, 1958.

Stageberg, Norman C. "Obstacle Words in Group Conference," *Journal of Communication* 2:82–87 (May, 1952).

Tobin, Richard L. "Communications," *Saturday Review,* 43:53–65 (Oct. 8, 1960).

three

•

Supervision and Improved Morale

In the suburb of Washington Heights some teachers were described as irritable, hostile, and almost unapproachable. Others simply went through the motions of teaching. Both groups spent less time than usual on lesson preparation, on evaluation, and on nonteaching activities. In the teachers' lounge, in the cafeteria, and in the corridors teachers would gather in small groups which vanished on the approach of any member of the administrative or supervisory staff.

The Johnson Middle School was staffed by a small group of highly motivated teachers. Among them was Miss Willard, just one year past her master's degree. She had a friendly disposition and worked enthusiastically with others in lively and interesting discussions. She gave no evidence of either hostility or apathy, usually going out of her way to encounter a member of the administration or supervision staff. She was always ready with a question about the new curriculum or some technological advance in teaching.

Two elements stand out in the above descriptions which provide clues to the study of morale. One is the situation, or the conditions under which teachers work; physical, social, economic, and psychological factors make a difference in morale. The other element is the person, who by activities and attitudes can affect students and colleagues. Supervision must analyze the problems of apathy and hostility and develop programs to improve social relations and morale. The Miss Willards may provide the means of building new faculty leadership. The challenge of assisting such a teacher to work with other faculty members will demand carefully laid strategies.

Morale

Definitions

Morale is the individual's state of mind or attitude conditioned by what he perceives to be the difference between his goals and his present situation (achievement, performance, or status). Morale depends on the extent to which goals are being achieved and so becomes an emotional, a mental, and in some instances a physical reaction to the job. In this context two factors are important in morale: present achievement as perceived by the individual, and the progress he feels he is making. Even though the gap is wide between the current situation and the goals, if the individual believes that his progress is satisfactory, his morale will be high.

A Progress Report

Henry Francois, a third-year teacher in Big City public schools, is excited about teaching and is becoming an exciting teacher. Rated only average while at the university, Henry knew what he wanted — to be the best teacher he could be. He was fortunate to be hired by Big City because this district had a plan to aid and encourage professional improvement of teachers.

In only three years Henry is well into a master's program which has already helped him in his classroom and will soon increase his take-home pay. In addition, his supervisor, Miss Barrett, has been of invaluable assistance. With her guidance he is developing a teaching strategy which is more effective with each passing week. Henry is gaining the self-assurance of a professional who knows what he is doing and why. He realizes he is rapidly moving toward his goal and his enthusiasm is high. Is Henry justified in having such a rosy outlook?

Groups of teachers, with group goals, react in a somewhat similar manner. If the faculty has been working on welfare programs such as better salary schedules, retirement plans, sick leave policies, or working conditions, the morale of the group will be conditioned by its view of the gap between what should exist and what does exist. The wider the gap, the lower the morale. The slower the progress toward the desired goals, the lower the morale. If the gap between anticipated income and present salary is wide, and progress is imperceptible, the group may become greatly disturbed, and, as a by-product, teachers may spend their energy on protests. Intermediate goals (teacher welfare and salaries) may become the supervisor's first concern in his relationships with members of the staff. However, he certainly must not stop at this point.

Social Climate

Social climate can influence morale because teachers are affected by social interaction. If this interaction has quality (if it is intellectually and culturally at a high level) and provides for contacts outside as well as inside the professional family, morale may be high. It is important to the intellectual and social life of teachers to have extensive contacts with many elements in the society and culture of which they are a part. From these contacts they obtain new ideas, new meanings and understandings, and they become more powerfully motivated to teach.

The Fuller Life

Supervisor Prokiev has many first-year teachers who annually arrive from all over the country, drawn to his district by the winter sports. Mr. Prokiev has long since recognized that this single interest alone will not sustain morale throughout the school year. He has, therefore, encouraged the young teachers to join together in several semiformal social groups which meet regularly and provide opportunities for socialization and intellectual stimulation. The groups vary each year with the interests of the teachers but they are always available.

Mr. Prokiev is wise in fostering such activities; he recognizes that without some replacement for the activities engaged in "back home," teachers will suffer as the boredom and lonesomeness of a stranger in a new city increase. In small groups members can come to support each other, increase communication, assist one another, and build morale together.

Teachers who are active in organizations often have a higher morale than those who are inactive. If the activities of the groups with which the individual is identified have variety and quality, appear to be valuable to society, and accomplish something worthwhile, morale tends to be good. The participant not only gives the group something of himself but receives something which is important to his larger world. If communication among one group and other groups within the community is poor, if communication is seldom sought or is tolerated rather than appreciated, the group has little or no morale-building value.

Isolation is an important factor in morale. If a teacher is assigned to some out-of-the-way room in the building, the supervisor should make a special effort to communicate with him, see that he receives acceptance. If the informal cliques leave him out, the supervisor should take him under his wing and develop a new informal group which includes him. The individual should be involved in committee meetings and projects of an appropriate nature.[1]

Economic Factors

Security provisions affect morale. As the teacher grows older, economic security becomes more important. The general pattern of living in America assumes that the family man, including the male teacher, or the career woman will accumulate some of this country's great economic wealth before retiring. Teachers who are forced to take a second job for economic reasons tend to reduce the day-to-day preparation needed to keep their courses current and alive. They constitute a problem for the supervisor.[2]

Another facet of the economic problem is the question of whether it is fair to continue to pay good, fair, and poor teachers alike. The single-salary schedule which developed during the thirties and forties was hailed as an answer to outdated bargaining practices, or salary schedules which seemed to discriminate among persons of varying age or marital status or because of teaching assignments. Yet now the single-salary schedule is being questioned, and some school systems are experimenting with variety in salary schedules.

In recent years Lloyd Trump and others have encouraged differentiated assignments according to different levels of expertise. Such a staff reorganization is being implemented in Temple City, California.[3] Specific discrete job descriptions indicate what is expected at each staff level. An identifiable hierarchy is established with teachers receiving a salary appropriate to the amount of re-

[1] Irving R. Melbo and David W. Martin, "Building Morale in Teachers of the Deprived," in *The Educationally Retarded and Disadvantaged* (Chicago: University of Chicago Press, 1967), p. 340.
[2] Adolph Unruh, "Can Men Afford to Teach?" *Phi Delta Kappan,* 33:138–139 (Nov., 1951).
[3] M. John Rand and Fenwick English, "Toward a Differentiated Teaching Staff," *Phi Delta Kappan,* 49:264–268 (Jan., 1968).

sponsibility they carry. Since staff members throughout the district were involved in drawing up the final plan, the administration of Temple City anticipates a high morale factor as a result.

The introduction of a different frame of reference, such as the teaching team, makes a differential salary schedule possible. A team may be composed of master teachers, career teachers, beginning teachers, intern teachers, and clerks. Also, multi-level salary plans have been suggested in the staff utilization studies of the National Association of Secondary School Principals. While proponents of these plans make vigorous claims for them, there are at present no carefully conducted studies of morale of people employed under these conditions.

The economic provisions attached to teaching include welfare benefits as well as adequate salaries. Some of these provisions are retirement programs, sick leaves, credit unions, insurance, hospitalization, travel allowances, and the availability of adequate housing at reasonable costs. These are important considerations, as the amount of attention given them by the professional organizations in recent years shows.

An Intellectual Basis for Morale

For teachers, the intellectual basis for morale is highly important. Most teachers value a satisfying intellectual climate. The first prerequisite of such a climate is a dedication to truth and objectivity in administrative and supervisory ranks. Supervisors must not under any circumstances shade the truth, or utilize descriptions which leave out important facts, or make decisions on the basis of personal likes and dislikes. They should avail themselves of the best ideas or alternatives the faculty is able to produce, giving appropriate recognition for those adopted.

One of the most important intellectual aspects of morale is that which has to do with a knowledge of goals. The nature of the objectives of education and their clarity and specificity affect morale. If people are unsure of where they are going, they cannot be very enthusiastic about getting there. Knowing where one wishes to go affects the choice of methods. Many teachers do not understand educational philosophy, the purposes of education in American democracy, or the differing values placed on education by the various classes in society. Many teachers have not clearly understood that they are supposed to be masters of methodology; still more have not developed a working theory of education for themselves. To the extent that these indictments of teaching are true, one may expect to find narrow views of education, misunderstanding of the general responsibilities of teachers, perhaps even ignorance of common procedures. Supervision must supply whatever is missing in the education of teachers; it may not shrug off this responsibility. Certainly, one approach to maintaining or improving morale is helping teachers to clearly identify professionally acceptable goals. Once the goals are identified, the supervisor can help teachers state them in language which imparts the intended meaning while at the same time delimiting the goals themselves.

In the past, teachers have often clung to ambiguously stated objectives. No one would oppose them, yet they offer little tangible and specific direction. Recent refinements in putting behavioral objectives succinctly now give the supervisor improved tools to aid teachers in formulating guidelines which are not only workable but achievable.

It is one thing to state goals clearly. It is another to decide whether they are reasonable. The tasks as represented and implied by goals must be feasible, perceived by the teacher as consistent with his career objectives. Lack of congruence with career objectives will generate frustration and dissatisfaction. The possibility for self-fulfillment must be evident, and progress toward self-realization should be manifest. If it is, commitment is likely to increase. If commitment is high, morale should be too.[4]

The teacher who is inclined toward a scholarly career is frustrated by the continued presence of the substandard, uncertified teacher. Even though the latter has been around for many years, he is becoming less tolerable today. Nor does it help matters when, in times of great demand for teachers, poorly trained and inexperienced persons are employed at the same salaries as well-trained and experienced teachers. The supervisor cannot be oblivious to these problems. He can, however, develop programs of inservice education for the substandard teacher. And he should be cognizant of the fact that poor leadership depresses the morale of the professional teacher still more.

Further, a situation involving both experienced and inexperienced teachers may be confused by inservice education programs which

---

[4] Melbo and Martin, *op. cit.*, pp. 335–340.

are improperly designed. Inservice education activities should be equally useful to both novice and veteran. Yet they sometimes bore the career teacher and are misunderstood by the beginner. At times they are identified by teachers as instruments created by the profession to control its members.

Working Conditions

If school schedules and job or community pressures utilize so much of a teacher's waking hours that he has little or no time for cultural pursuits or recreation, his morale will sag. Supervision cannot be effective if teachers do not have time to plan and to initiate improvements in instruction. Rounding out a full day at school with paper work after dinner as a regular routine will not produce a readiness for more professional growth activities after school.

Supervisors must help provide time on the job for some of the professional duties which the school values, then encourage productive use of the time thus allocated. New buildings are designed to include teachers' workrooms and lounges so that teachers can work and relax away from the constant need to be both teacher and parent surrogate.

If supervisors are concerned with improving teacher morale by changing working conditions, they can take action along several lines. They can, if they suspect morale is low, conduct periodic surveys to investigate the possible reasons. Perhaps a cross section of the faculty would provide a sufficient sample. A good practice might be to involve a teacher committee in making the survey.

Adequate instructional supplies, aids, equipment, and clerical help in recording data, scoring tests, duplicating materials, and obtaining information to be used in committee work are vital in building morale related to working conditions. When capable teachers spend their time on clerical work rather than on intellectual work, or when they find their efficiency curtailed by shortages of instructional materials and equipment, they have reason to be dissatisfied. Other practical considerations include the reduction of class size, reduction of the number of class preparations, elimination of unnecessary committees, extra-class assignments, and routine school chores. On the other hand, it builds morale to have teachers participate in committees that are developing school policies, or examining and revising school practices, and be able to observe their recommendations going into effect. This is one concern of teacher groups and negotiating councils today that can have considerable effect on teacher morale.

The supervisor who is aware of the implications of working conditions will be constantly seeking ways to "involve" teachers. He will solicit their ideas, suggestions, and critical analyses prior to announcing a major course of action. He will, in essence, attempt to get everyone to come to a general agreement and commitment on planning and policy development rather than try to gain support for decisions previously made in isolation at the top of the hierarchy.

The Cost of Low Morale

No one knows just how great the educational waste is when boys and girls are exposed daily to teachers whose morale is low. Pressures tend to build up frustrations, and prolonged frustration may lead to hostility toward the school, toward certain people associated with the system, and toward students. Unless the hostility is somehow reduced (by better communication, participation in decision making, grievance mechanisms, group work), it mushrooms into aggression. If aggressive behavior is met with the imposition of new controls, the entire cycle of frustration, hostility, aggression may be repeated with greater intensity. Increased frustration results from suppression and leads to more intense hostility, which, in turn, leads to more aggressive behavior. If suppression continues to be the only response to this situation, the individual may go underground. He may exhibit hostility and aggressive behavior toward his colleagues. He may try to form a nucleus of sympathizers to assist in his aggressive acts. So the splinter group evolves. If one such group is evident in the faculty, others may well be present. The supervisor will probably now be completely ineffective in his attempts to improve instruction, and the pupils will be the losers. Pupil achievement is definitely affected by the morale of the teacher.[5]

Shortages Lead to Problems

Supervisor Smith faced the most difficult challenge of his long professional career. It was not his responsibility alone, of course, but he felt a strong pressure to protect the instructional level of the

---

[5] Lester W. Anderson, "Teacher Morale and Student Achievement," *Journal of Educational Research*, 46:693–698 (May, 1953).

district in any way he could. It had been a particularly hard year for the district. Three elections had been necessary to get an operating levy established so the budget could be set for the year. Uncertainty, combined with eventual budget cuts, had lowered morale throughout the entire staff.

Mr. Smith knew that the problem would be aggravated next year when shortages of supplies and equipment were felt in all classrooms. The superintendent was discussing the issue with his line administrators, seeking solutions for the district. Mr. Smith intended to place this item high on the agenda of the curriculum council at its first meeting in the fall. He further planned to call several meetings with key staff members throughout the district to search for possible solutions. In such a situation, many heads are preferable to one, and staff morale must be improved.

Under the circumstances, how is it possible to keep the faculty from becoming discouraged?

Identifying Low and High Morale

Danger Signals

The professional supervisor must be constantly alert to the problem of morale, whether it is related to only one individual faculty member or to a group. Such clues as these may be indicators of low morale:

1. The general distribution of grades given, unusually high or unusually low.
2. The frequency with which grievances arise, either from an individual or from the group.
3. The incidence of tardiness, of teacher and/or pupils.
4. Faculty absences from work, committee meetings, faculty meetings, appointments with members of the staff.
5. The number of requests for special permission to be out of the building during the free period, to use certain equipment or apparatus, to turn grades in one day late, etc.
6. Reluctance to turn in reports. Unwillingness to assume extra duties.
7. Repeated loss of supervisory or administrative bulletins.
8. Resistance to any change or suggestions for change.
9. Evidence of gossiping, bickering.

10. Teacher turnover, resignations, transfers, and dismissals.[6]
11. Evidence of waste: wasting class time, frequent loss of materials, lack of preparation and planning, neglect of or refusal to use auxiliary services.
12. Low scores by students on standardized tests.
13. Frequent excuses and alibis or excessive use of sick leave.
14. Evidence of hostility or aggressive behavior.
15. General negative teacher reaction.
16. The beginning of splinter groups or factions within the staff.
17. The use of the silent treatment.
18. Exhibition of frustration.
19. Increasing use of the grievance mechanism.
20. Criticisms of colleagues or supervisors.
21. Unfavorable comments about the school or community.
22. Clandestine meetings of the faculty.
23. Health problems, personal problems.
24. Lack of personal responsibility for property, duties, etc.

Once the supervisor has identified a situation in which low morale seems prevalent, he should carefully review the available evidence. Thoughtful analysis may very well suggest the source of the difficulty, thereby indicating possible steps to be taken toward its alleviation.

Late Again!

Supervisor Brown gradually came to realize that something was amiss in one of the high schools of his district. When written reports were asked for, the reports from this school could be expected late or incomplete. If his office received any calls concerning memos, at least one call would come from this building.

Mr. Brown had been too occupied with the implementation of the new math program to devote much time to individual buildings. But his work was slacking off a little and he determined to take a good look at his "problem school" to see what could be done to help. He called the principal and arranged to visit the next day. Could it be that the appointment of the new principal last year from out-

---

[6] NEA Research Division, "Teacher Morale," *NEA Journal*, 55:55 (Dec., 1966).

side the district had upset some of the faculty? Could there be a morale problem in this school?

Evidence of High Morale

Generally speaking, high morale is found in people who are secure, unafraid, productive, and loyal. It is manifested in numerous ways. Teachers are cooperative. They are eager to get on with their work, to take a part in the staff meetings, or to do some little extra chore for some one on the staff. They are constantly improving themselves, their methods, and their knowledge, through a variety of means. Enthusiastic teaching is another bit of evidence. Staff members who have high morale regard teaching as an adventure, and their attitude and demeanor reflect this view. They are constantly exploring different areas of human interest and activity, looking for rich and usable instructional resources. They continuously create original learning materials for pupils They initiate studies, look for problems that need solutions, design experiments in methodology, and use reports on educational research. When, in class after class, such behavior is observed, the supervisor should expect excellent morale and be able to recognize individuals who have it.

People characterized by high morale are generous with praise for colleagues, show complete objectivity in cases requiring opinions or judgment, and frequently use plural pronouns (*we, ours, us*) rather than singular forms (*I, mine, me*). They have a constructive, positive, helpful attitude toward problems. They vicariously enjoy the successes, recognitions, awards, and good fortune which come to other members of the faculty. They compliment each other privately and publicly, and defend each other when defense is indicated. They invite visitors to their classes and eagerly share their best ideas with other classroom teachers. Their written reports are submitted on or ahead of time. They advertise their school and community at every opportunity. This attitude is infectious.

In schools in which faculty morale is high, teachers make excellent use of all the auxiliary services because they know the process of instruction is thereby enriched They call freely on the supervisor for his informal and formal evaluations of their work and request his ideas and assistance for improvement. Such teachers are at ease with department chairmen or in the presence of principals and superintendents. They often organize small groups for social or professional purposes, usually inviting staff members from several departments in the school. They do not need the security of like-minded groups or cliques.

Recent Studies of Teacher Morale

Twenty school systems were surveyed between 1949 and 1957 by the Division of Surveys and Field Studies, George Peabody College for Teachers, to determine what factors affect teacher morale. Reporting on the returns from the surveys, Harap found that the most common causes of poor morale were inadequate salaries, large classes, poor administration, lack of a daily period of relaxation, unsatisfactory plant and buildings, lack of teaching materials and equipment, absence of democratic procedure, lack of cooperation between the board of education and the public, impoverished social and recreational life, and inadequate tenure provisions.

Harap studied one school system in depth in which morale was good. Characteristics of this system judged to be concomitants of strong morale were high regard for leadership, both in the system at large and in the individual schools; a relatively good salary schedule; a considerable number of small classes; short but welcome periods of released time for conferences with parents; a professional atmosphere; and a record of several years of consistent educational progress in the school.[7]

Studies by Wynn and DeRemer showed that the quality of administration is a powerful determinant of faculty morale; that there is a high correlation between teacher morale and the quality of pupil-teacher relationships; that there is a strong relationship between teachers' morale and their perception of their principals and boards of education; that convergence of role expectation is associated with high morale, and divergence with low morale. Wynn recommends the application of sophisticated research methodology to probe relationships between teacher morale and such variables as acts of administrative behavior, aspects of personnel policy, new ventures in staff utilization, and organizational characteristics.[8]

In an extensive survey of the professional literature from 1944 to 1961, Metfessel and Shea have identified fifty areas of teacher frus-

---

[7] Henry Harap, "Many Factors Affect Teacher Morale," *Nation's Schools,* 63:55–57 (June, 1959).

[8] D. Richard Wynn and Richard W. DeRemer, "Staff Utilization, Development, and Evaluation," *Review of Educational Research,* 31:399 (Oct., 1961).

tration which the writers feel are often overlooked as contributing factors to low morale; they include inadequate physical facilities and materials, lack of auxiliary or supportive services, overload of teaching and extra duties, lack of democratic leadership, personal aspects, and community conditions including unwillingness to support the school system in terms of ability to pay.[9] Supervisory behavior is also related to morale.[10]

In an ambitious research study Redefer and a group of associates at New York University developed a unique opinionnaire that yielded a Morale Tendency Score, and studied faculty morale in twenty-four school systems involving more than five thousand teachers. Several generalizations were established: (1) Morale and quality of education are closely related; (2) a teacher's morale and his supervisor's rating of him are closely related; (3) salary and salary schedules, although important, do not wholly determine the individual's or the faculty's morale; (4) "problem" schools do not necessarily cause poor morale; and (5) morale is not closely related to marital status, sex, age, grade-level assignment, or socioeconomic status of the school community. Teachers who scored high on Redefer's Morale Tendency measure also rated these values high: They (1) would encourage both sons and daughters to go into the teaching profession; (2) would place teaching higher in the community's esteem; (3) had more positive attitudes toward professional colleagues; (4) had fewer personal problems of meaninglessness, of loneliness, or of unsatisfactory dealings with authority; (5) got more satisfaction from teaching; (6) carried on more research to improve their teaching; (7) had taken more professional studies in the last five years; (8) had joined, voluntarily, more professional organizations; (9) participated more actively in professional organizations; (10) felt less fatigued at the end of the school day; and (11) were less bothered by routines and professional ruts.[11]

Good morale is definitely related to good salaries and satisfaction with the leadership of a school; low morale stems from low salaries, diminution of professional status, and lack of materials. Schools

---

[9] Newton S. Metfessel and John T. Shea, "Fifty Often Overlooked Areas of Teacher Frustration," *American School Board Journal,* 142:16–17 (June, 1961).
[10] Arthur Blumberg and Wilford A. Weber, "Teacher Morale as a Function of Perceived Supervisory Behavior Style," *Journal of Educational Research,* 62:109–113 (Nov., 1968).
[11] Frederick L. Redefer, "Factors That Affect Teacher Morale," *Nation's Schools,* 63:59–62 (Feb., 1959).

that maintain high morale have less teacher absenteeism and greater creative productivity. School administrators and supervisors can best build morale by keeping lines of communication open between themselves and staff and by setting good examples for creativity. Democratic administration will offset other factors tending to produce low morale. Specific means of achieving good morale include a staff relations committee, an open-door policy, and a unifying school project.

An opinion poll conducted by the Research Division of the National Education Association in 1966, reported the factors that encourage teachers and those that discourage teachers. Teachers become discouraged when the attitude of parents and pupils is negative and encouraged when it is positive. Adequate instructional materials, staff to support the work, and funds to underwrite the program operate as morale builders; if these are inadequate, as inhibitors. Good administration was fifth among the factors which encouraged teachers, but poor administration was third as a cause of discouragement. Salary was an important factor in morale.[12]

Chase sampled over two thousand teachers in forty-three states and found that autonomy in one's work was very important to morale (freedom to plan and the opportunity to participate in educational planning, setting salaries, and providing adequate facilities).[13]

It is something of a mystery how teachers manage to keep their morale up when one considers the great variety of pressures on them. There is a constant insistence on efficiency; teachers now work longer days and years, prepare more reports and do more paper work, and take part in more inservice education. There are pressures from state agencies, from federal project directors, from the school's hierarchy to modify objectives, to use video tapes, to use new curriculum guides, to help in the tax campaign, and finally to evaluate and be evaluated. All these things, coupled with a long list of requirements and regulations, do not leave much autonomy, unfortunately. As if in self-defense, teachers in Chase's study added two factors to the maintenance of morale: opportunities for participating in decision making and excellent leadership.

---

[12] NEA Research Division, "Teacher Morale," *NEA Journal*, 55:55 (Dec., 1966).
[13] Francis S. Chase, "Factors for Satisfaction in Teaching," *Phi Delta Kappan*, 33:127–132 (Nov., 1951).

Implications of Teacher Morale Studies for Supervision

Such findings clearly point to a strong relationship between morale and quality of instruction and imply a challenge to supervision. The summary below consists of (1) factors causing low morale and (2) suggestions for improving morale. The latter could form the nucleus of a significant inservice program.

Factors Causing Low Morale	*Suggestions for Steps Toward Improvement*
Financial and personnel practices and policies are unsatisfactory.	Teachers, supervisors, administrators, lay persons work cooperatively to solve basic financial problems.
Salaries are inadequate; sick leave and retirement programs poor; recruitment practices poor. Overload on the job includes too much extracurricular duty, too much clerical duty, and insufficient time to plan and prepare adequately, or to teach. Promotional policies are unsatisfactory. No subventions for out-of-town meetings are offered. Merit plans are imposed. There is no adequate scheme for recognition of good teaching, little security, and no recent (or only nominal) increment in salary.	Attention is given to views of all parties. Consultants are brought in. Salary programs of comparable school systems are studied. Adult education in the economics of education is promoted. Aides, lay helpers, and instructional secretaries assist teachers with clerical work. Time is allotted to do the job of preparation, and excellent use is made of communication. More autonomy for teachers is provided. Financial help, from lay groups, PTA's, business and industry, is made available. Fringe benefits are increased.
Physical plant, facilities, materials are inadequate.	Teachers are included when physical facilities, materials, and equipment are being planned and purchased.
Instructional supplies are hard to obtain, the library is out-of-date, mimeographing and duplicating services are inadequate, test materials are minimal. The teachers' work-	Physical facilities are built or remodeled to meet the demands of new curricular developments, are custom-made

Factors Causing Low Morale   *Suggestions for Steps Toward Improvement*

room is inadequate and lacks reference books and materials. Plant facilities are unsatisfactory, and audio-visual equipment is not available when needed. Parking space is scarce.

for each subject and each grade level. An instructional materials concept expands the former library concept. Teachers have opportunities to become aware of the new electronic media and how to use them; new printed matter and instructional materials of all kinds are publicized and made available for screening and use by teachers. Plans are developed for soliciting nonschool support for equipment.

Strong, democratic educational leadership is lacking.

Team or cooperative attitudes of teachers are missing. Inservice education is seen as leading to salary increments rather than professional development. There is lack of leadership in improving instruction, and lack of immediate and long-range goal orientation. Faculty and staff have too many isolates. Administration is poor. Participation in policy development is nonexistent, and expected leadership behavior is not in evidence. There is little confidence in professional leaders. Communication is impeded. Goals and aims are not clearly defined, nor is it apparent that they may be achieved.

Attention is given to development of leadership and use of group dynamics.

Teachers participate in selection of persons for leadership positions. Programs of orientation and growth are initiated for leadership personnel. Two-way communication is developed, up and down and laterally within the school; cooperation in decision making involves all who have a contribution to make; action is taken after all involved understand what has to be done and have been asked for their help. Teaching is seen as a collective effort so that sharing and teamwork predominate rather than development of star actors. Sensitivity training is used. Small informal groups can be morale builders.

Factors Causing Low Morale	*Suggestions for Steps Toward Improvement*
Community conditions contribute to poor teacher morale.	Attention is given to school-community relations.
There is lack of an appreciative attitude on the part of the parents and community; community is unwilling to support the schools in terms of ability to pay. Attitudes of pupils are poor. Opportunities for intellectual, cultural, and social interaction are poor. The community attempts to dictate what is to be taught, and to control teacher behavior in private life; teachers are not permitted really to belong to their community.	A thorough study is made of the field of communication and school public relations. Personnel are assigned leadership in this area. Every employee of the school sees himself as a responsible, well-informed public relations agent for better cooperation. Lay citizens and school representatives cooperatively establish the goals of the schools.

Supervision which considers these factors and diligently tries to improve the situation will at the same time be contributing to better staff morale. When teachers recognize that they are actively involved, that their ideas are carefully considered, that discernible progress is being made, their morale should rise.

Causes Relate to Effects

Newly appointed supervisor Ira Tate, after only a few days on the job, recognized that the morale of the teachers in the district was not good. As he continued to learn the intricacies of his position, he determined to attack directly the morale factor as his first major task.

He polled the teaching staff and identified a group of competent teachers who were willing to serve on an advisory committee. Mr. Tate reasoned that he must first provide the machinery and set the stage for the teachers themselves to determine what must be done. He would then do all in his power to make it possible for the ensuing recommendations to be carried out by the teachers themselves whenever possible. In the meantime, he outlined his plan to the superintendent and received assurance of support from that quarter. Was Mr. Tate really doing enough to "get at" the morale problem?

Summary

Morale is the individual's state of mind or attitude, conditioned by what he perceives as the difference between his goals and his present situation. The social climate in which teachers operate affects their morale. The kinds of groups in which they participate and the nature and quality of their activities do too.

Economic factors are important in the development of morale, and numerous ways to reward the creative teacher or group leader are being tried. A satisfying intellectual climate aids morale. The working conditions under which the teacher is asked to function also play a part.

Low morale is costly. It is accompanied by frustration, hostility, and sometimes aggression as well as lowered productivity. There is a close relationship between morale and the quality of instruction. The supervisor should be alert to signs of low morale and should be prepared to initiate action for improvement when needed.

Problems for Group Discussion

Analyze the following situations. In each, identify supervisory principles representing sound theory, if any are included. What are the basic elements which made a difference? How would you have approached the situation?

1. The principal held his faculty meetings in the little theater with its theater-type fastened-down seats. The room was rather dark and created an audience atmosphere. Smoking and soft drinks were not permitted. The net results were limited interaction and maximum direction from the principal.

The supervisor noticed the undesirable atmosphere and suggested to the principal that the next faculty meeting be held in the cafeteria so that the teachers could face each other around tables to discuss ideas. He also asked to have coffee and soft drinks available and proposed that the faculty be permitted to smoke. The result was a marked improvement in the quality of the meeting. The principal noticed the better teaching morale and patterned his future faculty meetings after this example.

2. The language arts supervisor, in a meeting with all secondary English teachers, discussed the district homework policy, indicating that many teachers were not complying with it. He failed, however, to explain how the policy should be interpreted and how the teacher could discover when he had assigned the correct amount of homework. He

did emphatically state that the teachers should correct their faults. As a result of confused directives, the morale of the English teachers dropped sharply. What new problems did the supervisor create for himself? How would you suggest he could get back on the track?

Selected Readings

Anderson, Lester W. "Teacher Morale and Student Achievement," *Journal of Educational Research,* 46:693–698 (May, 1953).

Blumberg, Arthur and Wilford A. Weber. "Teacher Morale as a Function of Perceived Supervisory Behavior Style," *Journal of Educational Research,* 62:109–113 (Nov., 1968).

Call, R. V. "Faculty and Morale," *Journal of Higher Education,* 29:267–271 (May, 1958).

Chase, Francis S. "Factors for Satisfaction in Teaching," *Phi Delta Kappan,* 33:127–132 (Nov., 1951).

Cook, Lloyd, and Elaine Cook. *School Problems in Human Relations.* New York: McGraw-Hill Book Company, 1957.

Harap, Henry. "Many Factors Affect Teacher Morale," *Nation's Schools,* 63:55–57 (June, 1959).

Melbo, Irving R., and David W. Martin. "Building Morale in Teachers of the Deprived," in *The Educationally Retarded and Disadvantaged.* Chicago: University of Chicago Press, 1967, Chap. XV.

Metfessel, Newton S., and John T. Shea. "Fifty Often Overlooked Areas of Teacher Frustration," *American School Board Journal,* 142:16–17 (June, 1961).

National Association of Manufacturers. *Case Book of Employee Communications in Action.* New York: Industrial Relations Division, NAM, 1952.

NEA Research Division. "Teacher Morale," *NEA Journal,* 55:55 (Dec., 1966).

Ogden, Lowell, and Emory Stoops. "Staff Morale — What Is It? How Do We Get It?" *Educational Administration and Supervision,* 43:487–491 (Dec., 1967).

Rand, M. John, and Fenwick English. "Toward a Differentiated Teaching Staff," *Phi Delta Kappan,* 49:264–268 (Jan., 1968).

Redefer, Frederick L. "Factors That Affect Teacher Morale," *Nation's Schools,* 63:59–62 (Feb., 1959).

Unruh, Adolph. "Can Men Afford to Teach?" *Phi Delta Kappan,* 33:138–139 (Nov., 1951).

Whyte, William F. "The Social Structure of the Restaurant," *American Journal of Sociology,* 54:302–308 (Jan., 1949).

Wynn, D. Richard, and DeRemer, Richard W. "Staff Utilization, Development, and Evaluation," *Review of Educational Research,* 31:399 (Oct., 1961).

four

•

Human Relations in Supervision

Supervision under some earlier organizational schemes proved unsuccessful partly because of poor human relations practices. Teachers rebelled against the secret memoranda, rating sheets, and authoritarian practices, which negated the ideals of human worth and dignity, freedom and equality. Many teachers thought of these practices as antiprofessional. Teachers often left supervisory conferences cowed but resentful, and perhaps less professional and less effective.

The training of supervisors, consultants, or curriculum directors today places strong emphasis upon the human relations point of view. This chapter briefly treats five major topics involved in human relations: some social-psychological concepts useful in supervision, some elements in human relations, bureaucracy, the use of ideals as a basis for human relations, and human relations in schools.

Some Social-Psychological Concepts Useful in Supervision

Recent studies in social psychology provide an abundance of suggestions for developing better human relations not only in supervision but in the entire school situation. The human relations point of view reminds one that education proceeds only through people and through interacting with people. For the supervisor, a knowledge of technical skills is not enough.

The supervisor today must recognize that he lives and works in a community made up of diverse groups and of individuals with a multitude of concerns, interests, and needs. His task is to coordinate the many divergent pressures and movements of individuals and groups in a common direction whenever possible. One thing above all else must be uppermost in his mind: He is operating in a social structure, with and through people. It is impossible for him to withdraw into seclusion and function at all effectively.

A few selected behavioral concepts described below illustrate the importance of interacting with people.

Social Orientation

A person becomes socially oriented as he becomes an accepted and accredited member of a society. A new participant must find common meanings.[1]

For a teacher, especially a beginner, social orientation includes learning as much as he can about the actual work of teaching as quickly as possible. He must also learn to interact with the local faculty and staff for he will find in such relationships many of his satisfactions. Too, he is being accepted into the profession and is expected to share its problems.

For the supervisor, social orientation includes the development of a satisfactory rapport with the school faculty. The present professional climate is cool toward an authoritarian supervisor, and it most certainly demands one able to put democratic principles into practice. Interaction programs operating within the social organization become, then, key ingredients in the supervisory function.[2]

Perception

Perception plays a major role in human relations. How people see themselves in given social contexts, and also how they see others in similar social contexts, is important in supervision. It is not enough for a supervisor to have a pleasing personality and to be highly competent. He must also be aware of the group's perception of him as compared with his own perceptions of his role and that of the faculty with which he is working, or he will experience difficulties

---

[1] Albert E. Scheflen, "Human Communication: Behavioral Programs and Their Integration in Interaction," *Behavioral Science,* 13:44–45 (1968).

[2] Robert J. Havighurst and Bernice L. Neugarten, *Society and Education* (Boston: Allyn & Bacon, 1962), pp. 75–85.

in effecting any significant changes in instruction or in the curriculum.[3]

The concept of perception is crucial to the successful outcome of the supervisor's mission within his district. Teachers will react to him and to the instructional program according to how they perceive him and his status position. At the same time, most supervisors tend to function in terms of the way they perceive teachers, themselves, and their particular role assignment. If all parties are aware of and in agreement with these roles, mutual harmony will prevail and progress can be expected. If there are discrepancies in perceptions, conflicts will develop and progress will lag. It becomes the responsibility of the supervisor to make certain that whenever possible these various perceptions are compatible and generally understood by all.

Anxiety

Old-style supervision rested on the hope of bringing results through stresses of anxiety and insecurity. Research indicates that high levels of anxiety uniformly depress performance and low or moderate anxiety sometimes improves it.[4] Logically, then, the normal anxieties of attaining mutually accepted goals should be more likely to produce desirable results than situations which involve personal threats.

Considerable research has recently tended to support the premise that the most effective operations in the long run are those in which low-trust unilateral decision making is replaced by high-trust participative decision making involving all components of the system. The modern supervisor will modify and neutralize objectionable anxieties of teachers by capitalizing upon strengths. The weaknesses of the teacher also suggest the "stuff" for mutual, long-range goals. A rational attack on such deficiencies will place the supervisor in a position to offer the greatest service to the teacher. The edu-

---

[3] Reba M. Burnham and Martha L. King, *Supervision in Action* (Washington: Association for Supervision and Curriculum Development, 1961), p. 39. Arthur Blumberg and Edmund Amidon, "Teacher Perceptions of Supervisor-Teacher Interaction," *Administrative Notebook,* Midwest Administration Center, University of Chicago, 14:1–4 (Sept., 1965).

[4] Philip J. Runkel, "The Social-Psychological Basis of Human Relations," *Review of Educational Research,* 29:324 (Oct., 1959).

cational supervisor can learn much from his counterpart in business and industry. Industrial and business research has led to modification of past practice, resulting in reduced anxiety on the part of workers, which, in turn, contributes to maintaining productivity. Gibb and others have provided a clear, positive position on emergent leadership for the supervisor which promotes increased concern for good human relations.[5]

Interpersonal Relations

The complexity of the interpersonnel relations involved in the supervisor's role begins to be apparent when one considers not only the formal groups but also the informal groups of which he may be a part. The following incomplete listing indicates the variety, number, and identity of these groups. It can be predicted that at some time a supervisor will be required to interact with

The entire school system	Boys and girls
The central administration	Nonteaching professionals (medical doctors, dentists, psychiatrists, speech therapists, other specialists)
Office staff	
Building staff (one or more)	
Secretaries	
Building administrators (principals, assistant principals)	
Consultants in the system	PTA and similar groups
Department heads	City officials
Veteran teachers	City employees (park and recreation, fire and police protection, etc.)
Younger teachers	
Various teacher groups	
Maintenance staff	County professional groups (health association, youth commission, etc.)
Bus drivers	
Cafeteria workers	
Board of education	State department of education
	Pressure groups
	Taxpayers
	Teacher aides
	Student teachers

How he meets these groups should be a direct reflection of his democratic educational philosophy and his acceptance of the importance of the good human relations attitude. The autocratic super-

---

[5] Jack R. Gibb, "Dynamics of Leadership: Defensive or Emergent," *Vital Speeches of the Day*, 33:375–380 (Apr. 1, 1967).

visor of yesteryear could not be expected to respond in a manner similar to the supervisor of today who recognizes and practices good human relations.

How to Reduce Anxiety

Stan Kent has been hired to replace retiring Supervisor Abe Moses and will report for duty August 15. Stan has all summer to prepare for the new position and he plans to use his time wisely. The shift from teaching senior English requires a major readjustment in many ways.

As he contemplates what approach to employ during his initial year as a supervisor, Stan resolves to keep in mind several things. First, he must provide for a broad pattern of interaction with all the secondary teachers. His own reaction to Mr. Moses' style was that there was entirely too much basic decision making within the confines of the supervisor's office. "This year things will be different if I have my way," Stan thinks.

Next, as he develops rapport with teachers, he intends to outline clearly what he feels are his charges as supervisor for the Elktown district. He is going to "level" with teachers and report on the conversations with Superintendent Tompkins when the two discussed the position prior to Stan's acceptance. Whether they all agree or not, he wants to be certain that the teachers understand what is expected of him and what he thinks his role is. They will then be less likely to consider him a failure if he neglects what they want done and concentrates on some other aspect of instruction. Stan considers this a method of establishing "life insurance" because he fully means to develop his program in concert with the teachers. The eventual result will be a welding of all ideas into a workable consensus.

Lastly, Stan wants to establish new working relationships with the teachers on a "more professional level." That is, he will attempt to stimulate teachers and encourage them to set realistic goals for their own improvement but will disassociate himself completely from Mr. Moses' pattern of writing evaluation reports twice a year for each teacher. He is firmly convinced that he will thus reduce the anxiety level to the point where something worthwhile can result and teachers will have less need for sedatives. Stan starts his preplanning by listing some of the groups which he should contact prior to the opening of the new term.

Does this represent the start of supervisory preplanning or fantasy on the part of an untried supervisor-in-name-only?

Common Applications of Human Relations to Supervision

Cooperation

Several research studies have shown that groups in which members perceive a facilitative interdependence manifest higher cohesiveness, greater interest in the group task, greater desire to complete the task, and higher morale than groups in which such perception of interdependence is absent. Studies have also shown that cooperative situations lead to greater productivity than competitive situations.[6]

Genuine cooperation is not manipulation; the faculty, therefore, will not necessarily do the supervisor's bidding. When each person makes what contribution he can toward the solution of a shared problem, and is willing to accept the result regardless of whether his ideas prevail, he is on the way to cooperation. The good supervisor is aware of the importance of strong cooperative endeavors in present-day educational practice and is constantly working to strengthen them in every way and at all times. The concept of mutual respect between two professionals is a far cry from the earlier idea of the superior-inferior relationship and is a major improvement in recent educational administration.

Cooperation has to be a two-way street. For example, the supervisor needs the assistance of teachers in order to put into operation any kind of revised curriculum program in the high school. Without the cooperation of the social science department, for example, he can scarcely accomplish his goal. At the same time, the teachers may feel unable to prepare behavioral objectives for themselves and their various courses. They should feel free to ask the supervisor for help in learning how to develop this necessary skill without fear of being "downgraded" on the next evaluation report coming from the principal's office.

Good Manners

Everyday good manners are a part of human relations.[7] Good manners consist of being courteous, gracious, friendly, and "slow to anger." They require humor, social sensitivity, and the discipline

---

[6] Bertram H. Raven, "The Dynamics of Groups," *Review of Educational Research*, 29:332–334 (Oct., 1959).

[7] John Dewey, *Democracy and Education* (New York: The Macmillan Company, 1923), p. 21.

of patience. They are achieved through perception of the other person's viewpoint and through genuine interest in the welfare and concerns of others rather than constant attention to one's own objectives. Being an attentive, courteous listener is definitely called for. The good supervisor is constantly attempting to improve his own performance.

Some inexperienced supervisors are fearful of exhibiting even basic good manners on the assumption that such behavior might be construed as weakness. They attempt to establish themselves in their new positions by being officious, arrogant, and generally obnoxious. The standard comment from teachers is, "He was a nice fellow when we taught together last year, but now he is different and I neither like nor trust what I see." A schism develops where none should be.

The Democratic Approach

The democratic approach is based upon group work, group responsibility, and individual leadership. It is shared authority.

Supervision should generate leadership within the group. Emerging leaders can carry much of the burden of improving the curriculum and the conditions surrounding learning. The supervisor should not fear competition from these leaders, for if he does he will quickly lose his effectiveness and dilute theirs. Rather, he should encourage the new leaders, earn their respect and cooperation, and weld them into a team. Teamwork is one goal of supervision; a team can accomplish more than one person.

Teachers are helped to become team members through team planning, sharing, and evaluating. Favoritism is avoided; each teacher is made to feel that his individual abilities, needs, and interests are important. Agendas for meetings are cooperatively planned. Credit for a job well done is given to teachers who did the work.

In schools in which supervisors use the democratic approach one can observe more pooling of materials, resources, techniques, and experiences in solving problems. Not only will the supervisor make use of democratic practices, but he will encourage teachers to do likewise in their classes.

Who Gets the Credit?

The physical education departments of the four high schools in River City sometimes appear to represent a mutual admiration society as they work with Supervisor Strong. When he is asked about the physical fitness program which has received so much national recognition, he immediately names the various teachers who developed the program and made it succeed. When in turn these teachers are interviewed, they repeatedly cite the support and assistance they had from Mr. Strong and indicate their fervent appreciation of his efforts on their behalf. First reactions sometimes are that this talk smacks of hypocrisy, but further investigation shows that all are sincere in their remarks and that a good example of democracy in action is present in River City.

Professional Ethics

Human relations are the core of professional ethics. Certain ways of behaving toward each other have become generally accepted in the profession and are normally expected. It is on the basis of these common expectations that administration is built and that interaction takes place. Professional ethics demand that all staff members be treated as peers, that public criticism of colleagues be avoided, and that confidences be respected. Everywhere, at all times, the supervisor works for the improvement of professional ethics.

The individual who learns of confidential matters, both personal and involving professional practices, and who shares them with others will never become a successful supervisor. Some people find it difficult to respect a confidence; no supervisor should fail to honor a confidence.

Likewise, it is very important for the supervisor to behave as a peer in his relations with teachers. A supervisor's "talking down" to a teacher can be as disastrous as a teacher's "talking down" to the senior English class. While this point seems rather elementary, it unfortunately has been the downfall of many would-be supervisors.

Recognition

Among the basic psychological needs is recognition. Sometimes people need recognition so intensely that they drive themselves to extremes in order to obtain it. Recognition properly accorded helps to maintain self-respect; it builds status within a given group; it provides job satisfaction.

Research bearing on human relations done at the Hawthorne Works of the Western Electric Company between 1927 and 1932 has been widely discussed in the literature of business administration and social psychology.[8] It led to many studies of informal social organizations and social hierarchies. We do not intend to describe these well-known studies in detail; our purpose is to draw some inferences for supervision.

In the Hawthorne studies, production was the constant factor while the variable consisted of changes in working conditions: introduction of rest periods, lunch breaks in the forenoon and afternoon, shorter days, changes in illumination, and others. But there was a difference in the type of supervision used in experimental and control groups. The first group was brought into the experiment in various ways and there was interaction between management and the group. The second group experienced no such interaction, and it quickly organized to resist management and to enforce its own standards. The first group was productive regardless of the changes in working conditions.

Subsequent studies of the Hawthorne data have indicated that nonphysical factors were operating: the importance to the individual of "belongingness" and of his membership in the group; the importance of recognizing the worker through direct communication, and through bringing him into the planning of work schedules. At Hawthorne the workers responded by turning out more work than the company thought possible. The lesson of recognition is one of the enduring results of these studies.

Recognition must be a basic component in the human relations program of the supervisor. In a day when money is so difficult for school districts to obtain and when there is so much pressure for increased salaries, personal recognition is more critical than ever. The status that the teacher can achieve within his building, his district, and his state can become vital to his professional self-concept and his attitude in general. Teachers who are doing outstanding work should receive appreciation and no one is in a better position to offer it than the instructional supervisor.

Shared Decision Making

A perceptive visitor to a school can soon sense whether the teachers are adequately represented in the decision-making process.

---

[8] George C. Homans, "The Western Electric Researches," in S. D. Haslett, ed., *Human Factors in Management* (New York: Harper & Brothers, 1951), p. 15.

If they are, the enthusiasm for the job that comes with sharing of responsibility and power will be evident. When teachers help to make important decisions on such matters as curriculum development, planning physical facilities, and setting up salary schedules, a cooperative attitude tends to permeate their classrooms. Their students also are often asked to share in planning and working toward improved learning.[9] The good supervisor will so plan his activities that teachers do in fact have the opportunity to engage in meaningful and purposeful decision making.

Too often the supervisor mistrusts decision making by teachers yet asks them for decision acceptance and support. Democratic supervision, however, contends that professionals who have the facts before them can be expected to make a reasonable decision. Supervisors who take this viewpoint will be willing to share the decision-making process with teachers and will agree in good conscience to the conclusion reached.

Empathy

Recently, much attention has been given to the necessity of maintaining an identification relationship with the teaching staff. Unless the supervisor can show empathy — that is, demonstrate the ability to "put himself in the other person's shoes" — he will always be somewhat ineffective. The kind of relationship expected today demands the mutual respect and acceptance of the various professionals — the classroom teacher and the supervisor especially.

Democratic Leadership Generates Problems

Mr. Brown was a strong advocate of democratic supervision. He realized that to achieve his goal, emphasis on good human relations was imperative. Accordingly, he set out to build a positive rapport with staff members throughout the district. He deliberately involved many individuals in the decision-making process. He actively cooperated with teachers and encouraged a cooperative relationship among all the teachers. He worked to establish an atmosphere in which individual achievement was recognized and encouraged. The words "my," "I," "they" became "ours" and "we." He tried hard to eliminate the feeling of teachers that when the supervisor made a suggestion he was really stating a dictum.

---

[9] Larry L. Cummings and Gary William Mize, "Risk Taking and Organizational Creativity," *Personnel Administration*, 31:38 (Jan.-Feb., 1968).

Mr. Brown knew that when the staff members recognized him for his capabilities, not for his supervisory position, he could really become effective. If Mr. Brown were new in this situation, how long would it take him to achieve his goals?

Bureaucracy and Human Relations

The following episode illustrates a situation which happens too often.

Bureaucracy in Operation

Mr. Queen was a social studies teacher in a large city system. Feeling that the textbooks and outlines given him for his course in American Problems were stale and academic, he suggested that a change in instructional materials was badly needed, but accomplished nothing. Desperate for relevance in the curriculum, he purchased thirty copies of a paperback at his own expense and passed them out to his class. Student interest began to improve, and Mr. Queen was convinced he was gathering evidence that a change in curriculum would be beneficial.

About this time the social studies supervisor visited the class and observed the use of the paperback. Without a word to Mr. Queen, the supervisor went to the principal's office, reported what he had seen, and reminded the principal of the system's rules on introducing materials into classes. The principal immediately called upon Mr. Queen and informed him he was breaking the rule which required that all instructional materials be approved by the Central Curriculum Committee; until that was done he could not use this paperback. Also, he said, he, the principal, had the authority to confiscate the paperbacks. However, the Central Curriculum Committee would meet during the summer months, and the paperback could be introduced for consideration at that time. Then the principal left to continue his appointed rounds.

Perhaps one should not be too harsh in his criticism of the principal in the episode above, for he too was bound by rules and regulations. Some principals would have solved the problem differently, but here we have an "organization" man. Since the supervisor reported the situation to the principal, the principal in turn could be expected to report it to the official at the next higher level.

Large school systems have more of the characteristics of a bureaucracy than small ones and are more resistant to change. Bureaucracies are impersonal in management and depend largely on rules to keep the system going smoothly and as efficiently as possible. The management jealously guards the decision-making function, delegating it carefully and providing the conditions and limits of operation.

The problem is one of deciding between efficiency and democracy. If each of a hundred social science teachers developed his own course in American Problems, the system might well receive considerable criticism of its inefficiency, especially from parents whose children transfer from one school to another. At the same time, democracy demands independence of action and some control by teachers over what they do in the classroom. Excellence cannot be accomplished by fiat, but just a few words can stop initiative, innovation, and the desire for progress. Innovation, if desirable, must be accompanied with security and autonomy sufficient to do the job.

A bureaucracy contains both formal and informal structures by means of which the work is accomplished. The two often reinforce each other and become antagonistic only when the goals of the individual member and those of the organization are dissimilar. In the episode above, the goals of the organization and the instructor were probably similar: quality instruction. In this case the supervisor could have initiated a small informal structure to conduct a program on a trial basis. He was, however, bureaucracy oriented. Hence his insistence that rules be followed to the letter.

The bureaucratic structure may well have denied Mr. Queen the opportunity of engaging in meaningful, creative work and developing greater self-respect. It is very possible that many other teachers in the same district have been "turned off" in a similar manner. Some big city systems are not very innovative but rather rigid and traditional. The productive supervisor attempts to find ways to resist inhibition through bureaucracy and to encourage originality in the classroom.

Ideals Form a Basis for Human Relations

The human relations point of view must be soundly established in supervision lest it degenerate into the usual platitudes. From a complex background of attitudes, appreciations, knowledge, concepts, and values, a philosophy of personal and social action emanates.

Seven ideals are here suggested as a basis for human relations in supervision: the use of reason and intelligence, community, participation, variety, human worth and dignity, freedom, and progress. The presence or absence of these ideals helps determine supervisory behavior. It is not to be inferred that this is a closed system; ideals may be added or eliminated.

The Use of Reason and Intelligence

The use of reason in solving educational problems contrasts with trial and error methods or decisions made on the basis of how one feels. Supervisors who utilize the method of reason must be open-minded, have a desire to seek the truth, and learn to suspend judgment at times. Most people find this process difficult when they are emotionally involved in a problem or in its solution.

It is by the use of reason that we distinguish between fact and rumor, between truth and rationalizations. Gossip and propaganda yield when attacked by reason. If the supervisor hears that Mr. Malcolm has lost control of his pupils, or that the new English teacher is not employing the approved course of study and units, he calmly pursues these stories until every scrap of information has been discovered. Then he sets about solving the problem in a methodical way, showing neither favoritism nor hostility.

In education, as in law or science, reason becomes a tool for solving problems and a social process (reasoning together) for directing progress. If one wishes to reexamine, as is periodically necessary, any of the educational platitudes, assumptions, or propositions, this is the only technique that will yield valid results. Research as a method of reason will be discussed in a later chapter.

Community

A community is a group of persons having in common certain characteristics, interests, objectives, language, and historical and cultural heritage. A community is held together by a variety of bonds: the perceptions individuals have of themselves and their groups, their region or locality, their economic and sometimes religious ties, and so on. The concept of community is useful in understanding the growth and development of the individual, for he is a part of some group and reflects some of its characteristics. His ideals and values are likely to mirror many ideals and values of the group in which he was reared. Yet a teacher's communities often widen from local and parochial to worldwide circles, and from the present to both the heritage of the past and projections of the future.

The concept is also useful for recognizing subgroups and sub-cultures. Within the larger society are innumerable smaller groups: the American Legion, the machinists' local, the community of scholars in an institution of higher learning, for instance. So also within any faculty there are smaller groups, cliques, and factions, whose members have in common such things as social class, amount and kind of education, types of skills, and objectives. Sometimes conditions of work or a belief that members have been discriminated against or otherwise unfairly treated will make the group adhesive.

The supervisor might originate and sponsor groups for a purpose. With others, he might prepare the objectives, suggest projects, provide rewards and satisfactions, and thus avail himself of the advantages of the activities of like-minded individuals. Advantages include support for his ideas, an entrée into the local communications network, allies in the change process. Once a beginning has been made, a group can be led to become a larger community of thinkers, innovators, or scholars. Yet the supervisor had best be careful to develop groups which have a direct relationship to their own destiny. If he does so, he is providing sound educational leadership.

Participation

Participation in the culture is the process by which an infant ultimately becomes a part of that culture as a functioning adult. As he begins to share in the folkways, the beliefs, the mores, the social, political, and religious actions and ceremonies of his group, he grows into social usefulness. Involvement usually results in personal satisfactions, personal and social identification, and a feeling of belonging. These in turn develop loyalty to the culture, give rise to vested interests in the society, and initiate development toward the guardianship function.

Much of the modern unrest in education comes from lack of participation. Teachers have for some years felt left out of the decision-making process and have determined to force the issue. Students likewise have felt their exclusion from the decision-making process and have shown their displeasure. In spite of the fact that leaders in education have been critical of the curriculum, of teaching methods, and of the administration, not enough basic or lasting change has been made. Many educators believe that the rash of tax referendum failures in recent years is due to a lack of genuine participation in planning and policy development by citizens and patrons of the school. While this is not the only reason, it is probably a very important one.

Learning, growing, and personality development are all influenced by participation in appropriate activities. Participation fosters strength of purpose, social skills, human understanding, and self-confidence. Teachers should be encouraged to grow in self-direction, in professional competence, and in the knowledge of curriculum. To this end they must be involved from the beginning in such activities as planning for curriculum change, planning for in-service education, and planning for and designing better methods and instruments for evaluating progress.

Marge Changes Her Approach

Marge Kraft was busily doing her preplanning for next year. As she reviewed her long-range goals for the junior high English department, she reflected upon her accomplishments as the English supervisor over the past two years.

Marge had been doing some reading and considerable thinking and had reached the conclusion that much more progress might have occurred if she had used a different approach with the teachers. To be quite honest, she had made up her mind without asking anyone else and had literally rammed through the last course revision on the strength of her own persuasive abilities. She still liked the outcome, for it had been an improvement in the curriculum, but she now had less faith in the tactics.

This year she would "lay her cards on the table" and start with an honest exploration with the teachers. They would help determine what was most needed and in which priority. She would truly involve the teachers.

Will such a technique really work in practice, or is Marge giving up her responsibility?

Variety

There are 340,000 kinds of plants, ranging from some so tiny that they escape the unaided eye to the giant sequoia. The animal kingdom's 800,000 species similarly range from small to very large, from simple to very complex organisms. In human society there are different cultures and hundreds of languages and dialects. Often the variety of individuals within a classification is greater than the number of classifications. People adhere to different customs, hold unlike values, and have distinctive needs, interests, and vocations. It is to one's own system of values, beliefs, and experiences that he must look for the bases of social and political relationships, hierarchical arrangements, and social control.

The intellectual wealth, the literature, drama, and other facets of the culture of a nation are largely dependent upon the talents of its people. Opportunities for specialization and differentiation, therefore, are to be sought and exploited. A great variety of specialties and talents provides security for a society because for any emergency or problem that may arise there are resources and expertise to be applied. If variety is a reality and is encouraged, civilization is assured of a constant stream of new ideas, developments, and discoveries. In the inservice seminar or in the classroom the discussion is enriched by different ideas and questions. Variety brings enjoyment, whether pointed toward the intellect or toward the senses. That culture which demands uniformity in behavior and thought is hastening its own demise.

The supervisor who sets out to identify differing talents of teachers or to locate teachers with unique approaches to teaching faces a challenge. College and university training has forced upon students a pattern of conformity during the preservice period. When most new teachers arrive at their first teaching position, they find a rectangular room with thirty-five chairs in neat rows, long formal corridors with more cell-like rooms opening into it, prescribed teacher behaviors, and certain important taboos such as "don't rock the boat." It is often next to impossible for the newcomer to try out creative ways of applying the theory he has recently studied at the university. In addition, there may be little or no opportunity to participate in the decision-making process, and communication channels may be choked with emotionalism. When one of the authors suggested that a teacher bring a specific matter to the attention of his immediate supervisor, the teacher said he could not because the supervisor invariably became angry about such reports and refused to discuss them. It is almost useless to look for imagination, ingenuity, or creativity in situations like this; the supervisor is far removed from a supervisory setting which will not only permit variety but cherish it.

Human beings exhibit an extraordinary range of differences; sometimes they become the source of jokes or even persecution in a society. They can also become the strengths of a society. Similarly among teachers, differences may cause ostracism from the group, persecution, and separation, but the wise supervisor will find out all he can about these differences and any possibilities of turning them into social strengths. For generations children have been classified, regimented, and certified at commencement time as young people who have learned to stay in line. The same type of conformity has been expected of teachers, who, when they learned their lessons well, became "professionals." Yet conformity does not produce the kind of society or education we need in a world characterized by variety.

Many teachers honestly feel that they dare not try new ideas in their classroom for fear of criticism from their "superiors." They strive to do things as much like their neighbors as they possibly can "so the students won't be upset when they move from one class to another." The alert supervisor must constantly work against such an attitude if he really envisions instructional improvement. Since change necessary for improvement can take place only through different teacher behaviors, he must stimulate experimentation at every opportunity. As more and more teaching techniques are attempted and found satisfactory, the coveted improvement may commence.

Human Worth and Dignity

A man is valued because he is a man, considered to be the highest development in creation. His upright position permits him to view the environment to his advantage, to use his hands (a special adaptation) freely, and to divorce his sensation and attention from strictly corporeal limitations. He experiences more sensations and emotions than any other creature. Above all, he is a thinking, reasoning being, with abilities to communicate ideas, to remember, to project, and to plan for the future.

Human worth and dignity requires that the individual be respected; that his personality not be violated; and that his responsibilities, personal and professional, not be abrogated by unilateral action from the outside. The supervisor who supports this position would never march into a classroom and assume command of the class without permission from the teacher who is in charge. Protestations by administrators and supervisors to the contrary notwithstanding, teachers are treated as second-rate members of the profession in far too many instances. In a confrontation between teacher and administrator, or teacher and board of education, the teacher will rarely be permitted to win. This bureaucratic practice is now paying off in lack of initiative, resistance to change, and increasing militancy by teachers.

In the Universal Declaration of Human Rights are these words:

> . . . recognition of the inherent dignity and of the equal and inalienable rights of all members of the human family is the foundation of freedom, justice and peace in the world . . . the people of the United States have in the Charter reaffirmed their faith in fundamental human rights, in the dignity and worth of the human person . . .

The ideal of human worth and dignity is the cornerstone of human relations, and the supervisor of the future must learn to honor it. Teachers and students have discovered the meaning and desirability of power and learned how to organize and use the power of a group to obtain further power. They will no longer hesitate to confront the autocratic supervisor or administrator with their demands and, failing to achieve them, may turn to sabotage or other forms of overt rebellion.

Supervisors "caught in the middle" between the authoritarian administrator and genuine concern for the dignity of the individual teacher cannot shirk their responsibility to the person. They must, in conscience, respect the worth of each teacher and strive to work with him in a fair manner. Their concern for human relations can sometimes neutralize the negative aspects of authoritarianism.

Freedom

Personal and political freedom characterizes the American way of life. Our ideal is that Americans should be free to move about the country as they wish, to choose their residences, clothes, food, or modes of transportation without restriction. Indeed, many people believe that freedom means lack of restriction, restraint, or control by someone or some agency. But freedom really means that Americans can take action, make decisions, and produce, distribute, and consume goods. They are able to establish organizations to provide health care, education, protection, and care of the aged. When Americans actively and constructively pursue their freedom to take responsibility for managing civic and social functions, and when they provide all with the opportunities to participate in decision making and to share in the good things of life, they need not fear restrictions, restraints, and regulations. Our freedoms can be preserved only if they are consciously utilized.

It is no different in supervision and curriculum development. Most recent curriculum innovations have come from outside the school because the freedom to innovate or to improvise was not utilized within the school.

Forcing Change

In the Adams Junior High School the curriculum had not changed for a number of years. It was extremely bookish. Teachers used the traditional recitation method. Many neighboring schools, however, were experimenting with new ideas. Since neither teachers nor chairmen of departments were interested in changes, the board of education forced the issue.

A new high school was designed with one entire floor devoid of interior walls. Only movable partitions allowed the area to be divided. The administration assigned this floor to the social studies department and announced that all social studies teachers would henceforth engage in team teaching. The freedom to choose from a variety of methods and class organizations was lost because the faculty and chairmen had not exercised their options in time.

The supervisor faces a difficult task in carrying out a board-administration mandate so arbitrarily established. Lack of respect for individuals was evident in the requirement that all social studies teachers participate in a team-teaching situation. Could this dilemma have been avoided?

Wherever it exists, the freedom to have a voice in decision making, the freedom to make choices, and above all the freedom to dissent must be exercised. These freedoms are needed by teachers and supervisors if they are expected to experiment, innovate, make changes, and take risks.

Progress

Not all change is progress, but there is no progress without change. Change is man's constant companion, for better or worse. When change is toward useful ends and is given appropriate and desirable directions by reason and intelligence, it becomes progress.

Supervisors who are interested in progress should try to develop certain traits among faculty members. There should be an attitude of accepting change, a willingness to examine new ideas and innovations. There should be anticipation and expectation that new things and new ideas are exciting and potentially useful. Embedded in this attitude toward progress is a human drive to advance, to improve, and to accomplish something just a little bit better.

People have different ways of estimating progress. Some rely upon the dropout rate at the high school, a comparison of standardized test scores, the number of merit scholarships, the percentage of high school graduates who go to college, or the survival rates of students once they get to college. Some supervisors believe progress is being made when the use of audio-visual equipment and materials has increased, or when teachers are using video tapes, tape recorders, independent study for students, and other newer methods. Instead a keen interest in progress should focus attention on improved evaluation techniques which use concisely stated criteria for making adequate judgments.

Defining Progress

It was time for Supervisor Franklin to submit his annual report to Superintendent Liken. Mr. Franklin and his secretary spent three days pulling together the necessary figures and eventually produced a narrative twenty-five pages long. In his summarization Mr. Franklin pointed out the reduction of dropouts, the favorable relationship of this year's standardized achievement scores to last year's, and his explanation for the figures. (His office had effectively improved the curriculum.) He also listed the number and types of meetings held during the year as well as the involvement of teachers as evidenced by the number of calls for audio-visual equipment and materials. He built a strong case for progress in the instructional program.

Should Superintendent Liken accept the assumption of progress based on numbers such as these?

Functions of a Philosophy

Mr. Frank Teal, the Assistant Superintendent for Personnel in the Valley Air Public School System, had an important job opening to fill. The board had agreed to add a supervisor for the secondary schools, on the recommendation of Superintendent Able. Frank knew just the kind of person he wanted to hire, if the salary would attract him. The new supervisor should have the usual credentials — master's degree, a good blend of content and professional course work, perhaps general knowledge in one or two areas in addition to his discipline. These were the easy parts.

The difficult one, and at the same time the most important, was the man's philosophy. Frank knew from many years of experience that unless an educational leader, such as a supervisor or principal, had a well-defined philosophy to guide him there would sooner or later be trouble. This new supervisor must have a deep concern for the human element in his job. He must always recognize the worth of every individual. He must not be rigid in his outlook but be ready to examine a given situation on its merits. A person with a strong conviction for such basic items as these could consistently make decisions to support his philosophy and could be counted on for a rational approach to supervision.

Application of Human Relations Concept to the Current Scene

Supervisors and administrators have too often mistrusted teachers and the public in general. They have resorted to decision making in a star-chamber-like setting which effectively eliminated undesired input by others. They were thus able to obtain their own ends without being forced to defend their judgments. Such practices efficiently produced top-level decisions but did little for basic implementation. It is difficult for those with power to voluntarily relinquish it, and many rationalizations have been advanced by supervisors for failure to involve teachers.

The supervisor who is dedicated to a democratic approach and concerned with good human relations perceives his role differently from the way the supervisor who is overly concerned with maintaining his authoritarian image does. The former recognizes the potential strength of teacher involvement. He makes every effort to encourage input and to evoke feedback from the initiation of a proposal to its eventual climax. He knows that his strength comes from obtaining support from the teachers' group as well as the administration. He recognizes the need for good human relations to generate consensus and build that support.

This underlying concept enables the supervisor to fit naturally into the evolving educational scene today. Teachers restive under authoritarian treatment and discontented with the entire process of instruction have taken steps to rectify these perceived iniquities. Organized teacher groups have been made to assume some of the power formerly retained by boards and administrators. Thus administrators and supervisors are finding it necessary to modify their arbitrary decision making in favor of greater teacher involvement. Sanctions have been imposed on districts and on states. Strikes called against districts have had far-reaching effects on the educational process. Teachers are now being heard as a result of drastic pressures.

Many states have legalized professional negotiation while school boards in other states permit it without specific legislation. Soon most states will have it in some form.

Thus a new day is dawning for the supervisor. With legalized professional negotiation, his role and his tasks will undergo considerable modification and redefinition. Teachers, either directly or through representation, will be very much a part of many types of top-level decision making, including curriculum development, inservice planning, and other matters at present decided elsewhere. Such items may find their way into the negotiations contract itself. The previous informal agreement of teacher and supervisor to undertake a project may no longer be possible. In fact, the decision either to undertake a project or to eliminate one may be made at the negotiating table. Perhaps "middle management" will thus be charged with carrying out programs it had no part in planning.

The sad commentary at this point is that the American ideals of democratic action may be mandated and circumscribed by contract rather than permitted to operate freely through existing structures. What should have been a natural democratic process, therefore, may well become legislated action. The rapport between supervisor and teachers attempting to act in a democratic manner may be sorely tried, for even the best practices in human relations will then have to be checked against the negotiations contract lest an association functionary be bypassed or a procedure instituted incorrectly. In some instances the supervisor will be inhibited; in others he will be encouraged to expand his activities. He is likely to become somewhat frustrated until he adjusts to his altered role. But the democratic supervisor will adjust far more swiftly and effectively than will the authoritarian supervisor.

Supervision and personnel administration as professional fields have some functions in common. Both seek to place the best person for performing a task in a position to execute it properly. If preliminary training of the individual is needed, the supervisor and/or the administrator will offer assistance. But under a formal contract, the method of providing the assistance will be spelled out in some detail. Even such simple procedures as selecting a person for a temporary job, or for the chairmanship of a committee, may have to go through a series of offices. Examples of formal operational procedures could be cited at length, each affecting the supervisor's method of operation to some extent. Other problems will plague him if the contract accepted by the teachers' group and the board includes agreements which in effect bypass or ignore the supervisor and his efforts to improve instruction. Such an eventuality could render his office ineffective or might eliminate him from the educational scene.

This problem is sure to arise when individuals continue to operate on an elementary level of human relations and will not accept or do not understand how to use the basic principles described in the present chapter. There will be tests of strength between two power structures — teachers' organizations and boards of education. How can the supervisor manage to stay out of the line of fire or protect some vital part of the inservice program from being torpedoed out from under him? Obviously he must work with both power structures.

The authors contend that the supervisor who has established good human relations and developed rapport with classroom teachers will survive in very satisfactory fashion and, in some instances, will be strengthened by the teacher support generated through these positive working relationships at the grass roots level. Programs originated and agreed to by teachers and by such a supervisor will eventually find their way into the negotiations contract. The supervisor then will have the power of the teachers' group behind the program he wants to develop. The successful test of his ability may well be his human relations program.

Negotiations Bring Dilemmas

The teachers' organization had just negotiated an agreement with the board of education. Several items pertaining to the operation of the instructional program had been detailed.

Supervisor Jenkins was in close contact with the leadership of the teachers' group regarding these items. He felt that a clear understanding between his office and the teachers must be established immediately and he was attempting to accomplish this mutual acceptance of the task ahead. It was obvious that some practices would be eliminated or greatly revised, but in the last analysis all were eager to provide the best instructional program possible.

Mr. Jenkins wanted to develop a strong rapport with members of the organization so his work with individual members in the classroom would not be curtailed. Is there danger that Mr. Jenkins might be classified as management, and if so, what problems will he encounter?

Summary

The educational supervisor of today must steadfastly maintain a human relations point of view. He should address himself to (1) social-psychological concepts which emphasize the need for interaction, and (2) common applications to supervision, including cooperation, good manners, a democratic approach, professional ethics, recognition, shared decision making, and empathy. He should recognize that bureaucracy presents both a threat and a challenge to human relations practices of supervisors. Several methods are available to him: appropriate recognition procedures, appropriate forms of socializing, shared decision making, and good listening techniques. Ideals of the American way of life should undergird human relations. Failure to recognize the above aspects of human relations will cause the supervisor serious problems, especially as legalized professional negotiation in education develops.

Problems for Group Discussion

Analyze the following situations. In each, identify supervisory principles representing sound theory, if any are included. What are the basic elements which made a difference? How would you have approached the situation?

1. The new supervisor was selected from within the district, largely because of his number of college credits. He was not notified until August. His first move was to announce a classroom visitation schedule. This seriously perturbed the older teachers, who banded together to resist his efforts. The younger, inexperienced teachers were torn between lining up with the older group and supporting the supervisor. What problems has the supervisor created?

2. The beginning teacher was having her problems. Her room was considered quite noisy by her neighbors. In a conference she admitted

to the supervisor that she did not know what to do. He gave her the benefit of his experience.

A short time later the supervisor met with the faculty on another matter. The "problem teacher" was absent, and the supervisor discussed her case with the faculty. Several suggestions and criticisms were brought by the group. Word of the conversation quickly got back to the teacher in question, who became upset and defensive. What principles can be utilized in working out better supervisory practices?

3. Meeting with the new English teachers before the start of school, the supervisor attempted to orient them to the district and to how he wanted them to handle the problems of instruction. One new teacher asked if she could have her students read books not listed in the course of study. The answer was an emphatic "No." How else might this teacher have been answered?

Selected Readings

Association for Supervision and Curriculum Development. *Fostering Mental Health in Our Schools.* Washington: The Association, 1950.

Benne, Kenneth O., and Bozidar Muntyan. *Human Relations in Curriculum Change.* New York: Dryden Press, 1951.

Blumberg, Arthur, and Edmund Amidon. "Teacher Perceptions of Supervisor-Teacher Interaction," *Administrative Notebook,* Midwest Administration Center, University of Chicago, 14:1–4 (Sept., 1965).

Bode, Boyd H. *Democracy as a Way of Life.* New York: The Macmillan Company, 1937.

Burnham, Reba M., and Martha L. King. *Supervision in Action.* Washington: Association for Supervision and Curriculum Development, 1961.

Conradi, Catharine. "Participating in Shared Child-Adult Activities," in *Fostering Mental Health in Our Schools.* Washington: Association for Supervision and Curriculum Development, 1950.

Cummings, Larry L., and Gary William Mize. "Risk Taking and Organizational Creativity," *Personnel Administration,* 31:38 (Jan.-Feb., 1968).

Dewey, John. *Democracy and Education.* New York: The Macmillan Company, 1923.

Gibb, Jack R. "Dynamics of Leadership: Defensive or Emergent," *Vital Speeches of the Day,* 33:375–380 (Apr. 1, 1967).

Griffiths, Daniel E. *Human Relations in School Administration.* New York: Appleton-Century Crofts, 1962.

Havighurst, Robert J., and Bernice L. Neugarten. *Society and Education.* Boston: Allyn & Bacon, 1962.

Homans, George C. "The Western Electric Researches," in S. D. Haslett, ed., *Human Factors in Management.* New York: Harper & Brothers, 1951.

Lane, Willard R., Ronald G. Corwin, and William G. Monahan. *Foundations of Educational Administration, A Behavioral Analysis.* New York: The Macmillan Company, 1967.

Laser, Marvin. "Toward a Sense of Community," *Journal of Higher Education,* 38:61–69 (Feb., 1967).

Lieberman, Myron, and Michael H. Moskow. *Collective Negotiations for Teachers: An Approach to School Administration.* Chicago: Rand McNally & Co., 1966.

Moskow, Michael H. *Readings in Collective Negotiations.* Chicago: Rand McNally & Co., 1967.

Pounds, Ralph L., and James R. Bryner. *The School in American Society,* 2nd ed. New York: The Macmillan Company, 1967.

Raven, Bertram H. "The Dynamics of Groups," *Review of Educational Research,* 29:332–334 (Oct., 1959).

Runkel, Philip J. "The Social-Psychological Basis of Human Relations," *Review of Educational Research,* 29:324 (Oct., 1959).

Scheflen, Albert E. "Human Communication: Behavioral Programs and Their Integration in Interaction," *Behavioral Science,* Mental Health Institute, University of Michigan, 13:44–55 (Jan., 1968).

Smith, T. V., and Eduard C. Lindeman. *The Democratic Way of Life.* New York: New American Library (Mentor), 1951.

Stinnett, T. M., Jack H. Kleinman, and Martha Ware. *Professional Negotiation in Public Education.* New York: The Macmillan Company, 1966.

Tompkins, Ellsworth. *Keystones of Good Staff Relationships.* Washington: U. S. Office of Education, Miscellaneous Bulletin No. 13, 1955.

five

•

Developing an Inservice Education Program

Many inservice programs are virtually useless. Often the program is made up of a day or two of preschool sessions devoted to welcome speeches and some cursory planning for the opening of school. Or there is a "professional day," consisting of general sessions replete with school choruses and a lecture, followed in the afternoon by small-group meetings and shoptalk. The general session speakers are usually the local superintendent, a board member, and perhaps a couple of outsiders to dilute the parochialism of the program.

Beginning teachers are seldom adequately prepared to undertake their professional responsibilities because preservice preparation is insufficient to produce the kind of teacher needed. There is great diversity in the preparation of teachers, with regard to both quantity and quality. The experienced teacher has the problem of keeping up with new developments which outrun his techniques and outdate his curriculum. Difficulties arise when the local district drifts for some years so that even the educational and instructional approaches of the experienced teachers are permitted to become obsolete.

The problem of being ready and able to move ahead with the changes that are sweeping education affects not only teachers but supervisors, administrators, and board members. Often teachers are set to make changes but are deterred by their administrators, who prefer "smooth sailing." Board members, for a variety of personal reasons but mainly from lack of proper education, may try to maintain the status quo. Therefore, a well-planned and organized inservice program should include supervisors, administrators, and board members.

Boards of education should be informed of the trends, innovations, and possible improvements in the educational program. Administrators and supervisors must know the requirements of planned changes in terms of staff and faculty, educational paraphernalia, and space. Without the support of these subsystems, the strategy for change miscarries.

Many school systems provide inservice activities and projects for their faculty, staff, and noncertified personnel. Such programs vary in quality and scope according to the ingenuity and imagination as well as the professional competence of the leaders. If the leaders' expectations are low, the effectiveness of the inservice program will probably be low. If leaders are provincial, ritualistic, and insistent upon the "organization man" image of their subordinates, the inservice program will be superficial and perhaps totally irrelevant. Modern, open school systems admit change and permit and often encourage divergent thinking. The well-planned inservice program becomes the vehicle by which the schools are moved from yesterday into tomorrow.

Inservice education, then, makes it possible for teachers, administrators, and others to keep abreast of social and cultural changes in the community and the nation, and of events as they occur abroad. It is an excellent way for all to keep current in subject matter and in new techniques of teaching. A continuous attempt must be made by the local school district to inform all staff members of innovations and experiments and to maintain an awareness of changes which may have value for them.

A Model for an Inservice Education Program

Some educators call any effort to improve instruction with the staff an inservice operation. However, a definite, well-planned program involves faculty members in developing purposes, activities, and methods of evaluation. The purpose should always be to enable staff members to work together and to grow professionally in areas of common concern. Inservice programs should be based on staff experience and training, nature of the pupil, population and community, status of curriculum development in the district, and other such factors. Their prime goal is to promote the continuous growth of teachers, including the elimination of deficiencies.[1]

Supervisors must see that inservice programs are developed and maintained in such a fashion that continual progress is recognized by the various components of the instructional team. Careful planning must precede implementation. While each program will, of necessity, be tailored to the local situation, it will in most cases have the three dimensions of the model described below.

The first dimension of the proposed model is concerned with professional growth. In each of four periods from preservice to professional maturity the teacher is learning certain competences and achieving certain goals. The second dimension, areas of knowledge (the content of the program), involves five major fields of study which have been selected because they contribute much to the understanding of the process of education, the school as a social institution, and the process of learning. Unless a program has something from each field to stimulate the intellectual powers of teachers, it is not likely to be a balanced program. The third dimension is motivation. Teachers must constantly keep themselves informed of new knowledge, the modification of methods, and new insights produced by research. At the same time, there are counterforces which demand time from the teacher's day. The desire to continue the activities leading to professional growth and increased competence is often reduced and sometimes eliminated by these counterpressures. Therefore, the supervisor needs to be familiar with the problems of motivating teachers even as teachers must learn to motivate pupils. Above all, the supervisor is a teacher of teachers.[2]

Winning Acceptance of an Inservice Program

When Hal Farmer was interviewed for the vacant supervisory position in Mill River District, he was asked to explain what he considered his major responsibility as the secondary supervisor. His immediate and emphatic reply was "the initiation and maintenance of an inservice program."

---

[1] Harold Spears, *Curriculum Planning Through Inservice Programs* (Englewood Cliffs, N.J.: Prentice-Hall, 1957), pp. 314–316.

[2] David Turney, "Beyond the Status Quo," *Educational Leadership*, 23:664–669 (May, 1966).

Hal could easily recognize the lack of favorable reaction to his statement and he sensed the usual negative feeling for inservice activities. He knew that he would be required to sell his position; at the same time he knew that he was right. This was the appropriate time to outline the model he had evolved, which served as his guideline for a district-wide program.

As he introduced the three dimensions of his model — professional growth, areas of knowledge, and motivation — he was careful to spell out their interrelationship and the importance of utilizing each to achieve adequate balance and he continued to pound away at his basic premise of the value of inservice education to the instructional program.

Hal Farmer was the choice of the personnel selection committee to become Mill River's next supervisor. Now he had to produce. Would the model help?

The Professional Growth Needs of Teachers

Teaching begins in the preprofessional period and develops as the individual matures. A program of guiding and stimulating all teachers to continue their preparation is necessary.[3] Let us, therefore, arbitrarily divide the professional life of a teacher into four periods, of indefinite length; some persons have been known to remain in the initial teaching period for many years while others have progressed rapidly toward the maturing period.

Such a categorization of teachers is more helpful for inservice education purposes than is the usual indiscriminate grouping which usually delineates the lazy teacher, the colorless teacher, the hypersensitive teacher, etc. The categories used in the model provide a basis for planning professional programs.

The four periods of professional growth are (1) the preservice period: preparation at the high school and college level; (2) the initial teaching period: similar to the probationary term though it may vary in length; (3) the security period: built upon the early years of experience; and (4) the maturing period: a continuing increase in competence and effectiveness. The professional needs of teachers vary from one period to the next; likewise their motivations change as they move through these stages, and even the sources of

---

[3] Ben M. Harris, "Inservice Growth — The Essential Requirement," *Educational Leadership*, 24:260 (Dec., 1966).

motivation change. Their philosophy deepens; with the passage of time it should explain more effectively the value systems of man and define with increased clarity human behavior and relationships. Since needs shift throughout these periods, so do the requirements for content in the inservice education program.

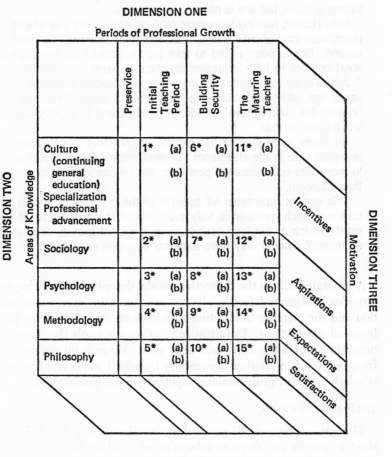

DIMENSION ONE

Periods of Professional Growth

	Areas of Knowledge	Preservice	Initial Teaching Period	Building Security	The Maturing Teacher	
	Culture (continuing general education) Specialization Professional advancement	1* (a) (b)	6* (a) (b)	11* (a) (b)	
	Sociology	2* (a) (b)	7* (a) (b)	12* (a) (b)	
	Psychology	3* (a) (b)	8* (a) (b)	13* (a) (b)	
	Methodology	4* (a) (b)	9* (a) (b)	14* (a) (b)	
	Philosophy	5* (a) (b)	10* (a) (b)	15* (a) (b)	

DIMENSION TWO

DIMENSION THREE

Incentives

Aspirations

Expectations

Satisfactions

Motivation

Fig. 1

A Model for a Program of Inservice Education

* Each of the fifteen cells may be filled with (a) independent studies and (b) group work. A large number of activities and projects can thus be generated.

Stages of Professional Growth

Wing A of McKinley High has four classrooms. The teachers who occupy these rooms, although teaching different subjects, have developed a strong positive relationship with one another.

Sally Simme is just out of the university. This is not only her first teaching position but her first full-time job. Sally is interested and willing to learn, but she is naive in many ways.

Miss Hunter, nearing retirement (she refuses to say just when), is recognized throughout the district as one of the best English teachers around. She is often asked to take part in special workshops and short courses to help interested teachers improve their techniques.

John Farley was graduated from the state teachers college three years ago, after completing his obligation to Uncle Sam. He has finished his "shakedown" at McKinley High and is rapidly turning into a good teacher.

Art Cobb, math teacher par excellence, is about to celebrate his twentieth year in the classroom. Several times Art has been invited to move into administrative positions, but he has elected to stay in the classroom.

This quartet represents all aspects of the profession, and in his own way each member is truly professional in every sense of the word. Which of the four periods of professional growth does each represent? Should they have identical inservice education?

A program built on the theoretical model described in this chapter provides background for developing sequences in inservice education and for meeting intellectual requirements and increasing professional satisfactions. Unfortunately, in some schools the inservice program is much the same year after year. There is no progression from one level to another demanding increased intellectual power, scholarly effort, or professional competence of the participants.

The Preservice Period

The preservice period, particularly at the college level, is too short to permit an adequate education of teachers in the complex world of today. The vast accumulation of knowledge and the continued rate of increase in knowledge have simply made the traditional four-year, 120-hour college preparation for teachers obsolete. The preservice period is not one of the supervisor's major areas of activity, but his interest in preservice preparation should be high because he must organize inservice education to supplement and complement the college training program. His experiences with beginning teachers could be utilized to improve the teacher preparation program.

Teaching Teachers

Every year Supervisor Myra Hagerty is invited to spend a day at the state university, expenses paid, as a consultant to the College of Education. Myra and several other supervisors from cities throughout the state contribute much to developing the teacher training program. At the same time, Myra keeps in touch with some of the newer developments which might otherwise be difficult for her to learn about. It has become a mutually satisfying and profitable exchange for the four years the program has been in existence. Should she take this much time away from the problems of her district which are her responsibility?

The Initial Teaching Period

This period of development has a clearly identifiable beginning point but may extend from one to a number of years, depending upon the person. In our opinion it generally covers from one to five or six years. Probationary periods under state laws usually last for three years but may run as high as five. During this stage the teacher dropout rate is quite high. One study found that 14 percent of first-year teachers left the profession, and the estimated rate for the second year was just as large.[4] Some reports indicate that for a given graduating class 50 percent of those who have gone into teaching will drop out in five years. So the probationary years are crucial both for the teacher and for inservice education. The supervisor is particularly concerned with the teacher's establishment of sound instructional practices, and the fledgling teacher is deciding whether to make a lifetime career of teaching or to move to another pursuit.

The beginner often has problems — with discipline, with routine and organization, with scoring and marking papers, and with curriculum development. In fact, the newer developments in curriculum

---

[4] J. Scott Hunter, "Turnover Among Beginning Teachers — A Followup," *School Life,* 44:22–24 (Apr., 1962).

are often unknown to him.[5] Moreover, he is desperately attempting to gain acceptance from the rest of the staff.

Reducing the Dropout Rate

Supervisor Sam Freeberg is much concerned with the problems of the young teachers in the Plainview District. This growing suburban area adds many new teachers each year. Naturally a large number of them are beginners just out of the university and need assistance to establish themselves in their classrooms. Sam has learned the hard way that if these people are not able to reach rather quickly at least a minimum level of performance, discouragement will lead to frustration and then to failure. Such a pattern loses potentially good teachers to the profession at a time when many more are needed. It also makes Sam's position more difficult as he continues to work with more and more beginners each year.

Since Sam considers this situation the key to his entire attack on the problems of instruction in Plainview, he is devoting much effort to helping these neophytes. A strong inservice program beamed toward new teachers has reduced the turnover rate in the district by 50 percent. Sam is working toward the figure of 100 percent. Is this a wise investment of his time and energy?

Building Security

The period in which teachers generally achieve certain kinds of security has indeterminate beginning and end points. Supervisors often describe a person at this stage of development as a teacher who has "know-how" or who "knows what he is doing." A few benchmarks help identify the stage.

This time of decisions and dedications covers roughly six to fifteen years of service. The probationary period is over; earlier goals have been achieved; tenure has been achieved. The individual finds satisfaction in a career devoted to seeking excellence in instruction. He

---

[5] National Education Association, Research Division, "First Year Teachers in 1954–55," *Research Bulletin,* 34:1–47 (Feb., 1956). John B. Stout, "Deficiencies of Beginning Teachers," *Journal of Teacher Education,* 3:43–46 (Mar., 1952). Melvin Tower, "Orientation and Inservice Practices in Ninety-One School Systems of the U.S.," *Educational Administration and Supervision,* 42:181–190 (Mar., 1956). M. S. Wallace, "Problems Experienced by 136 New Teachers During Their Induction into Teaching," *North Central Association Quarterly,* 25:291–309 (Jan., 1951).

finds security in his convictions and commitments and views every task as an opportunity. Such a person has both professional and personal security which controversies cannot shake. He seeks ways to improve his own background, increase his knowledge, and bring reality to his teaching. He has been busy with additional studies and advanced academic preparation so that he will qualify for additional increments and higher salary levels, as well as more stimulating types of work.

Change Is Everyone's Responsibility

Mrs. Valentine regards the development of a revised English curriculum as the major thrust of the secondary English teachers next year. It is obvious to her that she alone can do very little, so she hopes for much faculty participation. She will attempt to involve all English teachers in the deliberations and feels certain that she will receive much assistance from them.

Mrs. Valentine is realistic enough to know that not all teachers are capable of making the same contribution. Instinctively she starts a mental list of those who will be of most help, who consistently can be counted upon to think through problems and reach sound solutions. The list includes a majority of teachers who have taught for over a dozen years, and in more than one district. These people represent the "solid citizens" with whom Mrs. Valentine expects to work most closely. Should she really expect to "shift the burden" to them, or should she do more of the task herself?

The Maturing Period

This category has been widely recognized.[6] Much supervision is provided by the mature members of the faculty; it is not limited solely to the individual who carries the title "supervisor."[7] Any member of the staff may assist teachers in developing a better learning environment for pupils.

---

[6] Robert J. Havighurst, "Rewards of Maturity for the Teacher," *Educational Forum*, 20:145–150 (Jan., 1956). Association for Supervision and Curriculum Development, *Toward Professional Maturity of Supervisors and Curriculum Workers* (Washington: The Association, 1967). Frederick Mayer and Frank E. Brower, *Education for Maturity* (Washington: Public Affairs Press, 1956), pp. 136–145.
[7] Kimball Wiles, *Supervision for Better Schools*, 2nd ed. (Englewood Cliffs, N.J.: Prentice-Hall, 1955), p. 7. See also our discussion in Chapter One.

The maturing teacher usually exhibits considerable depth in most phases of his professional life. He is likely to be highly competent and to feel quite secure in the performance of his duties. He may also be at home in various aspects of American culture: art, literature, music, history, sociology, and/or politics. Most important, he is a specialist in his field.

The attitude of the mature teacher permits him to accept change as one of the dominant processes in life rather than as a threat. Change comes rapidly at times and it may come unexpectedly. Therefore, a part of the teacher's security in his profession lies in being alert to change. He has an air of constant expectancy; he recognizes that research will find new answers to problems, new bases for understanding behavior, better explanations of motives, and neater descriptions of perceptions. He is always at the point, intellectually, of suspecting common assumptions, methods, and rule-of-thumb procedures. He looks for verification of information and theory. He has achieved the understanding of and has accepted the concept that a teacher never "arrives." He thrives on curiosity, on intellectual bouts with concepts, relationships, and ideas.[8]

Utilizing Faculty Resources

Mr. Robert Keister is the senior teacher in Lincoln High. He is three years from mandatory retirement, yet his age has not slowed his activities or dulled any of his senses. The state and national associations know of Mr. Keister and he is often invited to participate in conferences. He has contributed several articles to their journals.

Mr. Keister has willingly assisted Supervisor Gregg with many workshops within the district. In fact, Mr. Gregg has said upon many occasions that Mr. Keister is his (Gregg's) right arm.

Mr. Keister enjoys helping younger teachers to become better professionals and he doesn't mind spending some of his time this way. He feels a certain amount of professional responsibility to help whenever he can. Should such activity be considered the responsibility of the "superior" instead of the teacher?

A properly developed program of inservice education should provide for a continuous growth of teachers from the probationary or early years through the period of the maturing teacher. The

[8] Muriel Crosby, *Curriculum Development for Elementary Schools in a Changing Society* (Boston: D. C. Heath & Company, 1964).

beginner needs assistance in getting under way. The teacher achieving security needs aid of a different type and much freedom. The maturing teacher needs additional challenges to keep up his interest and support and to retain his enthusiasm. He can provide invaluable service by helping the beginner or occasionally the experienced teacher solve a problem. The maturing teacher group represents the greatest resource the supervisor could possibly have — if a satisfactory working relationship is maintained. However, should the supervisor, through arbitrary or unreasonable practices, alienate this particular segment of the faculty, his road will be rocky. While the experienced staff members can be of great assistance to the supervisor, they also know many subtle ways to plant roadblocks if they find such to their advantage.

Changing the Format

Mr. Stevens, the newly appointed supervisor, was perfunctorily assigned the task of "preparing the program for the preschool workshop." Upon inquiry he learned that this referred to a five-day period when the professional staff reported just prior to the arrival of students for the fall term. Previous sessions had consisted of large meetings in one centrally located high school auditorium, where speakers talked to the assembled staff members on topics ranging from the inspirational "it's great to be a teacher" type to the "you've got to raise the district test score averages if we are going to pass the next bond issue" preachment.

Mr. Stevens suspected that these meetings were not well received. It was easily determined by talking informally to a few teachers that most resented the time "wasted" in them. It was well known that many teachers went fishing and shopping instead, at the risk of being docked a day's pay.

An outline for an entirely new format began to emerge, and Mr. Stevens took his notes back to the superintendent for approval. His plan consisted of diverse activities beamed toward discrete groups of teachers. First, those new to teaching would join experienced teachers new to the district for an orientation to the district and to the community. Then the first-year group would receive specific assistance on handling the detail work necessary to get school started. In some instances an opening unit was prepared for their use the first two weeks of class until they could get their "feet on the ground."

The experienced teachers new to the district joined the other experienced staff for a workshop. Problems of operation were dealt with: "How can we improve on the reporting process?" "How should we handle the homework this year?" and the like. Time was also set aside for teachers, meeting with the others in their disciplines, to prepare instructional materials for use during the year. Mr. Stevens contacted some of the respected master teachers to assist in the various activities, and the money usually paid the speakers was spent instead for supplies for the curriculum workshops.

The local educational television station agreed to tape the superintendent's annual address to the staff on the "state of the district." The station also agreed to transmit the speech twice — once at a designated time during the day when all staff members were in their respective buildings and could watch it there as a group and once during the evening when the patrons of the district could view it. Each building principal acted as a group discussion leader, and the staff groups informally reacted to the remarks of the superintendent. It was hoped that many of the interested citizenry would listen and thus become better informed on the problems of the district as well as some of the recent accomplishments.

A follow-up evaluation by Mr. Stevens indicated that teachers throughout the district overwhelmingly supported his efforts and desired more of this type of "useful" activity. In the evaluation, what specific questions would be appropriate?

Areas of Knowledge

The second dimension of inservice education concerns content: continued attention to the intellectual life of the teacher, support for scholarly endeavors, and assistance in raising pertinent questions related to teaching and learning. The teacher-scholar represents perhaps the ideal; this is a level difficult to attain, but to move in that direction should be the purpose of every teacher. The supervisor can be of assistance in numerous ways. The good supervisor will find himself constantly immersed in the pursuit of greater professional excellence — his own, the teachers', and the pupils'.[9]

The curriculum for the continuing education of teachers can be drawn from a number of disciplines including the following: (1) culture: gaining an understanding and appreciation of one's

---

[9] Lois Williams, "The Consultant-Teacher Transaction," *Educational Leadership*, 23:541–545 (Apr., 1966). Earl Johnson, "The Human Dimensions of Supervision," *Educational Leadership*, 18:222–227 (Jan., 1961).

own and others' cultures; (2) sociology: understanding society, the social processes and institutions, urban living, the big city; (3) psychology: developing an understanding of learning, individual differences, personality, perception, motivation; (4) methodology: achieving increasing professional competence; (5) philosophy: developing a philosophy of education and life.

Culture

Culture may be thought of as the total life of a people. It embraces all that people in a given society do, think, feel, believe, desire, and fear, plus the various ways and media used to express their thoughts, feelings, and so forth. Included are all the artifacts, ideas, institutions, behaviors, customs, and traditions of a people. Four years of college preparation do not allow time for the study of many worthwhile courses related to one's own culture plus that of others. What one has learned of the material and nonmaterial components of culture, the symbolic expressions of it, and its influence upon the lives of individuals greatly enhances his understanding of human beings. He perceives more clearly the folkways, customs, and mores not only of his but also of other cultures.

The teacher's own field, be it history, mathematics, science, or whatever, is a part of the cultural area. An undergraduate specialization is only the beginning of depth in a given discipline. The model of inservice education is based on the assumption that a teacher will continue studying and specializing in his chosen field beyond undergraduate requirements. A challenging aspect of education is the constant accumulation of new knowledge. Changes necessitate constant reading and study to maintain professional and technical competence.

The scholar-teacher should keep abreast not only of the new ideas in his own field but also of outstanding developments in other fields. The supervisor too needs to be aware of new ideas in several areas. In fact, besides keeping up with the new information useful for the teachers, he must often seek it out and make it available to them.

Continuing Education

One of Supervisor Barth's most difficult tasks is keeping current in his field. As the science supervisor in Commerce City, he works with fifty secondary science teachers of varying ability, training, and interest. Had it not been for the various institutes, Mr. Barth is convinced that the program would have deteriorated long since to an unacceptable level. The fields of science are moving so rapidly that no one man should be expected to keep abreast of all changes.

Mr. Barth has resorted to providing digests of material in each of the areas of science to the appropriate teachers in the district. He attempts at least to skim this material himself before distributing it and relies on department chairmen to catch important items he has overlooked. He is not particularly proud of his efforts in this direction but feels that he is "holding his own." Is it realistic for the supervisor to even try to educate teachers who are supposedly already trained?

Sociology

In the preservice training program there is no time to study thoroughly or to observe firsthand such processes as social integration and disintegration, acculturation, and assimilation, which are carried on by people and, in their absence, by means of symbols. The impact of folkways, mores, habits of speech, dress, and communication is very real. Society may impose its will on the individual, punishing him or rewarding him in various ways. It may withhold protection or deny him information, security, or identification with the group. On the other hand, it may accept, encourage, and reward him. A continuing study of social processes, including a study of social class, delinquency, urban development, social disorganization, and the like, becomes background for understanding the school and its role in the social order. Such exploration may be formal or informal, as demonstrated by the class project detailed below.

A Class Project. Schools are sometimes criticized for being middle-class institutions managed according to middle-class values. A recent graduate supervision class made up of high school principals, supervisors, and teachers undertook to test this view. First of all, after much discussion, members of the class categorized themselves as members of the middle class. Then, by consensus, they drew up a set of ten values and ranked them as follows:

1. Education	6. Respect
2. Cooperation	7. Sociability
3. Wealth	8. Health
4. Talent	9. Worthy home membership
5. Service	10. Leadership

The second phase of the project was to submit this system of values to an elementary school class, a ninth-grade class, and a twelfth-grade class for students and teachers to rank on a scale of 1 (highest) to 10 (lowest).[10] The elementary school was situated in an area inhabited by professional people, managers, and independent store proprietors. Twelve teachers and twenty-four sixth-graders produced a coefficient of correlation (rho) of .465. At the junior high school level in a similar community but with a somewhat more heterogeneous population the coefficient of correlation was .295. The subjects were thirty ninth-graders in art and eight junior high school teachers. The senior high school was located in a community made up largely of laborers, semiskilled workmen, machine operators, and office workers. Here the coefficient rose to .565. The sample consisted of twenty-seven pupils in twelfth-grade social studies and six instructors.

It was concluded from this experiment that schools were surely oriented toward middle-class values and were probably indoctrinating pupils with them. The coefficient of correlation was lowest at the junior high level, which finding seems reasonable if one accepts the idea that the early teens are a time of conflict and rebellion. It was also found that the values might be ranked differently by pupils from either lower- or upper-class families.

The study alerted these supervisors-to-be to problems of values and motivation for learning. It resulted in considerable discussion and much serious thinking and reading about social class, class structure, class values, and the school in the social order. The supervisor must understand the origin of values, and what implications they hold for the development of an inservice program.

Psychology

There are several aspects of psychology which underlie and have special relevance to teaching. The teaching process is based on such concepts as maturation, intelligence, and transfer. Most students of education and psychology will agree that the fields of perception, motivation, learning, and emotions are important. To these might be added individual differences, personality, adolescent or child growth, and perhaps theories of psychology. Little of this con-

---

[10] Unpublished classroom data cited as an example of action research which could be done by a faculty.

tent is available at the undergraduate level because of a crowded academic program. An excellent place either to continue such studies or to begin them is the inservice education program.

Most teaching personnel could profit handsomely from a study of the individual — how he behaves, thinks, learns, and what his needs are. Without such a background, teachers must resort to guesswork or trial and error and may never become competent professionals. Few will rise above the level of "recitation hearing."[11] Lacking a rationale for pupils' interests, likes and dislikes, and changing attitudes, and having little or nothing of a scientific approach to learning, a teacher could hardly be expected to develop a theoretical framework or to conceptualize the process of teaching. He will be less than effective if he has neither a sound educational theory nor the ability to adapt what he does have to his own local situation. Supervision should guide teachers into asking the kinds of questions necessary to get at the heart of the educational process. As teachers are helped to plan the inservice program they need, basic psychological principles with their implications for good teaching should be included.

For example, supervisors often work with a group of teachers in a preplanning session, prior to initiating an inservice program. The intent is to assess properly the local need and thereby to provide activities which will be of most worth to the teachers involved. Many teachers when asked to suggest programs will immediately request the "nuts and bolts" sessions which give them specifics, but little thought may be given to the intangibles that provide guidance and rationale for the total teaching sequence. It is then up to the supervisor to raise the appropriate questions with the teachers in order to ensure adequate consideration of psychological concerns. What is the maturation level of these students? Are we taking into account what we know of the individual and his many needs as we design our program? Should we refresh ourselves on what sound educational theory says should be done to make certain we are moving in the right direction?

Methodology

Almost every day, with teachers, the supervisor must face the problem of techniques and methods. He will find the development

---

11 Elmer R. Smith, ed., *Teacher Education: A Reappraisal* (New York: Harper & Row, 1962).

of teachers' methodologies at various levels, ranging from poor to excellent and from elementary to advanced.

The novice is particularly interested in the application of knowledge to the classroom situation. What methods are best? Are there different ways of teaching? What are they? How does one teach thirty children of greatly varying abilities? How much can one assign to a class? How fast do pupils learn? How often should papers be graded?

The teacher may rely, for a time, upon the traditional methods of lesson assignments and recitation, book reports, etc. But modern methods make much use of information about students, their educational and social backgrounds. More attention is being given to pupil interests and motivations. Attempts are being made to bridge the gap between students' objectives and the educational objectives of the school. Many teachers are experimenting with machine teaching, programmed instruction, independent studies, self-help of various kinds, tapes, and other techniques. The range of individual differences of pupils, frequently spanning as much as three grades below and above the normally expected level, calls for the use of all sorts of methods.

One experimental approach involves the use of as many media as possible, all focused on a given concept. Critical questions are asked; materials are gathered, classified, analyzed, and evaluated. The culminating activities make use of slides, pictures, tapes, reports, demonstrations. From the point of introduction of a new lesson, unit, or project, and continuing throughout the entire life of the activity, including the closing phases, various media are brought into play so that the class is vastly different from the traditional recitation.

The classroom is rapidly coming to be the center of many research studies and projects. Both sociologists and psychologists, in addition to supervisors and professors of education, are rediscovering this rich source of research problems.[12] It has been found, for example, that the teaching act is divisible into many elements, each of which can be observed, measured, and described. Interaction between teacher and student certainly can be described and the results noted.

The supervisor must be a student of method. It is imperative that his knowledge of psychological principles and educational theory be solidly grounded in appropriate techniques. While he will con-

---

[12] Robert J. Schaefer, *The School as Center of Inquiry* (New York: Harper & Row, 1967).

tinually seek and disseminate new ideas, he will also encourage teachers to consider carefully the learning process in their own classrooms so as to strengthen constantly the total instructional program. A properly developed inservice program for a school district will provide opportunities for teachers at all stages of professional development to ask relevant questions and search for better answers. At the same time, the master teacher can be enlisted to support the supervisor in strengthening the skills of the novice.

Sharing Professional "Know-how"

Jim Taylor considers himself fairly proficient in methodology. His six years in the classroom were considered worthy enough to ensure his election to the new supervisory position created last year.

In spite of this strength, Jim feels he has much to learn. He has made it a practice to search the district for methods and techniques which are new to him.

There are several ways he can disseminate these new methods throughout the district. When appropriate he passes the information by word of mouth. Sometimes he arranges a conference between two teachers. On occasion he helps a teacher obtain released time to observe a successful colleague in an actual teaching situation. When it is feasible to schedule a half-day workshop, he invites the teachers to demonstrate exciting methods to their peers.

Thus new, creative methods of teaching are circulated through the district, and many teachers benefit from the techniques devised by a few. Is it professionally ethical to give away the methods which make one an outstanding teacher?

Philosophy

Teachers will scarcely have time during the preteaching period to make a thorough study of philosophy, but it is useful to know something besides hearsay about philosophy. The process of interpreting a philosophical statement, elaborating upon its meaning, and applying it to teaching, curriculum development, and school management can be very rewarding, and opportunities to explore it should be provided in the inservice program.

A popular way to study philosophy is to collect statements on educational philosophy from various school systems, analyze them, and then synthesize the elements into a new statement. A major pitfall of this method is that, while everyone may favor the generalized statement, it does not necessarily evoke the attitudes and actions needed to improve an instructional program. Too often it is filed away, and teaching goes on in the same old way.

Another approach to developing a philosophy is to ask questions. The faculty comes together for discussion and tackles one or two questions at each sitting. For example:

1. What is education? What is the purpose of education?
2. What is a school? What is a school supposed to do?
3. What is learning? What are the results of learning?
4. What is knowledge? What is the ultimate reality?
5. What are values? How do people develop them?

Once some of these questions have been considered, and tentative ideas have been developed, teaching may take on a different meaning. Concepts are refined, terms are redefined, and perception of significant terms such as *ends* and *means* becomes more meaningful. The work on curriculum, or the workshop on the improvement of methods, becomes an intellectual challenge rather than just another meeting.

Much philosophical literature can now be purchased in paperback form, including ethics, logic, systems of philosophy, and the works of individual philosophers. The supervisor could arrange to provide copies for use of teacher discussion groups. It might be more useful to supply a competent leader for discussion groups, or a qualified lecturer who could present an organized, short series of lectures introducing the faculty to the essence of philosophy and stimulating a study of it. A carefully organized program dealing with this topic should be so designed that teachers will feel its strength and positive effects but not resent the entire operation as "more busywork from the central office."

Coming Around to Philosophy

Supervisor Brown is quite aware of the impracticality of forcing teachers to upgrade themselves. Yet he deeply feels the necessity of some district-wide effort and he knows that he must provide the leadership. The board of education requirement of six semester hours of university credit each year is of only limited help. The salary increments for work beyond the bachelor's degree, especially the large one for the master's degree, are more useful. However, often the teachers get "locked in" to a degree program established by the university and are unable to take work which would prove more valuable to his district.

With the approval of the building administrators, Mr. Brown called an exploratory meeting of all department chairmen. He outlined his reasons for desiring a broad attack to upgrade the district staff in general. He invited comments, suggestions, and reactions from the group. They had many suggestions of things they felt needed attention. A priority list was established, assignments were agreed to, and a broad inservice program was initiated with great enthusiasm as being "something worthwhile — not busywork."

Mr. Brown admitted that many of the items with high priority had not been on his original list. He was quite willing to start with them, however, inasmuch as they represented the judgment of the chairmen. But he wondered whether any of the forthcoming discussions would involve philosophy. What do you think? How could he best inject consideration of philosophy?

Motivation and the Inservice Program

The third dimension of inservice education pertains to motivation. It is common knowledge that teachers differ vastly in motivation. Some exhibit a tremendous drive for self-improvement and improvement of the work of the school. Others spend great portions of their time and energy on nonschool tasks. The motivation, the personal thrust, and the concern about professional matters in education form a necessary dimension of the inservice program. It would be ideal if all professional personnel were interested in continued self-improvement, in increasing the effectiveness of the school, and in the progress of the profession, but this is not likely to be the case.

There are numerous schemes to stimulate the less motivated. One is the single-salary schedule with its recognition of advanced professional study, degrees, etc. Another is extra pay for professional activities, such as participating in preschool workshops. A third is financial support for those wishing to attend summer school or to take a specific course in a college or university. Others are fringe benefits, merit raises, and promotions.

Recently there has been a new trend in teacher evaluation. Schools are experimenting with the classification of teachers in such a way that the career teacher, or the master teacher, receives a higher salary. No one scheme has yet evolved, and experimentation will probably continue. This trend is in a transition period; it seems inevitable that the whole field of educational economics will receive a thorough airing in the next decade. Many attempts will be made to tie economic incentive to quality instruction, with levels of expertise being identified and reimbursed accordingly. Hitherto untried practices will gain prominence as the demand for sufficient funds continues to plague the profession. Alternate methods of financing will no doubt play an important role in the development of salary schedules. In any event, the supervisor will be in the center of the action and will be called upon to make the new incentive program workable.

In this context, the problem of motivation is a significant one for the supervisor, and several questions will arise to worry him. (1) How does one get all teachers to behave in an enthusiastic manner about their work and their profession? (2) How can one motivate people of varying backgrounds and varying aspirations to do similar tasks? (3) Should all staff members be regarded as equally dedicated and be expected to devote equal amounts of time to their teaching assignments? (4) What is the role of the supervisor in the administration of incentive schemes, or in the evaluation of teachers? (5) How will he evaluate instruction without evaluation of the instructor?

The Nebraska Symposium on Motivation in its publication *Psycho-Physiology and Motivation* noted that motivation was a combination of forces or drives within the individual which cause him to initiate activities, direct his actions purposefully, and persist in his goal-oriented behavior.[13] In the yearbook *Fostering Mental Health in Our Schools*, motivation was described as an inner drive consisting of such factors as the individual's biological, personal, social, and emotional needs.[14] His ambitions and aspirations, as related to his perceptions of the world in which he lives, add to the strength of his motivation.

Motivation is often divided into two types. One is intrinsic, the inner drive, with its biological or organic basis. Hunger, thirst, weariness are examples of inner states which give rise to activity.

[13] Donald B. Lindsley, *Psycho-Physiology and Motivation* (Lincoln: University of Nebraska Press, 1957), p. 48.
[14] Association for Supervision and Curriculum Development, *Fostering Mental Health in Our Schools* (Washington: The Association, 1950), p. 170.

Psychological needs which tend to spur the individual include the
needs for acceptance, independence, and achievement and the drive
to find fulfillment in socially approved ways.

The other type of motivation is extrinsic. It arises from external
pressures and socially acquired (learned) needs. "Keeping up with
the Joneses" is learned. Social values of status, prestige, money,
achievement, and reputation are learned. Since an individual grows
up, lives, and works in a society of people, it matters to him what
they think of him. Thus praise, reproof, recognition, acceptance,
demands, etc., may be used to initiate action or to condition behavior.

We are mainly concerned with social motivation in supervision;
however, not all persons respond to the same stimuli. Some examples of what motivates people follow:

1. Drives for status and prestige.
2. The need for security.
3. The need to identify with certain groups.
4. The need for recognition: holding an office, a title, a position
   in the hierarchy, a degree from X College.
5. Rewards, merits, bonuses.
6. Drives created by competition and social facilitation.
7. The need for success, the drive to achieve.
8. Winning social acceptance.
9. Knowledge of progress, or of success.
10. The desire to do something worthwhile.
11. The desire to contribute to progress.
12. The need to build a career.
13. Ethnic attitudes and compulsions which require one to "get
    ahead."
14. The need to be engaged in an intellectual task, or challenge.

There are also negative aspects to extrinsic motivation. Sometimes
criticism motivates people, although they may consider it unreasonable. One might prepare a long list of ways in which
teachers have been reproved or punished. Reproof creates an
avoidance pattern; actions which bring reproof will be discarded.

Reproof may also result in avoidance of the supervisor or lead to frustration and inordinate anxiety. While some anxiety can be beneficial and even desirable, an undue amount will have negative results. The wise supervisor will be tactful and constructive and attempt to achieve his ends through positive approaches rather than negative reproof.

Some teachers respond to positive incentives. The supervisor will be alert to find new ones or to combine old ones in new ways. He may find it useful to start teachers with one or more of these "primers":

1. They should help plan and administer the orientation program.
2. They should participate in curriculum evaluation, planning, construction.
3. They should help develop administrative policies or instructional policies.
4. They should be a part of a research team or a study group.
5. They should be given opportunities to develop leadership.
6. They may be given recognition by being asked to assist others, coach the young professional, share their knowledge, etc.
7. Their advice and ideas should be sought consistently.
8. They should be placed in charge of certain phases of the inservice program.
9. They may be assigned to teaching via television.
10. They may be the major lecturers or the head teachers in a team teaching project.
11. They may assist in developing the instructional materials center.
12. They may teach others how to make the most efficient use of instructional secretaries.

Cory's study pointed out that certain incentives are especially effective with beginners in the profession.[15] Supervisors and administrators in many school systems have teamed up to develop a

[15] N. Durwood Cory, "Incentives Used in Motivating Professional Growth of Teachers," *North Central Association Quarterly*, 27:398–407 (Apr., 1953).

motivation-producing orientation program for the new teacher. The following practices have been found useful:

1. Employing subject matter consultants during the preschool conference to help beginners improve their subject matter background.
2. Planning sessions with a supervisor or assistant principal, who teaches the beginner how the local school operates.
3. Developing a survey of the teaching resources available in the community and the methods of employing them in teaching.
4. Assisting with the understanding of the course or courses, use of a syllabus, and development of the unit.
5. Discussing the new teacher's role in the faculty and promoting the sense of belonging.
6. Furnishing complete information on salaries, extra pay if any, increments, etc.
7. Initiating a frank discussion of all rules and policies, using a teacher's handbook if one exists.
8. Providing information about books, supplies, equipment, and how these may be requisitioned.
9. Discussing the various ways in which the new teacher may participate in important matters related to his job, his profession, and his community.

It is difficult to describe how motivation is improved, especially that of professionals. Macdonald believes that teachers must be made aware of alternatives to existing practices if they are to improve.[16] The supervisor should be prepared to make available a variety of alternatives for consideration and investigation by the teacher. More important, he should be skillful in helping teachers to recognize the need for change and therefore to develop a desire to seek alternatives. He should stress intrinsic types of motivation.

If appropriate insights into the behavior of the individual can be gained, a beginning on teacher motivation can be made. A tactful study should be initiated to find a pattern which the super-

---

[16] James B. Macdonald, "Helping Teachers Change," in *The Supervisor: Agent for Change in Teaching* (Washington: Association for Supervision and Curriculum Development, 1966), p. 5.

visor can utilize to advantage. He needs to (1) observe a given teacher to determine if possible why he acts as he does. This opens the whole range of intrinsic and extrinsic motivations, which are carefully studied for evidence, and (2) hypotheses are developed relating behavior to possible causes. Then (3) the supervisor collects all data by means of observations, a review of the confidential files, conversations and interviews with people who know the teacher, and any other sources of information available. (4) He analyzes the data in relation to his hypotheses and decides whether he is on the right track. He has the choice of changing methods, changing hypotheses, or staying with his present line of procedure at this point. (5) If he decides he is on the right track, and his data seem accurate, he continues his studies and formulates his approaches to the teacher on the assumption that he can be helpful, and with confidence that he has opened new doors to the understanding of a valued member of the faculty.

One might propose some additional methods of instigating behavior. For example, the supervisor should encourage new ventures by the teacher, creating opportunities for expression or action if present ones are inadequate. Social pressure of public and professional opinion may be used in some cases. Success in the venture should be a reasonable possibility. A task that is too difficult and complex causes anxiety or apathy or frustration and thus only dampens motivation. At the same time, the supervisor should prepare the teacher for, and help him to accept, possible failure. He can point out the temporary nature of failure. After all, Edison developed the incandescent lamp only after a great many failures. The supervisor must emphasize that failure is to be expected if one is attempting something genuinely new and should be accepted.

Utilizing Faculty Resources

Mr. Trevor, science supervisor for the district, was becoming concerned with the caliber of science instruction. In too many instances teachers were obviously out-of-date in their field, yet some teachers were antagonistic to any sort of change and actively resisted efforts to help them improve. He knew he must do something to get at the problem, but what?

He invited all the science teachers to an exploratory meeting. When almost half failed to appear, he was not at all surprised. The meeting was devoted to considering the possibilities of generally revamping and updating the secondary science curriculum of the district, taking into account recent developments in the various fields. Some of the teachers had recently attended institutes and were eager to move in this direction.

The ensuing months were spent in preparation. During the summer many teachers were able to attend other institutes. In the fall the new program got under way with considerable district recognition and obvious support.

Before the year was out, the success of the new program began to affect the dissident teachers, as Mr. Trevor had hoped. Several who had at first ignored the department efforts began to take an interest and expressed a desire to join the others. Peer pressure had achieved what authoritarian dictate could never do. How else might Mr. Trevor have approached this problem? Suppose there were no institutes at all?

Providing a Functioning Program of Inservice Education

If Mr. Trevor happens to be a generalist, responsible for the instruction in all subjects at all grade levels, his task will be difficult — one of providing proper balance and adequate coordination among the disciplines. If he is responsible as a subject matter specialist for only one discipline throughout all grade levels, his task will be somewhat more concentrated and specialized but no less challenging.

Selection

The supervisor must recognize the variety of needs and deficiencies among the staff, and the special interests which are present. He will wisely select those needs, deficiencies, or interests for possible inservice concentration which are most prominent and which can best be handled within the framework provided by his district.

How should he attack this problem? Is he sufficiently knowledgeable to arrive consistently at the best answers by himself or must he seek help? If he considers himself inadequate, of whom does he ask assistance? The prudent supervisor will not hesitate. He will turn to the teachers. In some instances he may take rough proposals to the staff for initial reaction and refinements. In others he will solicit from the faculty a list of problems, suggested directions, and procedures as a first step. Then he can develop programs based on the desires expressed by the teachers, and he will develop them cooperatively with the classroom teachers so that the finished product is as much theirs as his.

The importance of this procedure cannot be overemphasized. Supervisors have too often been accused, and with reason, of superficial diagnoses and arbitrary prescription, the result being an inservice program imposed upon the staff which irritated nearly everyone. In fact, such methods will add to teacher unrest. Education today calls for something better.

Typical Programs

Summer courses at the university are a popular result of this joint planning. The individual's academic background is strengthened, and the pressure to attend inservice courses eliminated. Sometimes the supervisor will be able to counsel the teacher as to the most appropriate specific courses and thus build up faculty strengths which can be utilized in inservice activities.

Various approaches to curriculum development can serve as excellent inservice activities. As strategies for curriculum revision are planned, pertinent questions regarding the purposes of education and the value of proposed changes must be considered. In the give-and-take of this forum, new insights may be achieved by the teachers involved and attitudes toward curriculum changes may be improved. The Portland, Oregon, school district has recently been utilizing small groups of teachers to construct course outlines. Inservice experiences for the teachers were excellent, and needed materials for use by other teachers were produced.[17]

From time to time the staff should reexamine attitudes toward and knowledge of the pupil as an individual and restudy the learning process in order to find new directions for education and/or reinforce existing programs. Such examination-in-depth renews teachers' commitment to provide students with better learning situations.

The continuing need to select up-to-date textbooks can be employed as a beginning of an inservice program. The teacher who will use the new text should have an interest in what it contains, and examining the possibilities can serve as a "refresher course" to acquaint him with new developments in his field.

---

[17] Victor W. Doherty, "Procedure for Growth," *Educational Leadership*, 23:247–251 (Dec., 1965).

Certainly orienting teachers to the instructional routine expected of them prior to the start of the school year is an important aspect of an inservice program. For example, they should know the legal implications of leaving a class unsupervised while getting supplies from the principal's office. They should be aware of legal requirements relating to the curriculum, attendance, and discipline.

Internal problems and practices regularly need attention from the professional staff. Solutions which were acceptable last year may be inapplicable to this year's problems. An increase in the number of the faculty, changing the goals of a department, changing interpersonal relations, and modified organizational rules are only a few causes of necessary revisions which will affect staff activities.

Procedures for marking and reporting and record keeping are recurring problems. There is increasing pressure for careful examination, selection, and proper utilization of new instructional devices including a myriad of "hardware" items, as well as the even greater number of "software" materials.

Opportunities for inservice growth are available in study programs, group study of school problems, community study of activities, school visitation, travel, workshops, exchange teaching, writing, and research. The following elements are important in a good inservice program for a school system:

1. Teachers are made to feel that they are an integral part of the administration of the school.
2. Opportunities exist for promoting teacher status.
3. Curriculum planning is carried on cooperatively by the faculty, administrators, and supervisors.
4. Research and experimentation by individual teachers and groups of teachers are encouraged.
5. New teachers are oriented to their positions and accepted by the faculty.
6. Teacher-parent cooperation and community support are helpful.
7. Salary policies recognize training, experience, and innovativeness.
8. Time is available for group activities and teaching projects.
9. Administrators are willing to accept new ideas.

10. Activities are carried on by the total personnel working as a team.

11. Lines of communication in any direction are open.

Problems Involved

In the past, many programs were carried on by teachers after they had finished teaching a full day. It is becoming increasingly difficult to operate a satisfactory inservice program in such a manner. Now and then use is made of the summer months, especially if production is involved.

School districts are searching for various alternatives which will provide the necessary time when the teachers are fresh and most productive. Solving this particular problem may be the supervisor's most important achievement because of the far-reaching implications for the entire instructional program. A combination of preschool days in late summer, followed by a few regular days throughout the school year is one workable scheme. Greenville County, South Carolina, has been scheduling an additional ten days of teacher time each year for several years and found the practice rewarding.[18]

After-School Inservice Programs

Pressure has been building throughout Big City District for more time — time to teach, time to innovate, time to improve professionally. Teacher groups, taking their cues from industry, have been insisting more and more that "management" address itself to these problems.

As a result of this pressure, administrators in Big City are reexamining their time-honored practices. Supervisors Miss Sally Jones and Mr. Al Kent, who have been attempting to operate in a democratic fashion and to work cooperatively and professionally with teachers, are very much aware of the items that need correcting. These supervisors no longer plan long inservice programs to be held after school in the afternoons. They are actively searching, with teachers, for other solutions which will enable teachers to come to the inservice sessions fresh and ready to give their best efforts to the task at hand.

---

[18] Gordon L. Smith, "Inservice Education by E.T.V.," *The Bulletin of the National Association of Secondary Principals,* 50:182–188 (Apr., 1966).

Both Sally and Al agree that there must be a better way and they have committed themselves to continue with a variety of pilot programs, looking for one which will satisfy the need. Are they being realistic in their approach?

Most solutions to inservice problems involve increased costs — pay for substitutes to release teachers or reimbursement to teachers for working other than during the regular school day. Supplies and materials are also necessary for a successful inservice program often in large quantities. With the normally tight instructional budget, these additional expenditures call for careful advance planning on the part of the supervisor. He must anticipate financial needs, often long before the money is to be spent, and, of course, be able to defend the projected expenditures as they compete with other budgetary demands.

Cooperative inservice projects such as faculty and staff meetings, teacher councils, study groups, workshops, demonstration centers, study clinics, orientation of new teachers, group excursions in the community, planned visitation and observation, and teacher committee work also require funds. Individual endeavors such as graduate study, research and experimentation, travel, interschool and intraschool visitation and observation, membership and participation in organizations, and constant self-evaluation must have adequate financial support. In the past it was sometimes possible to operate an inservice program at faculty (or participants') expense, but this arrangement cannot continue.

The federal government has set aside funds for some inservice programs. A part of the money is to be used by the individual states for planning, pilot projects, enriched academic programs, continuing adult education, specialized instruction, and assistance to those working in remedial programs. With such financial help, individual school systems have set up many incentives for teachers in the form of better salaries, sabbaticals, leave allowances, funds for substitute service to relieve teachers for special workshops, bonuses for advanced professional study, compensation for preschool and postschool conferences, provision for necessary study time, and so on.

Some federal funds are made available to the state departments of education to be distributed in an equitable fashion. Some are allotted directly to individual districts. Some provide all or most of the necessary expense, while others require matching funds from the local district. Regardless of which device is utilized, the intent usually is to initiate improved practices or to offer greater resources than are available locally. The supervisor who is knowledgeable about such funding can often mount a stronger program in his district. Indications are that this support in some form or other will continue.

As the supervisor is able to work out the directions to be followed and the problems to be tackled in a joint endeavor with the teaching staff, he will be launching what can develop into a successful, profitable inservice program. In the process of attempting the new and untried he will, on occasion, fail. If he attempts nothing, he most

Areas of Interest	Levels of Interest or Knowledge		
1. Organizational Theory and Practice	I	II	III
2. The Learning Process			
3. Sensitivity Training			
4. The Research on Teacher Classroom Behavior			
5. Newer Curriculum Approaches			
6. Bureaucracy: Structure and Function, School and Society			
7. Newer Methods: Multimedia			
8. Interaction Analysis			
9. Humanizing the Curriculum			
10. Life Skills in School and Society*			
11. Science for Life and Home			
12. Multidisciplinary Programs			

* A.S.C.D. Yearbook, 1969.

Fig. 2

A Suggested Inservice Schedule

certainly will fail. His is both an opportunity and a challenge to find ways of involving increasing numbers of the staff on important instructional questions in a manner not only acceptable but exciting. If he maintains a successful inservice program, he is more likely to be a successful supervisor.

Figure 2 represents an inservice program developed by a supervisor and a faculty in a suburban district. It was arranged to provide for needs, interests, and levels of sophistication. It could be revised in many different ways.

Summary

This chapter describes a model for an inservice education program. The first dimension in the model consists of the periods of professional growth: preservice, the initial teaching period, the security period, and the maturing period. The last three are times for inservice education.

The second dimension consists of the areas of knowledge, the content in which continued learning is necessary for the growth of the professional person. These include culture, sociology, psychology, methodology, and philosophy, and from them teaching constantly draws new ideas and sustenance. Their use in teaching, interpreting, elaborating, and comparing is crucial in developing understanding.

The third dimension involves motivation. Supervisory practice is concerned with both extrinsic and intrinsic motivation. However, intrinsic types of teacher motivation are more desirable and should be sought.

The supervisor should examine the entire inservice program of his district. Care must be exercised to initiate programs which the recipients can accept as needed. Equal care must be applied to planning for necessary costs and for suitable times in which to offer the programs.

Problems for Group Discussion

Analyze the following situations. In each, identify supervisory principles representing sound theory, if any are included. What are the basic elements which made a difference? How would you have approached the situation?

1. The new superintendent has begun an intensive program of reorganization and curriculum improvement. One of the major thrusts will be inservice programs aimed at changing sterile teaching methods. Many of the older teachers deeply resent such "interference," feeling that their years of experience should relieve them of "rubbish" of this kind. The supervisor has the task of implementing the wishes of the superintendent in the face of their open dissatisfaction. How should he proceed?

2. The science supervisor attempted to ascertain how well the newly introduced science course was progressing. He quickly learned that some of the older teachers had virtually abandoned it for their established methods, saying that the new course was too difficult for their students. He knew that many had not been keeping professionally current and suspected that they were unprepared to handle the new material and were returning to the old comfortable way in self-defense.

He attempted to solve the problem by calling a meeting of all teachers involved and invited them to participate in a summer workshop to rewrite the new course in the light of their experiences of the current year. Two science educators from the local university had agreed to assist the group, he told them. He also indicated that participants would be paid by the district. What advantages and disadvantages can you see in this procedure for starting a program?

3. The supervisor had worked diligently to acquire a respectable amount of audio-visual equipment for his district. It soon became evident, however, that his efforts were not appreciated. In building after building he found the equipment collecting dust in remote corners. He held a meeting with teachers representing each building and began to study ways of getting the equipment into use. How might this be done best? How might your solution relate to an inservice program?

Selected Readings

Association for Supervision and Curriculum Development. *Perceiving, Behaving, Becoming.* 1962 Yearbook. Washington: The Association, 1962.

Association for Supervision and Curriculum Development. *Fostering Mental Health in Our Schools.* Washington: The Association, 1950.

Association for Supervision and Curriculum Development. *Toward Professional Maturity of Supervisors and Curriculum Workers.* Washington: The Association, 1967.

Boring, Edwin, Herbert Langfeld, and Harry Weld. *Introduction to Psychology.* New York: John Wiley & Sons, 1947.

Cory, N. Durwood. "Incentives Used in Motivating Professional Growth of Teachers," *North Central Association Quarterly*, 27:398–407 (Apr., 1953).

Crosby, Muriel. *Curriculum Development for Elementary Schools in a Changing Society*. Boston: D. C. Heath & Company, 1964.

Denemark, George W., and James B. Macdonald. "Preservice and In-Service Education of Teachers," *Review of Educational Research*, 37:233–243 (June, 1967).

Doherty, Victor W. "The Carnegie Professional Growth Program: An Experiment in the In-Service Education of Teachers," *Journal of Teacher Education*, 18:261–269 (Fall, 1967).

Doherty, Victor W. "Procedure for Growth," *Educational Leadership*, 23:247–251 (Dec., 1965).

Harris, Ben M. "Emergence of Technical Supervision," *Educational Leadership*, 22:494–496 (Apr., 1965).

Harris, Ben M. "Inservice Growth — The Essential Requirement," *Educational Leadership*, 24:260 (Dec., 1966).

Harris, Chester W., ed. *Encyclopedia of Educational Research*. New York: The Macmillan Company, 1960.

Havighurst, Robert J. "Rewards of Maturity for the Teacher," *Educational Forum*, 20:145–150 (Jan., 1956).

Hunter, J. Scott. "Turnover Among Beginning Teachers — A Followup," *School Life*, 44:22–24 (Apr., 1962).

Johnson, Earl. "The Human Dimensions of Supervision," *Educational Leadership*, 18:222–227 (Jan., 1961).

Lindsley, Donald B. *Psycho-Physiology and Motivation*. Nebraska Symposium on Motivation. Lincoln: University of Nebraska Press, 1957.

Macdonald, James B. "Helping Teachers Change," in *The Supervisor: Agent for Change in Teaching*. Washington: Association for Supervision and Curriculum Development, 1966.

Mayer, Frederick, and Frank E. Brower. *Education for Maturity*. Washington: Public Affairs Press, 1956.

National Education Association, Research Division. "First Year Teachers in 1954–55," *Research Bulletin*, 34:1–47 (Feb., 1956).

National Society for the Study of Education. *Inservice Education*. Fifty-Sixth Yearbook, Part I. Chicago: University of Chicago Press, 1957.

Schaefer, Robert J. *The School as Center of Inquiry*. New York: Harper & Row, 1967.

Smith, Elmer R., ed. *Teacher Education: A Reappraisal*. New York: Harper & Row, 1962.

Smith, Gordon L. "Inservice Education by E.T.V.," *The Bulletin,* 50:182–188 (Apr., 1966).

Spears, Harold. *Curriculum Planning Through Inservice Programs.* Englewood Cliffs, N.J.: Prentice-Hall, 1957.

Spears, Harold. *Improving the Supervision of Instruction.* Englewood Cliffs, N.J.: Prentice-Hall, 1953.

Stout, John B. "Deficiencies of Beginning Teachers," *Journal of Teacher Education,* 3:43–46 (Mar., 1952).

Tower, Melvin. "Orientation and Inservice Practices in Ninety-One School Systems of the U.S.," *Educational Administration and Supervision,* 42:181–190 (Mar., 1956).

Turney, David. "Beyond the Status Quo," *Educational Leadership,* 23:664–669 (May, 1966).

Wallace, M. S. "Problems Experienced by 136 New Teachers During Their Induction into Teaching," *North Central Association Quarterly,* 25:291–309 (Jan., 1951).

Wiles, Kimball. *Supervision for Better Schools,* 2nd ed. Englewood Cliffs, N.J.: Prentice-Hall, 1955.

Williams, Lois. "The Consultant-Teacher Transaction," *Educational Leadership,* 23:541–545 (Apr., 1966).

six

•

Establishing a Favorable Environment

If all the objectives of supervision could be consolidated into one major objective, it would be to create optimum conditions for learning in every classroom. One might think this could be accomplished with relative ease. All one needs is a good teacher and books — and the problem ceases to exist. However, the situation is more complicated than it first appears because so many people are involved, each different from the rest, because learning itself is a complicated process, and because of the complexity of the modern classroom and school environment.

As the supervisor sets the stage for an improved environment for learning, he comes into contact with a variety of people, each of whom views learning from a unique perspective. It then becomes the supervisor's task not only to deal with these divergent viewpoints but to take into account the material ingredients he has at hand to produce the most effective learning environment possible. He must consider the physical environment, the climate for learning, the teacher, the administrator, and himself.

The Physical Environment

It has long been known that physical comfort helps to create a satisfactory atmosphere. Therefore, physical distractions generated by uncomfortable temperature, lighting extremes, noise, monotony, etc., should be reduced to a minimum. Often a teacher who has learned to live with a poor situation will require the encouragement and assistance of the supervisor to discover (1) a reason to change and (2) a solution.

The supervisor should take the lead in working with architects so that adequate provision for the instructional program will be made in new or remodeled buildings. Very often, the architect's creative design and knowledge of education can prevent problems from occurring. Lack of understanding of the educational use of a facility may cause the architect to "build in" future difficulties for instruction as he deals with some other design question of concern at the moment. Educators and especially supervisors must take the responsibility for seeing that such potential problems do not go unchallenged. Often school officials do much better in planning classrooms for vocational and technical subjects than for academic subjects. Many new school buildings evolve along traditional lines, on obsolescent assumptions, and in apparent ignorance of the present or future instructional program. In general, factories and homes have been much better designed than schools for the functions they were to serve.

An Exciting Environment for Learning

An exciting environment is based on three imperatives: (1) Broaden the stage for learning; bring the world into the classroom. Introduce students to the multisensory classroom with the power to create interest. (2) Develop the environment in such a way as to feed young people's curiosity and interest. Provide much to see, to feel, to operate, and to hear — an environment that simply cries out, "Touch me!" or "Lift me, and examine!" and "Try me out — turn me on — push the button!" (3) Make learning itself exciting and satisfying. Encourage students to engage in processes because they want to know.

Regardless of the discipline taught, rooms should be laboratories in which discovery takes place. Dioramas, models, or mock-ups of all sorts might be present or in the construction stage. One corner of a room might be given to growing things, as students learn botany and biology; phototropism, photosynthesis, geotropism, etc., could be observed. A museum might be created illustrating the times and customs of the period of history or countries under study. In the spring a menagerie, botanical garden, experimental garden, or mini-zoo could be developed and studied. Perhaps models demonstrating city planning, or models of airports showing a better flow of planes, autos, and pedestrian traffic would intrigue some.

Various skills are important in such a learning environment: writing descriptions, plans, letters, and other communications;

drawing designs or preconstruction pictures, painting, and sculpting; composing poems, articles, essays, short stories, and musical pieces. Layout and design are needed by nearly everyone; these skills are related to how students plan their own learning environment.

A favorable learning environment places much emphasis on processes. Mastering processes is a much higher order of learning than mastering facts, but it makes learning facts easier, faster, and more meaningful, and the facts are retained longer. Such learning aids communication, both encoding and decoding, since it is meaning rather than information which is being transmitted.

Some of the processes utilized by students in an exciting learning environment are:

Selecting the events or phenomena to be explained, materials to be used, tools needed, and perhaps partners in the work.

Gathering and collecting data according to a plan or design.

Observing the phenomena, reading about them, inventing instruments and situations to make closer observation possible. (In social studies, creating opinionnaires, structured interviews, social class scales, etc.)

Measuring, weighing answers, scaling responses for statistical treatment, and recording measurements accurately.

Analyzing data, the process itself, the results; form, style, and plot in literature; structure of experiments and knowledge.

Classifying and developing order among ideas, data, and relationships. Once order has been established, other types of intellectual activity can go on. Classifications make the organization of work possible. Organization makes possible the setting of priorities and orderly procedures.

Generalizing, arriving at conclusions, and justifying conclusions on the basis of evidence. Verifying conclusions and noting their limitations.

Interpreting results (scientific, social, artistic), extrapolating and interpolating when these processes are indicated. The student shows the relevance of his findings, and it is not the teacher who is required to do so each time the question comes up.

Evaluating in a variety of ways. Students learn to ask procedural questions as well as value questions.

Such an environment builds its own tensions for learning; it bristles with opportunities. The traditional role of teachers is not adequate in the exciting environment, nor is the traditional role of supervisors. Supervisors have great responsibility in the development and maintenance of a vital environment.

Analysis of Space

The supervisor might improve learning conditions by engaging in a cooperative study of the physical environment with teachers. Thousands of classrooms could be improved simply by a little work, a minimum of supplies, and a lot of imagination.[1] An enterprising, tactful, responsible supervisor may assist teachers by (1) finding ways to make classrooms and halls neat and attractive; (2) presenting the administration with existing problems and possibly with some solutions; and (3) explaining to the maintenance staff and the custodian what would make conditions better for students, including sanitation, lighting, ventilation, etc.

The skilled supervisor will systematically analyze classrooms, identifying the programs going on in them and determining whether the space available for these programs is being utilized. He will try to learn if needed space actually exists or can be obtained. With the aid of the teacher, he can propose modifications of existing space. A school building is simply an arrangement of space to be used in the teaching-learning activity, and how it is used should depend on a prior analysis of instructional activities. Supervisors should assist teachers in making the best possible use of space allotted them or obtainable by them and thus maximizing the learning potential.

A Supervisor Plans Facilities

Mr. French was the district supervisor of health and physical education. He could recite many problems which the physical education department would always face in the existing schools because of improper facilities. He was more than pleased, therefore, to be appointed to the committee to prepare the educational specifications for the next senior high. Membership in this important committee provided an opportunity to explain the instructional program in physical education, particularly its unique aspects.

As the architects converted the educational specifications into drawings, Mr. French continued to study the plans and to serve as liaison between the architects and the physical education staff.

---

[1] Nathaniel Cantor, "The Multidimensional Contexts of Learning," *Educational Forum*, 22:229 (Mar., 1958).

Limited funds kept some requests from materializing, but many improvements did result from this close working relationship, most of which cost little if anything to incorporate. When the building was finished, the physical education facilities were well suited to the instructional program, and the staff was extremely pleased with the working conditions. Was Mr. French's time well spent? Or should he have been supervising instruction?

The Climate for Learning

In the effort to get at the "stuff" of learning, a concerted attempt must be made to discover the basic elements of the process of learning. Specifically identified items of behavior can be coped with; general concepts of learning cannot. By developing criteria for learning which can be measured, observed, and reproduced, the teacher, aided by the supervisor, can more readily deal with otherwise nebulous situations. The learning process then moves from the intangible abstract into the identifiable specific.

Skillful teaching is a complicated act, composed of numerous elements, some of which have not yet been identified. It is in the classroom that modern research in methods must be undertaken, using instruments designed to probe the common professional assumptions, practices, and prejudices. The supervisor must be an astute observer of the instructional scene if he is to help teachers in their daily tasks and with their recurring problems.

Berman discusses the close relationship between inservice programs and programs for students.[2] This is a significant point for the supervisor working with teachers. If he provides opportunities for teachers to function effectively, they in turn will be more inclined to provide similar opportunities for students.

The importance of involvement (participation) at all levels cannot be overemphasized. As the supervisor works with teachers to set up a healthy environment for learning, he must make himself a model for the teachers to emulate. The human element in the learning environment is crucial.

Emotional Factors

The social and emotional climates of the classroom are related to productivity and to the quality of interpersonal relationships. In a

---

[2] Louise M. Berman, "A Third Dimension Makes the Difference," *Educational Leadership* 21:280 ff. (Feb., 1964).

laissez-faire climate (lack of leadership from the teacher), learning effectiveness breaks down. The authoritarian climate tends to keep classroom interaction and intercommunication to a minimum. Competition for status in the eyes of the teacher, the principal, or the group leader rises sharply, and anxiety becomes widespread in a group sponsored by an authoritarian leader.

The effects of leadership and of teacher personality on the social climate of the class are faithfully reflected in the productivity and interpersonal relationship of the class members. A good classroom atmosphere is achieved by the teacher who makes proper use of learning incentives in a climate which is neither laissez-faire nor authoritarian. The student gets into the work quickly, sustains his interest in productive learning until the work is finished, and forms good relationships with his classmates.

The emotional climate is influenced by the emotional health of the members of the class and particularly that of the teacher. For example, a class often behaves nervously when confronted by a nervous teacher. A supervisor observing this phenomenon might be especially concerned if he also observes that a teacher ridicules, isolates, or overstimulates students. Noting that a teacher is too short with students, or unreasonably demanding of them, the supervisor can be fairly sure that the emotional climate of the class is less than desirable. Does the supervisor find quarreling, moodiness, fighting, cheating, name-calling, defacing of property, nail-biting, excessive laughing without sufficient reason, and perhaps tics and twitches in students? Does he detect lack of harmony or resentment, vindictiveness, or a general negative and defeatist attitude in teachers? These and related behaviors may be indicative of poor emotional climate. The teacher needs assistance and encouragement to change the classroom atmosphere. In contrast to such symptoms, a healthy learning environment actively fosters creativity, enthusiasm, interest, excitement about learning, and self-control.

Tina Presents a Problem

Miss Hinley always had mixed feelings when she visited Lincoln Junior High. Two young English teachers presented such contrasts. Miss Hinley found herself drawn to Alice Orr's room because so many exciting things were always taking place. It was invigorating and stimulating to see students so eager to learn, happily working, yet serious about what they were doing. And, of course, Alice herself was always bubbling with enthusiasm. Certainly this teacher was competent and well-adjusted! But just down the hall was Tina. Her room was dull and listless by comparison. Miss Hinley was forced to spend much more time with Tina. There had been progress over the year — even Principal Bark had acknowledged that — but in view of her efforts Miss Hinley felt that it was unreasonably slow. "Tina is better organized these days and she has done something about the looks of her room since the last visit, but she is still using those nervous mannerisms as much as ever. She almost dances around the front of the room when she makes her assignments, and she waves her hands and arms until the students begin to get restless. The worst part of all is the way her voice rises in pitch and intensity as she becomes nervous."

Naturally her students mirrored Tina's nervousness and misbehaved. Miss Hinley took a deep breath to steel herself for the expected and opened the door of Tina's classroom for another visit.

Teacher Expectations

The best teaching-learning situation is one in which there is an attitude of questioning in an atmosphere permeated by positive human relations. Questioning is not solely the prerogative of the teacher or it would eternally frustrate the learner. Questioning by the pupils is most important. It matters not how simple the question. The sole criterion is: Does the knowledge called for move the learner forward? Numerous questions from pupils are the sine qua non of teaching. They become the guidelines of method and of content. They are basic to curriculum construction. They represent pupil interest and pupil motivation. To ignore them is to teach in a vacuum.

Questioning, however, will give little positive stimulation or intellectual satisfaction in the absence of effective human relations. When this omission is noted, the supervisor should call it to the attention of the teacher. Applying the principles of human relations to learning and to building wholesome attitudes, teachers and supervisors alike will find the following worthy of sober reflection (to apply the list to supervision, the word *teacher* may be substituted for the word *pupil*):

1. Every pupil has intrinsic worth.
2. The pupil is a complex individual.
3. Individual differences exist in all human traits.
4. The pupil reacts as a totality to a given situation.

5. Adjustment to society and to social conditions is a continuous process.

6. Pupils can and do think for themselves, a fact often overlooked by teachers.

7. Motivation and perception are the key factors in adjustment.

8. In a democracy, self-determination, within limits, is the right of every individual, and therefore planning and evaluation are imperative in cooperative learning situations.

9. Individual pupils should be studied and understood and effectively taught in the light of their environment, their social and psychological conditioning, and their behavior in this environment.

10. The ultimate goal of education should be effective, efficient citizenship.

11. Every human being (pupil) has a need to achieve and to be recognized.

12. Each pupil should have opportunities for growth and self-improvement.

13. Each pupil has the need to belong, to be a member of the group, to be an "insider," as it were.

14. Each pupil needs many opportunities to contribute to the lessons, to the discussion, to the progress of the group.

15. Each pupil should have the right (by virtue of his participation in the learning process) to know what the institution (teachers especially) expects of him (objectives) day by day.

16. Each pupil should have the right (by virtue of his partnership in the learning contract) to know whether he is progressing, and to what degree.

17. Each pupil should have the right (by virtue of the purposes of education) to be given only worthwhile, highly productive assignments within the range of his abilities and capacity to perform.

18. Every pupil should have the right (by virtue of the teaching-learning contract — assignment or project) to have his work carefully (professionally) inspected and evaluated.

19. Every pupil should be evaluated against himself — his own ability and capacity — rather than against a peer or sibling.

20. Every pupil should be regarded as a unique combination of attitudes, abilities, skills, intelligence, understandings, insights,

stamina, perceptions, and motivation. Teaching a roomful of thirty pupils is one of the most complicated of social processes known to modern culture.

21. In terms of participation, the special abilities and interests of pupils should be utilized in the interests of effective learning.

22. Rest and recreation after periods of hard work and strain should be provided for all.

23. New pupils should be introduced to the group and to the work by the teacher and a selected group of older pupils.

24. No pupil should be allowed to become a hermit, or to become routinized into monotony.

25. Every honest inquiry merits attention, and every child's questions should be given honest attention.

The supervisor should assist teachers in improved use of questions in their classrooms. At the same time, he should encourage the practice of wholesome human relations. In the final analysis, it is the teacher who, more than any other one person or thing, establishes the climate for learning. A major function of the supervisor should be to provide support and incentive as well as leadership and encouragement in making the climate for learning favorable. One of his basic objectives should be to locate and emphasize new methods of improving the learning climate.

Challenging the Supervisor

Supervisor Green is having a good year. In fact, this has probably been his most exciting year in the profession. He has found a group of classroom teachers in one of the high schools who are not only professionally competent and energetic but intellectually inquisitive. They have taken upon themselves the challenge of stimulating a group of "slow learners" by following sound learning principles. It was their idea and they have sought his assistance, so he has been feeding them reading materials, particularly research studies of all kinds which might have relevance to the problem. Together they have determined the goals for their classes and agreed upon several rather general courses of action. Many old methods have fallen by the wayside and many new techniques have been tested as the teachers continue to look for better ways to work with these students. A constant interchange and a running dialogue have kept the teachers interested in the project. More importantly, however, the students themselves have had a "new awakening" and are making much greater progress than anyone had dared to anticipate.

Mr. Green would be the first to admit that he did not originate the idea but that he had become a willing participant. How would you evaluate Mr. Green's experience in terms of values and priorities in supervision?

The Role of the Teacher

In public education, as conceived in the United States, the teacher is accorded an important place in the learning process. He is the prime mover in the development of optimum conditions for learning. Since many persons affirm this principle and communities generally support it, one might reasonably expect that every kind of aid possible to enhance the teacher's work would be made available. Unfortunately, this is not usually the case. Communities want good schools, and people say they want a quality education for their children, but they then often deny the teacher (1) *materials* needed to teach and to challenge learning, (2) *a salary* that would permit concentration on the job of teaching (including growing on the job), (3) *time* to do the work (all sorts of additional assignments and interferences are permitted), and (4) some clear *directions* or goals (he is pressured by both professional and lay — often uninformed — leaders, sometimes toward conflicting directions).

Excellence in teaching is dependent upon excellence in other institutional departments: library facilities, administration, ancillary and supportive services, financial support, academic provisions, policies of personnel administration which do not stress money, tenure, politics, or community "leadership," and other extraneous factors. Excellence in methods requires that time be made available for study, for planning, for research, and for experimentation. Supervisors should point out at every opportunity that teaching methods must be equated with methods utilized by the highest professions in the community (as exemplified by the surgeon perhaps) rather than with methods identified with the lowest of community services (as exemplified, say, by the baby-sitter). Such a positive emphasis on excellence in support for teaching might contribute to morale of teachers and promote esprit de corps. Without such encouragement, the supervisor certainly runs the risk of apathy or even of a defeatist attitude among the teaching staff.

The Classroom Climate

The teacher, as we have said, controls many of the qualities which make a good climate for learning within the classroom. He must plan ahead to set up worthwhile learning situations and he should consciously strive to develop an appropriate climate for learning.

The classroom should be a place where horizons are widened, where the student sees beyond his everyday world. These elements should be present:

1. The heart of the school program should be experiences which interest and challenge boys and girls. Vicarious experiences must be based on sufficient firsthand experiences to have meaning to the learners. Knowledge is important, but must be related to action.

2. Many learning experiences should be generated from home and other out-of-school situations. Living and learning at school in turn should be designed to help the child to think and act better in his out-of-school living.

3. School experiences should be consistent with the physical, emotional, intellectual, and spiritual needs of children.

4. A controlling purpose must be that each child shall have the opportunity to grow and develop to his optimum. . . .

5. Differences in the way children learn and achieve must be recognized. Genuine respect for individual differences in all phases of personality and ability calls for an informal classroom atmosphere in which children learn from one another and where questions of boys and girls are welcomed by the teacher and other adults. Learning materials of varying degrees of difficulty are essential. . . .

6. The criterion of achievement should be growth in desirable behavior characteristics, desirable action in performing the tasks of daily living now and in the future. . . .

7. Evaluation, a process of decision-making that is indispensable to effective learning, should be an actual part of teaching. It includes determining values, identifying and clarifying purposes, and arriving at judgments of results achieved which are supported by evidence. . . .[3]

[3] Association for Supervision and Curriculum Development, *Creating a Good Environment for Learning,* 1954 Yearbook (Washington: The Association, 1954), pp. 275–276.

One of the qualities needed by teachers is an insatiable appetite for knowledge. Needed too is a constant curiosity about things and people, changes, inventions, scientific experiments, accompanied by a critical attitude that inquires, "What are the implications?" Teachers should want to examine results.

The supervisor must not leave the development of teacher curiosity and its fulfillment to chance. He must deliberately fan the flames to keep away the chilling effects of complacency. If teachers cease to ask new questions and to search for better answers, ossification will most certainly set in. Moreover, the supervisor should encourage others to carry on projects stimulating to the staff members. He might promote philosophical discussions; he might provide written materials to help the staff find answers to questions as they occur; he might assist individuals to conduct research on previously untried practices.

An Opportunity to Be the Leader

Sam Hendricks dismissed his last class of the day more perfunctorily than usual and quickly made ready to leave his classroom. Sam's normal pattern was to tidy up leisurely, collect his papers from the day's classes, and meet the inevitable group of students who came back to the room to talk.

Today, however, Sam was going to the meeting of the Curriculum Council, and he was already reviewing in his mind how he would make his presentation to that group. Supervisor Imholf had suggested almost two months ago that the council consider new programs or pilot projects which might demonstrate other ways of teaching and learning. Sam and his friend Hank Jennings had spent several evenings over many pots of coffee and had worked closely with Supervisor Imholf exploring a possible variation in teaching economics which would involve students and teachers directly in the community and get them out of a textbook-only approach.

Now they had perfected their proposal. They were certain that it could work if it were just given the chance. The agenda for today's meeting included "Proposed Pilot Project in Economics — Sam Hendricks and Hank Jennings, Bartlett School." Sam was an excited young teacher ready to present and defend his first curriculum proposal.

The Teacher Must Constantly Improve

Whether the schools approve or not, they are in one phase of the greatest technological revolution in education that man has yet experienced. The teacher of tomorrow able to operate successfully in these changed circumstances will have to be a person of many talents. He must learn to be a scholar, he must learn to communicate, he must understand counseling, and he must have a positive personality. He must know how to use the new materials and be acquainted with the new methods. Above all, he must be able to coordinate a variety of talents and resources and focus them on his teaching-learning process.

Methods are not simply mechanical, automatic, electronic, chemical, or biological. They are psychological and social, based on communication, interaction, rapport, experience, maturation, sequential activities, organization, and personality. This is the reason machines will never displace the teacher.

It has been said that learning is a complex process. Can it then be argued that the methods of teaching are simple? The more sophisticated teachers in the public schools today utilize various techniques. They must, for emotionally involving the learner is a difficult task requiring keen insight into the learner and his life. Free and open-ended exploration of problems, the search for meaning, for relationships or causal connections, the development of the ability to suspend judgment, and the practice of independent thinking are facets of the complicated process of teaching.

Utilizing the social background and the empirical knowledge of students in order to enhance continuous, sequential learnings is not a task to be entrusted to the inadequately trained, unprofessional, and unqualified teacher so often employed by a board of education as a stopgap. He will always be recognized by the profession as an opportunist and not as a professional. He is not competent to treat the classroom as an organizing center for learning, much less to create optimum conditions for learning. This pseudo professional presents a special challenge to the supervisor.

One supervisor of considerable experience noted that the optimum climate for learning today is analogous to the attitude of cosmonauts and the preparation inside a space vehicle programming a landing. All systems are tuned to reentry and landing in a given area. This is the goal of the systems. In learning, all systems — social, psychological, and instructional — are oriented toward an educational objective: changed behavior on the part of pupils and teachers.

When optimum conditions prevail, supervisors report an air of excitement among pupils at the thought of excursions into unknown territory. The classroom with its books, magazines, projectors, radios, television sets, experimental equipment, and construction materials becomes a glamorous, attractive, and inviting situation with kaleidoscopic possibilities for new experiences and for igniting new interests.

In this exhilarating world of fantastic reality for the learner (the truth being stranger than fiction since its inventor is infinitely more ingenious), the master teacher contrives experiences that act as catalysts of reality. Given an atmosphere of freedom and spontaneity, and a sense of order and purpose both in what he is trying to do and in the universe, the pupil becomes preoccupied with learning. The value of administratively planned incentives (scores, marks, rewards) pales into insignificance in light of the discoveries pupils and teachers make for themselves.

Keeping Teachers "Sharp"

Miss Sara Smith is the newly appointed supervisor for the language arts in the district, and Miss Smith is frustrated. For the past five years she has taught senior English and before that, for more years than she cares to remember, junior high English.

This new position represents both a step into the unknown and a terrific challenge. She believes she knows what needs to be done, but will the other teachers accept her efforts toward improvement? She hopes so, and the superintendent thinks so.

There are two major objectives which Sara has established for herself, with the blessing of the director of instruction. She must provide a great deal of support and direct assistance to the new, nontenured teachers who are just developing their teaching patterns and who need help and reassurance. In addition, she must work with the experienced teachers, but in a much different way. They will need support of a material kind — supplies, materials, etc. — to accomplish the task they have set themselves. They will also need encouragement and stimulation to test constantly their teaching procedures in the search for improvement.

Sara is aware that as we become complacent and self-satisfied we also tend to become sloppy in our work, and a deterioration usually sets in. She is firmly convinced that even the best teacher tends to become less sharp, and less effective, and just a little lazy unless he encounters some individual challenge. She has no intention of presenting a threat to the teachers, but she wants to help them "stay sharp." Her immediate problem is what to do.

Sara decides to start by outlining her ideas for the entire group and concentrating at first on those who express an interest. Would a successful beginning with this group make the desired impression on the rest?

The Role of Administration

The administrator must have the ability to work with teachers and laymen so that the best possible educational plans will be formulated and executed. Improvement of instruction is recognized as one of the major responsibilities of administration. Principals can render the best service to their faculties by assisting teachers to grow intellectually, providing orientation programs, initiating effective inservice education, avoiding making decisions for others, encouraging initiative and experimentation, and creating a friendly, relaxed, democratic atmosphere.

The classroom climate may, indeed, depend upon the administrator. The geographical and organizational distance between the superintendent and the teacher increases as the system expands. Even if he wanted to help teachers directly, it would be impossible. He must provide this assistance through his staff and through well-designed inservice programs.

When administration is related to teaching and learning, one of its functions becomes that of ensuring that the teaching-learning process shall not be disturbed or unreasonably terminated. Constant interruptions of students and teachers at work for various activities, needless assemblies, etc., are inimical to learning. One teacher was heard to remark recently on the lament of another, "His work suffers so many interruptions that he actually teaches only four hours of the five per day allotted him in the schedule." Administration has failed to perform its protective function when such conditions prevail.

The administrator has certain special problems in developing optimum conditions for learning. The first is the procurement of competent, qualified, and intellectually alert leaders for the supportive positions: directors, coordinators, consultants, supervisors, department heads, psychologists, social workers, teachers of reading, counselors, speech therapists, etc. It is the responsibility of the administrator not only to provide as many qualified persons to fill these positions as possible but to make sure that they understand the interrelationship of the positions. Competition among staff members will then be kept to a minimum and all can better work together to accomplish the goals of the district.

Second, it is the administrator's duty to provide, to the limit of the budget, supporting materials and supplies and the clerical assistance needed for instructional purposes. Few school districts have actually given the instructional support needed to develop excellence. Too often administrators have acceded to fiscal pressures and settled for less. Today with the new potential available through electronics and through the revolutionary increase in materials, the instructional program can be greatly improved by the judicious expenditure of funds. The wise administrator will seek the advice of his assistants, including the supervisor, before encumbering his budgeted funds. In this manner he will be acquiring those items that are most needed and will be put to fullest use.

Third, the administrator should see to it that each pupil is challenged to the limit of the student's abilities. Collecting thirty or thirty-five pupils in a classroom under the direction of a "teacher" will seldom suffice. Instruction has to be on their level. Hence, he will study grouping and use it until better administrative methods are invented. He will be constantly working with his staff to discover how to utilize their strengths and minimize their weaknesses.

Fourth, the extracurricular program must be made to serve its proper purpose. It is neither the ultimate in education nor the doormat. It should consist of experiences for pupils which the school cannot provide in the regular class situation. Its main objectives are effective citizenship, a personal commitment to civic betterment, and a well-rounded individual. It trains leaders, makes intelligent followers, and opens consideration of avocations, hobbies, recreation, and personal development. With all the furor for intellectual development, extracurricular activities become more, not less, important.

Fifth, the administrator concerns himself with the improvement of the personnel, both certified and noncertified. He should depend upon his supervisors for leadership and information. He should support an inservice education program and throw the resources of the system behind its leaders. Almost every school district of fair size mounts an inservice program of some kind, and for numerous reasons: (1) orientation, (2) increasing knowledge in a subject matter area, (3) improving competence in professional skills (testing, making tests, scoring, marking, statistics, evaluation, textbook selection, curriculum development, unit construction, etc.), (4) induction into the problems of accreditation, certification, teacher education, unionism versus the NEA, and self-determination (including the policing of the profession), and (5) general intellectual and professional stimulation.

Sixth, every administrator is always and forever concerned with improving educational opportunities for the community. He is constantly engaged in community-wide public relations projects, the purpose of which is to raise the quality of education. Since he is very often the director or the coordinator of such a program, it is in accordance with his competence and leadership or the lack of it that in some districts the school levy is passed with an overwhelming majority while in others it is defeated. The levy determines how much money is available for the materials center, for clerical help, for special personnel, for inservice education, and for the down-to-earth necessities. The school levy determines whether Johnnie will get individual attention, whether that speech teacher will be employed, or that social worker, or that psychologist. This is a heavy burden on the administrator. Yet he can turn to the staff, the teachers, the entire system to help him put over his point with the public. He had better do so. For if he tries it alone, the community must hold him responsible if he fails.

Finally, his most important problem is the recruitment of the best teachers available. All his other provisions will benefit the pupil very little if poorly educated, incompetent teachers are employed. Whether he or someone he delegates does the recruiting, the person doing it should study teacher education programs and institutions. He should know where strong instructional programs are to be found, where programs are adequately staffed with professional personnel, and how applicants for teacher education are selected.

Selling Versus Participating

Adjoining districts were scheduled for tax elections on the same day. The administration in District A assembled on one page "tax facts" which gave the bare essentials of the tax proposal. This was read at several PTA meetings just prior to the election date and it was also made available to the local press. On election day everyone sat back and waited for the proposal to be passed. It failed by a large percentage.

The administration in District B first arrived at the amount of its tax increase after much public debate both within the professional staff and in the community. Not only could anyone interested in finding out know the particulars; many felt that they had personally played an active part in arriving at the final decision.

When the election date was set, the administration carried on an active campaign throughout the district. Voting areas representing large groups which had in the past not been strong proponents of school issues were treated with special care. Lay volunteers and members of the professional staff tried to reach all voters and to "sell" those inclined to vote "no" as well as those who were undecided. A particular effort was made to keep the teachers well informed so they might clearly understand the proposal in its entirety and could in conscience support it. For example, all teachers were well aware that approval of the tax proposal meant not only the long-awaited salary boost but improved equipment and supplies for more class-rooms in the district. As one might anticipate, District B voters easily approved the proposal.

Administration Works with the Board

Someone has said that the most important task any school board has is the selection of a superintendent. But it is also true that the most important task a superintendent has is the education of the board, collectively and individually. Board attitude and policy are critical aspects of developing optimum conditions for learning. There must be genuine concern for buildings, good salaries, and libraries. The vast fields of methodology, instructional materials, and special service personnel are entirely dependent upon the level of understanding a board has of the function of instruction and the problems of providing mass education.

Boards must have adequate and proper information to make policy decisions about curriculum, supervision, teaching, and instructional services. Not many board members have the educational background or professional understanding necessary to analyze these functions, and not many would be willing or able to give the time needed to become competent to do so. But they do need to know of and usually are interested in the conditions necessary for a quality program. The superintendent is the crucial person in this matter of educating the board. To be sure he will do only some of the instructing of the board; more of it will be done by his trusted professional lieutenants, including his supervisors.

The supervisor may suggest ways and means through which the board can inform itself. Board members can attend professional conferences even though they are not professional educators. They can be formed into teams and urged to attend meetings of the National School Board Association, the American Association of School Superintendents, the National Association of Secondary Principals, the Association for Supervision and Curriculum Development, and perhaps others. It should be pointed out to board members that representatives of boards in nearly all states can travel to such meetings at district expense; once they know this, board members are not so reluctant to attend.

In most states, the state department of education will provide consultants free of charge to assist in the education of boards. Specialists in school administration and other fields are available through the local universities. All school board members should be familiar with certain periodicals of educational significance.

More time should be spent in board meetings on the curriculum, the special services, and the results of the instructional program. Often boards concentrate on financial matters or building construction problems, as though these were their main considerations, or the ultimate purpose of the school. Probably they know more about these fields than about technical problems of instruction and curriculum and therefore feel more comfortable dealing with such familiar items.

One function often ascribed to the board is that of interpreting to the community the educational needs of youth, programs required to meet these needs, and the results of the programs. This is the point at which there must be close cooperation between administrator and supervisor. Not only can they reinforce each other, but individually they can identify personnel who are uniquely qualified to make reports, give demonstrations, and provide the evidence to assist the board in executing its functions.

The Supervisor Develops His Role

Mr. Quick is one of the "new breed" of administrators. He is personable, self-assured, competent, with a new degree in administration from a noted university. He has been assigned the principalship of the largest, and oldest, senior high in the district.

A cursory study indicates to him that there is much work to be done before he can expect to have an outstanding operation. He recognizes that he must get as much specialized assistance as there is available to work with him. He takes several "first steps" to recruit this assistance.

1. He meets with the central staff in his building — first the vice-principals, then the department chairmen and counselors. He describes his goals and ambitions for the school and listens to their comments and suggestions, most of which fit into the plan he is developing.

2. He meets with the district supervisors to identify the competences and specialties needed by teachers to be assigned to his building. This information will be transmitted to the personnel office so a search can be instituted by the district recruiters. He knows that unless he has teachers with expertise it will be impossible to accomplish the goals he has set.

3. Mr. Quick now settles down to work with his staff and with the instructional supervisors. He is aware of the support and technical assistance available only through these specialists, and he recognizes his own limitations both in time and in detailed knowledge of all the disciplines. Has Mr. Quick learned how to use the assistance available throughout the district to the best advantage?

The Role of the Supervisor

Providing the best possible conditions for learning is a challenging task for the supervisor and one that will require the use of a system of priorities. He cannot attack all problems at once and he cannot help all teachers simultaneously. Recent pressures have so increased the supervisor-teacher ratio that it becomes extremely difficult, if not impossible, to find time for individual teachers.

Luckily, the supervisor has strong allies in most administrators and boards of education. Since these people are aware that their decisions directly affect the quality of education, the supervisor is in a position to launch a program aimed at the orientation and education of the administrators, the board, and the community. In this endeavor he has another ally: the attitude of the public, which is demanding better schools.

A supervisor renders a variety of services. He constantly seeks fresh approaches to the task of helping teachers to teach better. He hunts up materials for classroom use of the teachers. He assists teachers to study youth and the problems of teaching subject content to them. He aids teachers to put various aspects of the curriculum into proper perspective since from his vantage point he has a clearer overall picture of the whole.

Helen Conserves Her Time

Helen Kane at one time felt strongly that her role as supervisor for the secondary schools included regular reading of a wide range of journals plus careful examination of new materials in the various subject areas. She read several hours each day (usually late at night) and much of each weekend.

As the number of journals increased, Helen found herself falling farther and farther behind. The unread stacks grew taller. In desperation, she finally realized that she was failing and made the difficult decision that she could not read everything available and do the rest of her job too.

After some study and a survey of what her counterparts in other districts had done, she put all materials and journals in the Materials Resource Center. Then the task of making such resources known to the teachers became her new responsibility. She arranged help for teachers who came to examine these materials to make the best use of their time.

As teachers throughout the district became accustomed to the new practice, Helen realized that she was much closer to her original intent of aiding teachers to become and stay knowledgeable, and her own time was being used to better advantage.

The supervisor develops an atmosphere in which teachers willingly cooperate with and assist each other. He encourages an attitude of curiosity about things professional, trends, and changes in certain phases of education, and through the inservice program arranges for continuity, sequence, and balance of offerings. He provides leadership in the study of problems and takes teachers' recommendations seriously in the development of the program. He cuts through red tape and helps get hold of needed instructional materials; he plays the ombudsman role.

The supervisor should make as definitive a study as possible of what constitutes an optimum learning situation in order to set up criteria for evaluating learning conditions in his own system. Surely it would be better to do this in cooperation with the faculty and staff because more people could profit from the study. It is the supervisor's task to devise unique and exciting ways of creating the best possible environment for learning.

Teachers have been steeped in the scholarly, objective world of the professor and his discipline. They often teach the child and adolescent as they were taught in college. They require from students many hours of homework, the reading of numerous paper-backs, the enduring of chores that defy persistence, all symbolized by students carrying loads of books and notebooks. These teachers need assistance in changing their approaches to teaching, in de-emphasizing marks and stressing learning, in reducing the anonymity in large schools or large classes by increasing opportunities for participation. They can learn to use many different kinds of materials and get away from the rigidity of a single text. They can learn to use evaluation (explanation and interpretation) and feedback rather than testing for marking purposes. They can learn to emphasize divergent thinking rather than convergent thinking. Perhaps with all this the learner can be removed from the assembly line and the school can recapture some of its human qualities.

There are other equally difficult tasks for supervisors if the classroom climate is to be improved. Overcrowding must be reduced in the interests of involvement and interaction. Rigid schedules must give way to flexibility to meet the challenge of the learning task. Every possible use should be made of the informal group to increase morale, productivity, and efficiency.

Summary

A primary objective of the supervisory process is the establishment and maintenance of a wholesome, fertile learning environment. The supervisor must be aware of and concerned with the physical conditions surrounding, supporting, and impinging on the learning process. He should set the tone for the climate for learning established by the teacher, the school, and the district and support teachers in their efforts to improve the environment for learning through innovation and creative teaching. The main ingredient in the learning environment with which the supervisor works is the teacher himself. The role of administration in establishing a satisfactory learning environment is very important, even crucial, to the eventual outcome.

Problems for Group Discussion

Analyze the following situations. In each, identify supervisory principles representing sound theory, if any are included. What are the basic elements which made a difference? How would you have approached the situation?

1. During the summer, the science supervisor prepared materials, ordered some new equipment, and set about obtaining information on new materials and new programs. In addition, he started a file of resource persons and field trip locations throughout the community. When school opened, all science teachers were invited to visit his office and explore the "resource center." At that time the teachers were shown how best to use the available material, information, etc.

2. Over a period of years, an elaborate testing program had developed in the district. The supervisor began to be aware of an undercurrent of protest among the teachers over the amount of class time used for testing and the way the pacing of the testing interfered with their instructional efforts. He undertook to study means of eliminating the negative aspects while retaining the positive portions of the program.

3. A social studies teacher is disturbed because her class is failing to achieve the behavioral outcomes hoped for. She is certain that the behavior she is seeking is possible, but her evaluation of the class shows she is not succeeding. The teacher approaches the supervisor with her problem.

Selected Readings

Association for Supervision and Curriculum Development. *Creating a Good Environment for Learning.* 1954 Yearbook. Washington: The Association, 1954.

Association for Supervision and Curriculum Development. *Perceiving, Behaving, Becoming.* 1962 Yearbook. Washington: The Association, 1962.

Berman, Louise M. "A Third Dimension Makes the Difference," *Educational Leadership,* 21:280 ff. (Feb., 1964).

Bruner, Jerome. *Toward a Theory of Instruction.* Cambridge, Mass.: Harvard University Press, Belknap Press, 1966.

Bruner, Jerome, *et al. Studies in Cognitive Growth.* New York: John Wiley & Sons, 1966.

Cantor, Nathaniel. "The Multidimensional Contexts of Learning," *Educational Forum,* 22:229 (Mar., 1958).

Davis, Robert A., *et al.* "The Teaching Problems of 1075 Public School Teachers," *Journal of Experimental Education,* 9:41–60 (Sept., 1940).

Dusel, William J. "Inservice Education for the Language Arts," *Educational Administration and Supervision,* 41:153–161 (Mar., 1955).

Miller, Starr. "Problems of Teachers That Can Point Up Needed Revision in Training Programs," *Educational Administration and Supervision,* 41:47–50 (Jan., 1955).

seven

•

Supervision and the Changing of Teacher Behavior

Teachers are not all alike, and the problems they present the supervisor with are many and varied, ranging from personal to professional. They have different styles of teaching, different degrees of competence, and different levels of awareness of what takes place in the classroom. They have their own rates of professional development and have reached various points along the road to maturity. Obviously, therefore, they require different kinds of attention. This chapter treats the methods a supervisor may use to help teachers change their behavior.

Counseling teachers and working with them on a one-to-one ratio has long been cited as a most valuable means of assisting them. Recently, Berman and Usery wrote that any major changes in the thinking and feeling (roots of behavior) of an individual frequently are the result of the influence of one person upon him.[1] Vergason cited individual aid as a way to improve teacher morale and to solve problems.[2] The interaction is personal and direct, based on the needs, interests, motivations, and patterns of thinking of the individual. When properly planned and conducted, these counseling situations become stimuli for changed performance.[3]

While it is true that the time necessary for individualized con-

---

[1] Louise M. Berman and Mary Lou Usery, *Personalized Supervision: Sources and Insights* (Washington: Association for Supervision and Curriculum Development, 1966), p. 1.
[2] A. L. Vergason, "Supervisory Conferences," *Bulletin of the National Association of Secondary Principals*, 34:245–251 (Dec., 1950).
[3] Robert M. Gagne, *The Conditions of Learning* (New York: Holt, Rinehart & Winston, 1967), p. 6.

ferences is difficult to come by, nevertheless the supervisor must make that time available for some teachers. Knowing when a conference is necessary and when other methods will suffice may well make the difference between an overworked average supervisor and a highly successful one.

Providing Personalized Assistance

The Stimulus Situation

The external stimulus situation may lead to the beginning of personalized assistance. External stimuli may take the form of pressure from the community to move through the curriculum faster or pressure from the school authorities to write curriculum materials or to provide objective evidence of pupil progress. They could arise in the classroom itself. The teacher's own motivations, values, and aspirations for his pupils represent his internalized stimuli. If the external stimulus situation conflicts with internal stimuli, such tensions may be generated that the teacher's efficiency is affected. If the two kinds of stimuli are consistent with each other, they will be mutually reinforcing.

The supervisor enters the picture for the purpose of helping the teacher analyze his situation and find new ways of behaving. This is a primary social situation in which the relationships are direct and communication goes on face to face. It requires good counseling techniques. In analyzing the situation, supervisor-counselor and teacher look for causes, influences, or alternative outcomes. This kind of professional help is a matter of fitting information and facts together in reasonable relationships or possible associations acceptable to the teacher.

For example, one highly motivated teacher may be so enthusiastic and so determined to succeed in new and creative ways that he tends to be ineffective in his teaching. Here the supervisor would attempt to assist the teacher to identify priorities and to establish a clear sense of direction for his innovations. Another teacher might represent the opposite attitude toward teaching, being uninterested in doing anything new or different. Here the supervisor would attempt to stimulate the teacher to develop a desire to venture. Alternatives should be presented in such a manner that the teacher can eventually select his own behavior pattern. It must not be imposed from outside if it is to be most effective.

The Role of the Supervisor

Every supervisor must learn the skills of a personal-professional counselor. They may be the combination that unlocks the problem and releases teacher initiative and talent. In his role as counselor, the supervisor may find that such professional problems as checking on the cognitive outcomes of teaching, or evaluating the quality of interaction in the classroom, or employing pupil interests in order to eliminate undesirable pupil behavior produce internal pressures on the instructor and threaten his personal morale. Sometimes teachers themselves can identify the causes for their lowered morale, but often they need the aid of a wise supervisor to adjust their methods and behavior patterns properly in order to remedy the situation.

It is quite obvious that the psychology of individual differences applies to teachers — and to their teaching. Some teachers stroll through their lessons day after day quite unaware of how inadequately they have conceptualized the field of teaching. In dealing with such a person, one might generate some dissatisfaction with the present status of his art of teaching. Increasing and intensifying stimuli from the outside may result in stepped-up desire and interest within the individual. This might be accomplished by comparing the results of his performances and those of others, by the use of demonstrations, or by providing time off for observations of carefully selected situations. Thus the teacher can see for himself the difference between his world and the professional world, and awareness of the discrepancy may prove the basis for changed behavior. There is also a danger that the contrast might supply the inadequate teacher with what he would interpret as a fixed answer.

Another generalized approach to changing a teacher's cognitive structure is to utilize such techniques as inspirational talks, exhortations to change, directed readings, short case histories, success stories, and vignettes of unusually successful teachers and school systems to raise the aspirations of the teacher. Gradually the acceptable pattern may come to mean innovation, change, progress, involvement, risk, supplementing the curriculum, varying the methods, and finding satisfaction from a comradeship with the avant-garde. But this approach may imperil morale.

Whatever the devices eventually utilized by the supervisor — and they should include more than one — careful consideration must be given to their selection. Perhaps the best is the conference with the individual teacher dealing with the teacher's conception of his problem. Holding such a conference implies a knowledge of the teacher and a thoughtful analysis of his problem. It also implies a mutually acceptable solution which is worked out cooperatively, not imposed. In the past, too many supervisors have felt compelled to provide *the answer* and have defeated themselves in the process.

Types of Approach

Personnel counseling is generally divided into three types. One of these is commonly known as directive counseling and consists in telling the other person what to do. Often ideas and practices are forced upon the teacher; the relationship between teacher and supervisor is then one of expert versus novice, professional versus beginner. The supervisor gives information and interprets data. He also interprets the approved practices, school regulations, and policies, then instructs the teacher what steps to take. The success of the treatment depends upon the teacher's willingness to accept and his ability to follow the supervisor's directions.

The second approach is known as nondirective counseling.[4] It is assumed that the major resources for the solution of the teacher's problems lie within himself. He needs a sympathetic ear so he can talk out his problems, all facets of them, to the smallest detail. He "lets his hair down" in the presence of the supervisor (the conference is held in the strictest confidence). From this stage of talking and analysis, the teacher is encouraged to make recommendations for himself. The supervisor in a skillful and studied fashion keeps the conference moving, but without being personally involved. He provides reinforcement, suggestions, interpretations, and information indirectly, letting the teacher make his own decisions.

Somewhere between these two lies a third approach which utilizes elements of both. It assumes that with some teachers the nondirective type is better while with others the supervisor needs to be more directive. The backgrounds and personalities of teachers are very important in their perceptions and in the expectations they have of supervisors. Sometimes a mix of directive and nondirective methods

[4] A. H. Maslow, "Self-Actualizing People: Psychological Health," in C. Gratton Kemp, ed., *Perspectives on the Group Process* (Boston: Houghton Mifflin Company, 1964), pp. 290–294.

in different proportions proves more effective than either approach alone.

The modern teacher is quite well educated, and both teacher and supervisor are presumably endowed with intelligence. Each has talents needed for solving the problem under consideration. In individualized supervision, the full range of the supervisor's philosophy is utilized. Good human relations and freedom pervade the atmosphere. Full use is made of two-way communication, participation in the process, and respect for the individual. Variety aids in understanding, reason is used in decision making, and progress is outlined and anticipated.

If the relationship between the supervisor and teachers is of the right kind, conferences will be initiated by teachers more often than by the supervisor. One index of the supervisor's success is the degree to which he is consulted. Is he needed? Is he sought after? Is he invited to observe classes?

Fundamentally, the individualized conference must be considered a continuation of teacher education, formal or informal, started in the preservice years. Just as the college or university employs the finest and best-trained professors it can obtain, so should the public school find the most talented, capable, well-educated people in the profession for the counseling approach to supervision. The trend is in this direction.

The supervisor who has developed a professional rapport with teachers will find that his conference time is in demand by those who desire his assistance because he poses no threat to their career but provides a sounding board for them to "talk out" their problems. They realize that as a fellow professional the supervisor is eager to help them help themselves. His aid might result in clarification of the problem itself, in the outlining of several alternative courses of action, in the provision of facilities or materials. It should represent something tangible that is not readily accessible to the teacher alone.

The Working Climate

Working with a teacher in a one-to-one relationship is not a simple matter of giving advice. The supervisor does not "straighten out" a teacher; any climate will do for this. The interaction required is teamwork. The supervisor must set up a working climate that implies the mutual interest of both himself and the teacher in the project. The supervisor accepts and treats persons as individuals.

He and the teacher are not attacking each other or impugning each other's actions or adequacy. If the supervisor has to impress the teacher with his accomplishments, constantly seizing every opportunity to fatten his ego, he is prejudicing the results. Teachers must be reassured as to the integrity and discretion of the supervisor. If anyone is to be "on the spot," it should be the supervisor because he comes into the situation under the assumption that he can be of service.

The climate should be of a permissive nature. The teacher should have complete freedom to talk, to express an opinion, and to ask any questions. There must be total freedom to disagree and to discuss any point. It might be easier for the supervisor to make comments on points rather than to raise additional questions. But questions can initiate the reflective thinking process, which is the beginning of change. The supervisor must learn the art of questioning. He can take cues from the statements made and from the countenance of the teacher, his manner of communication, changes of expression, gestures, etc. One of the most difficult of supervisory behaviors, but part of the real world of the modern supervisor, is to solicit, accept, and utilize teachers' ideas.

It is hard for the neophyte supervisor to establish a working relationship with teachers. He has to learn to pace himself and the tempo of the interview. Often he is either too eager to "get something done" (after all, he has other business to conduct) or completely nondirective and willing to wait until the teacher can solve his own problem regardless of the time consumed. Yet some constructive deliberation at this stage may very well pay off in productive results later. The more experienced supervisor will invest extra time here to ensure the long-range quality of the conference results.

Other Approaches to Changing Behavior

In addition to individualized assistance, discussed above, group process has been used effectively for problem solving and for changing individual behavior; it is described in Chapter Nine. Travel is another agent of change. The one most important factor is knowing exactly what change is to be made. This requires the supervisor to develop behavioral objectives for his own work.

Other approaches make use of audio-visual equipment and video tapes. Micro teaching, as developed at Stanford University, is characteristic of this general procedure. Tapes are used to present models or to compare good teaching with poor teaching. Micro teaching involves concentration on one technique (opening a lesson, teacher reinforcement of pupil response, etc.) for a short lesson (five to ten minutes). The performance is carefully analyzed, criticized, and then replayed with planned modifications. Evidence supports the assumption that behavior can be changed by such methods.

Supervisors have found special instruments to study interaction very useful in helping teachers change their behavior. Two of these are the Flanders Interaction Analysis Technique and the OScAR4V system.[5] Both are concerned with teacher behavior and provide schedules for behavior analysis. Having carefully recorded teacher-pupil interaction, supervisor and teacher can examine what kind of behavior may have hindered or disrupted learning and what kind seems to have facilitated it. With these data before him, almost any teacher could improve his interaction pattern.

Two additional approaches hold promise for success; the supervisor must be intimately associated with them when used. One is I-B-F supervision, developed by William Hill, director of the Xenia (Ohio) Center for Educational Programming.[6] "I" stands for image, the kind the teacher has of himself and of the role he thinks he is playing as a teacher. "B" represents the behavior he believes necessary to establish and maintain the image he wants. And "F" represents feedback from a number of sources which tells him how well he is doing. With adequate supervisory assistance, each of these three major elements may be analyzed and redesigned cooperatively. A program aimed at changing behavior is then launched.

The second approach is the use of shock treatment, similar to that used in psychotherapy. Gordon Klopf, drawing on the work of Leham, Hoyt, Neugarten, and Berrin, describes the characteristics of adulthood.[7] Adults are generally more restricted in their outlook, more preoccupied, and more concerned with comforts and conven-

---

[5] Donald M. Medley and Russell A. Hill, "Dimensions of Classroom Behavior Measured by Two Systems of Interaction Analysis," *Educational Leadership*, 26:821–824 (May, 1969).

[6] William M. Hill, "I-B-F Supervision," *Clearing House*, 43:539–541 (Nov., 1968).

[7] Gordon J. Klopf, "Helping Adults Change," in *The Supervisor: New Demands/New Dimensions* (Washington: Association for Supervision and Curriculum Development, 1969), pp. 19–27.

iences than children, and they have routinized their behavior. Some dramatic intervention in the usual pattern of behavior may be called for in order to broaden the adult's awareness, modify his commitment, and enrich his experiences. Perhaps a change in physical surroundings is indicated, such as a new room assignment for the teacher or shifting the assignment of the teachers next door so that he has new neighbors. A complete change of instructional materials in the department, including eliminating the textbook and moving to expendable materials, might be tried. Perhaps a change of daily schedule starting with the time of arrival and continuing until the time of departure would provide a "jolt." The "jolt technique" has often been used by administrators who decide to retain someone on his present salary for next year instead of giving him the usual increment. However, unless the teacher knew exactly what behavioral objectives were in question, such a technique might serve no purpose except to arouse resentment toward the administration.

In some districts, especially in the large schools, teachers complain that they do not have freedom to teach. The curriculum is prescribed, they say, and so many variables are controlled from the central office that teachers could not make changes even if they wished to do so. While these allegations contain some truth, there is at least a degree of freedom in even the most bureaucratic school.

Innovative teachers often perceive openings in the armor of the hierarchy. They are less inhibited, less constricted, less enculturated than conformists. And this raises the question of how enculturated teachers and supervisors are. To what extent are teachers predisposed by their education to resist change? Is it possible that inservice education reinforces stereotype behaviors?

The individualized and nonprescriptive approach to changing teacher behavior dramatically separates modern supervision from the traditional, authoritarian approach. Supervisors who persist in prescribing and proscribing exact patterns for teachers demonstrate a limited understanding of the teaching process. They likewise have little comprehension of today's education and will inhibit more creative teaching than they will free in the classroom. Instead, teacher and supervisor together must identify the objectives of instruction and attempt to analyze the teaching act in a logical, rational manner, searching constantly for means of improving the end product for that *individual teacher.*

Stimulating Self-Improvement [8]

If there is any risk involved in making changes, it is a mutual risk, the consequences resting with both teacher and supervisor. Teachers often feel secure in what they have been doing and are doing. Any change arouses anxiety and tension, which in turn may cause undesirable behavior such as overcompensation, emotionalism, or overemphasis on detail.

People have to learn how to make changes. The spirit of confidence must be established in teachers; only then will they try out new ideas. Boxed in by policy statements, red tape, rigid communication lines, or an authoritarian supervisor, teachers learn not to try to venture into new territory. Indeed, there are teachers who no longer even recognize opportunities for improvement because they have not been permitted to seize them in the past.

Change — not just any kind of change but calculated change — should be represented as an adventure upon the seven seas, and as exciting because the outcomes are not all known. Varying the input into the teaching-learning process and checking the results carefully should be stressed. In this way applied research may become an integral part of teaching, and of the teacher's professional repertoire.

Rewards for self-improvement are not to be neglected. The supervisor must provide support. He must be complimentary when genuine effort is exhibited and offer constructive suggestions when the effort seems to founder. Teachers should be encouraged to use what freedom and initiative they have — to build upon what they have done. They can be introduced into the excitement of experimenting, or anticipating outcomes, or being aware of outcomes that were not expected. There is also great satisfaction in knowing that one is growing in competence and knowledge, in the ability to conceptualize teaching in broad terms, and that one is not a victim but rather an initiator of change. Such knowledge reinforces the desired change and encourages repetition.

As stressed in earlier chapters, the prudent supervisor seeks to remove the threat of possible failure and the fear of risk taking. He

---

[8] Arthur W. Combs, "Fostering Self-Direction," *Educational Leadership*, 23:373–376 (Feb., 1966).

recognizes that it is normal for anyone to continue doing that which is understood and is considered relatively pleasant. He also is aware that the unknown can be very menacing to the less adventuresome. Opportunities must, therefore, be provided for teachers to try out as much innovation as they personally can cope with, while the supervisor ensures continual support and necessary encouragement. The supervisor who is able to accomplish this delicate task may in time find teachers growing on the job in discernible and productive ways.

Finding Satisfaction in Teaching

From the work of Maslow one can construct a model of rewards for teacher behavior at different levels of personal need and professional maturity. Early in the teaching career, certain economic and physiological needs are very important. They are followed by so-cial-psychological needs and finally by the need for self-realization. This model is of potential value to the supervisor, provided he is able to identify the level of a teacher's development.

The Order of Rewards

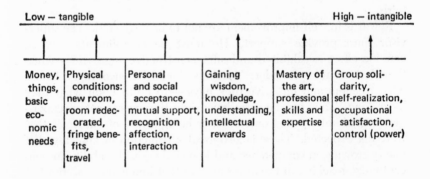

Low — tangible					High — intangible
Money, things, basic economic needs	Physical conditions: new room, room redecorated, fringe benefits, travel	Personal and social acceptance, mutual support, recognition affection, interaction	Gaining wisdom, knowledge, understanding, intellectual rewards	Mastery of the art, professional skills and expertise	Group solidarity, self-realization, occupational satisfaction, control (power)

The Supervisor Is Supportive

Mr. Coland, social studies supervisor for the district, has been working with a large number of the history teachers this year, studying the inclusion of a new, potentially controversial unit in the curriculum. Under his leadership the teachers have selected the content and relevant materials and reached a consensus on the general approach to be taken in the classroom.

Many supervisors would stop at this point and turn to other problems, Mr. Coland speculated, but not he. There remains one important step to complete the operation. He must work closely with the two teachers who will actually teach the unit. On the one hand, he is genuinely interested in what they will do. At the same time, he is aware that they have certain reservations due to the possible controversy attached to the subject and the fact that this is a pilot operation. From time to time they will need advice, encouragement, or perhaps even protection from community critics, although both are master teachers.

Mr. Coland knows that backing the teacher is one of the supervisor's responsibilities, as is encouraging bright, new, innovative teachers. He has adjusted his calendar to reserve time for this assignment. Was his decision a proper one, or should he step out of the picture at this point?

Dimensions of Teacher Needs and Problems

If the supervisor is to individualize his work with teachers, he must understand their needs and problems. One of the authors of the present book recently studied this subject, attempting to identify what items were of most and of least concern to teachers. Results of the study are presented here in some detail, not only for their intrinsic interest but to indicate the kind of investigation a supervisor might carry on in his district and with the teachers he supervises.

Problems of Teachers

Eighty-five teachers working for the master's degree were questioned about teachers' problems. Representing twenty-three different school districts in a metropolitan area, these teachers, some of whom were preparing to be principals, were quite frank and free in their discussion of problems. Their suggestions were classified into professional and personal problems for the purpose of further insight for the supervisor.

The larger category comprised personal problems, which were of several kinds. One type centered mainly on personality. According to the subjects in the study, some teachers have high-strung personalities and are incapable of working with children. Some suffer from ill health or are upset by illness in their immediate families. Some are discontented with the neighborhood environment or with their present status in life. Some are self-centered, social climbers, jealous, or too social and easygoing.

The financial situation of teachers seemed more serious than most supervisors apparently assume. It ranked second in importance among the personal problems of concern to teachers. Over 10 percent of the sample indicated that debts, financing college for children, carrying the responsibility for older relatives at home, and constantly providing for baby-sitters and housekeepers gave rise to stress among their colleagues. These conditions contributed to personal insecurity and sometimes to inferiority feelings.

Lack of income resulted in a considerable amount of moonlighting on the part of teachers. Some found attending night school a drain on their financial resources, but necessary to qualify for promotion. A few were so highly motivated that they were not only holding a full-time job but moonlighting and attending night school at the same time. Obviously this kind of drive and activity could create tensions within the individual as well as in his family.

The survey revealed thirty-eight "outside factors," not specifically personal or economic problems, which cause dissatisfaction among teachers. Most frequently mentioned were clerical duties involving too many official forms, chaperoning students at parties, and the multitude of extraclass duties. Many complained of the mountains of paper work, record keeping, grading of tests, and reading of compositions. The lack of job descriptions for teachers and their assistants was cited as a source of irritation.

These factors led to unhappiness because teachers did not have time to work with pupils. They reported a lack of free periods. In general, the fact that policies on individualized instruction were not implemented was deplored.

Respondents from several school districts complained about inadequate facilities and lack of audio-visual equipment and instructional materials. They spoke of much overcrowding, large classes, and little help with management of these problems.

High on the list of "outside factors" was the matter of leadership. Teachers complained about the poor quality of administration and about the absence of supervisory help. There was criticism of administrative policies which were not implemented and which, from the point of view of the teachers, were not consistent. The arrangements for grouping pupils were reported to be poorly structured. There seemed to be no assistance with problems from either supervisors or principals. In a few cases high turnover of competent administrative and supervisory personnel added to the teachers' frustrations. Frequently there was no grievance procedure. Good work was often unrecognized.

Self-Realization

From the data, it appears that some teachers are forced into conflict with the organization or the "establishment." This condition exists in other organizations and has been described by Argyris[9] and Presthus.[10] Argyris found four kinds of behavior among those who were in conflict with conditions imposed by the organization: quitting, becoming apathetic, taking a defensive attitude, and moving upward in the organization. Presthus classified such individuals as persons who were indifferent, those who were ambivalent, and those who were upward mobile. This classification should be expanded slightly to include such behaviors as apathy, and even withdrawal, on the one hand and aggressive-positive actions on the other. Upward mobile teachers rise in the hierarchy within their own system or to a more responsible position in another system.

Such a variety of possible behaviors in a faculty indicates the need for careful analysis of the individual teacher's conduct. Perhaps some teachers should leave the profession and be guided into other useful, satisfying work. Perhaps some are needlessly defensive. Perhaps upward-bound teachers should be helped to conquer organizational blockings.

It is, therefore, in order to examine both the symptoms and the causes of maladjustment. The treatment the supervisor prescribes for teachers exhibiting behaviors such as apathy, indifference, or ambivalence might be heavily loaded with concern for motivation and purpose. Those demonstrating aggressive but positive behaviors, or who are upward mobile may need only facilitating and supporting assistance from the supervisor. The problems encountered at these levels are vastly different.

Several of the respondents indicated that some teachers lack self-realization in the teaching job. This comment was made in different contexts. Maslow has pointed out that the mature person is one

---

[9] Chris Argyris, *Personality and Organization: The Conflict Between System and the Individual* (New York: Harper & Brothers, 1957).

[10] Robert Presthus, *The Organizational Society: An Analysis and a Theory* (New York: Alfred A. Knopf, 1962), p. 258.

who has achieved self-actualization or self-realization. It would be tragic if their profession were for many teachers inadequate as a meaningful career.

Yet over 15 percent of this sample of teachers noted that some of their own colleagues had no professional interest in their work and exhibited considerable apathy. Certain of their acquaintances demonstrated a lack of motivation, a lack of professional attitude, a lack of enthusiasm for good teaching. A few were identified as old teachers who had lost their drive and were ready to retire. Some were perceived as defensive about their professional growth; they saw no need for inservice education or continued work at the college level. A few evidently did not want to teach and therefore had low morale. Certainly such teachers will never find in teaching any measure of self-realization without expert professional assistance.

Professional Concerns

Probably the item which cropped up most frequently in the responses related to the teachers' lack of preparation in both academic and professional areas. There seemed to be a great need for knowledge about the school's goals, the philosophy of the district, and the philosophy of the administration. The complaint was made that teachers do not really understand teaching techniques, how to grade, how to use modern classroom methods, and how to utilize grouping procedures effectively. They often knew very little about the learning process or how to help students who have difficulty in learning. One-fourth of the subjects were concerned with what should be done about curriculum and wanted to know how to build a meaningful curriculum, how to plan wisely for a variety of abilities, what subject matter should be utilized, and how to present instructional materials. There seemed to be considerable need for information on how to use audio-visual aids and how to vary classroom techniques. Some teachers indicated that their colleagues' methods were outdated but admitted they did not know what to do about them. Frequently the lack of professional education was cited.

Some subjects reported that teachers in their schools resisted change, lacked organization in their work, and were rigid in the way they approached their work and in the ideas they applied. There was a lack of creativity, of talent, and of effective communication and interaction with students. Teachers who did not have the know-how in terms of modern methods also lacked confidence to forge ahead on their own.

These conditions affect the relationships of teachers with their students, with colleagues, and with other adults. Nearly 18 percent of the people in the sample stated that teachers had problems in relating with students. Some teachers do not accept students as individuals and are not really interested in helping them. They do not understand the limitations of adolescence and are too rough on students. They lack rapport with students, are unable to relate to and empathize with them, and do not know how to motivate them to do good work.

Regarding teachers' attitudes toward their co-workers, the respondents reported suspicion, gossiping about colleagues, and lack of cooperation. Several said their colleagues disliked their principals and were opposed to present school policies. Others, they reported, felt it was almost impossible to get along with administrators, and some were caught up in departmental jealousies.

One item often mentioned was lack of discipline and class control. Quality of discipline varied from one room to the next, and individual teachers were often inconsistent with their own pupils. Some teachers used peculiar methods of discipline, which sometimes frustrated pupils as they moved from one teacher to another.

A few additional problems will round out the dimensions of the difficult job undertaken by the supervisor when he assists individual teachers to change their approaches. Several times it was indicated that teachers needed help in finding the correct placement of pupils who had been transferred to their classes. They were unsure about how to evaluate student work. Some teachers were misplaced or misassigned. Schedules were said to be full of conflicts. There was no time for planning, and there was a lack of democracy in staff meetings.

One obtains the impression from surveys such as this that teachers are often driven from one thing to another, hastily moving about the building, performing their various chores. Their complaints that they cannot meet the needs of every student or have no time to undertake the solution of individual problems seem quite legitimate. If, on top of all these difficulties, the administration insists on innovation and change, obviously there will be much resistance on the part of teachers.

One question raised in the study was: Is anyone available to whom teachers can go for assistance, and if so, who? Half of the teachers interviewed reported that the principal was the only person available. A very few said that they had a department chairman or a supervisor or a consultant. The remainder obtained help from colleagues or from a guidance or counseling director, and some even turned outside of the school to lay persons.

Another question with regard to the type of help obtained brought some interesting responses. Such help as was available was most often described as dealing with administrative or organizational problems — reducing the teacher load, manipulating class sizes, working on the schedule, and record keeping. A few teachers received help with general problems, sometimes with discipline, public relations, and the use of equipment. Some felt they had the support of their administrators and were frequently encouraged to develop a better atmosphere for learning, or perhaps given suggestions related to pupil placement and grouping.

Fully one-fourth of the respondents received no help from their supervisors or principals although they were permitted to discuss their problems with these people. The result was that only occasionally did teachers receive advice that was of any value. Officials often listened to teachers' stories of their frustrations but offered no assistance.

Although teachers got some guidance in the field of general curriculum problems, only a very few supervisors were able to help them improve their competence in a subject matter area or find better techniques of lesson programming and materials selection in a specific subject. A few supervisors were good at generalized troubleshooting in the content and methodological areas and sometimes they explained the theory of instruction. Some teachers were taught how to use enrichment activities and teacher aids, and how to score papers and grade pupils' achievement.

Finally, teachers were seldom assisted to develop better relationships and empathy with students, with parents, and with other members of the faculty. The need, however, is there and should be carefully considered by the supervisor.

Almost half the schools were cited as having no supervisors and hence no supervisory assistance as such. Teachers from these schools who had problems almost uniformly turned to colleagues or to other adults for aid. This is horizontal communication in a hierarchy. A few teachers sought answers in their university textbooks or professional magazines. Examination of the problems encountered by teachers who had no supervisory assistance showed them to be much the same as those described for the total group.

One can conclude from this survey that some teacher problems are likely to go unsolved for a long time, and the teachers may become frustrated to the point of leaving the profession. If there is no time, or opportunity, for the exercise of creativity or autonomy, teachers will scarcely experience self-realization in their jobs.

If the situation described by these teachers exists in other geographic areas, it is obvious that a good supervisor is actually worth many times his salary! As he learns to apply the techniques of counseling and interviewing and then develops a program cooperatively with teachers, implementing plans effectively and efficiently, there should be considerable improvement in the attitude, the morale, and the productivity of teachers.

The supervisor will always be forced to fight the pressure of time, and he will probably question his ability to devote the necessary time to personal conferences. Yet teacher acceptance of him and of his program is imperative. To achieve this acceptance some individual conferences must augment the work done with groups. Without such balance, the group activity will become less effective.

Types of Help Wanted by Teachers

Is the supervisor capable of giving the kind of assistance that teachers say they need? Has he studied his own staff to see what its needs are?[11]

Five general problem categories may be identified. The supervisor who is aware of these categories will develop strategies to deal with each of them:

1. Individual personal problems are related to status in the faculty and prestige of the position. They have to do with satisfaction in one's work, attitudes toward the profession and/or job, and family or social relations.

2. Materials of instruction, including audio-visual materials of all types as well as graded materials in print which are especially

---

[11] J. W. Getzels and P. W. Jackson, "The Teacher's Personality and Characteristics," in N. L. Gage, ed., *Handbook of Research on Teaching* (Chicago: Rand McNally & Co., 1963), p. 506.

designed for newer trends and ideas, present teachers with problems. Few teachers know what community institutions, organizations, and individuals from various areas of human activity are available as resources for instruction. Teachers ask how supplementary textbooks and library books can be obtained in sufficient quantity to cover a wide range of interests and a wide range of difficulty in content. Problems of materials of instruction will require the supervisor to practice the fine art of cutting red tape and of running interference in staff meetings or budget hearings!

3. Methods of instruction appear in many guises. Teachers' needs often are related to new techniques of teaching. Questions arise as to how to organize and use group techniques; how to cope with individual differences in a large class; what to do with problem pupils; how to teach when rooms are over-crowded; how to evaluate teaching effectiveness; how to grade a child in a class which has a very broad range of ability; and what the advantages and disadvantages of using programmed instruction are.

4. Professional problems comprise a large category. There are the usual ones of seeming lack of recognition for honest endeavor and hard work, of insufficient income, of the absence of opportunity for promotion. There are also problems of pressures to join professional associations coupled with teacher perceptions of these associations as inadequate. The teacher shortage which lowers standards and devalues both advanced training and investment in education is seen as a problem. Merit rating, endless and often useless committee work, the lack of professional unity and professional leadership are real concerns. Fractionalized leadership, diverse opinions, and many voices which presume to speak for education cause confusion within the ranks. To counteract such anxieties, the supervisor must provide insights and teach the process of synthesizing viewpoints and engaging in constructive action.

5. Finally, teachers want and need intellectual and cultural outlets. The wide world of general education (readings and studies in all areas of knowledge[12]) and the cultural pursuits of a people must be opened to him if the teacher is to remain intellectually satisfied with the challenge of his profession. The supervisor might prepare bibliographies or point out good

---

[12] See Chapter Five for a discussion of the scope of inservice education.

books and good magazine reading. He might advertise dramatic productions, operas, musicales, lectures, discussion and study groups. In a community fortunate enough to have a college, a university, or an extension division the supervisor should be aware of the educational opportunities so that he may keep the teachers informed.

Meeting Diverse Needs

Jerry Popovitch, the secondary supervisor for the Big City schools, had been concerned for some time with a problem expressed in various ways by many secondary teachers. A ground swell of desire for assistance had become apparent in the district. Some teachers wanted help with instructional materials. Some were interested in better teaching methods. Some desired more organized cultural activity with fellow teachers.

Jerry had been pondering how he could meet all these needs. His intention was to prepare a loose structure designed around the materials resource center recently opened by the district. Teachers interested in preparing materials could work there with the necessary supplies and equipment. The large meeting room could serve as the central location for those interested in methodology. The central professional library might be augmented with items teachers might like to check out for their own pleasure, such as paintings, records, magazines, and light reading. (A cooperative arrangement with the public library could solve that one.)

In the resource center, with plenty of coffee and a friendly, relaxed atmosphere, perhaps teachers could get acquainted more informally and develop outside cultural interests together. It seemed worth trying and Jerry was ready to suggest such a plan for the consideration of the secondary teachers.

Is this kind of problem of sufficient importance to take up supervisory time or should it be left to the welfare committee or a similar group?

Preparing for the Personalized Situation

Prior to a scheduled conference both teacher and supervisor should prepare themselves for the meeting. The teacher may review his problem, gathering all possible information and reexamining any records he has. Most of all, he should prepare mentally to face himself with an open mind.

The supervisor should gather all the information and background material he can on both the teacher and the problem. He might review past records, conference notes, and a general history of the teacher. Why have this conference? Are the purposes clearly in mind? He should reflect on his own status and role in the counseling process. He might list ways of achieving the purposes as he understands them. How does he perceive the teacher? How does the teacher perceive his role?

If both parties have taken the time to prepare themselves and are committed to making a conscious effort to find some answers, definite progress may result. If either or both are unwilling to expend the effort needed to make preparation, or if either is unwilling to accept the necessity for the meeting, a satisfactory solution may be extremely difficult to find. The supervisor should be willing to take the initiative in most instances.

Use of the Interview

The interview, which is a form of communication, is a means of obtaining information. It is a way to get inside of and adequately identify the problem. Not everyone can effectively conduct an interview. For example, one must not drive for preconceived answers or well-phrased statements from the interviewee. The validity and reliability of information is influenced by the objectivity of the interviewer. If he interposes ideas, he may be identifying with the interviewee. The supervisor must not place the teacher in a defensive position or in a suspicious mood or the information obtained is likely to be invalid, invented to meet the demands of the situation.

There are at least two general reasons for using interviews: first, to obtain information to be used in personalizing supervisory assistance; second, to gather information to evaluate the supervisor's own services to teachers, and to appraise the inservice education or supervisory program. It is best, of course, if both teacher and supervisor know in advance what the subject of the interview is to be. Too many conferences are called without a stated purpose or a forwarded agenda. This is a wasteful practice and contributes to general confusion.

Perhaps several individual conferences with different people will reveal the presence of a problem common to a number of persons. In such an instance, a group can be formed for the purpose of working together, with obvious saving of time and effort. Group work should be included among the techniques for changing the behavior of individual teachers.

Use of Records

It is time-consuming to keep records on all interviews, but record keeping can be very useful. The supervisor's notes may be brief but they should be carefully thought through. It is also time-consuming to study these records before the interview. However, the difference between the results obtained by those supervisors who do and those who do not is analogous to the difference between the competent professional analysis and the routine "advice" of an acquaintance. Records can stimulate thought and help one decide what questions to ask. Therefore, a good system of records can lead to a structured interview and hence to a more effective use of the time of two busy people.

Records reveal what gaps may exist in the available information. They help to fix attention and to keep interviewer and interviewee objective. They reduce repetition of questions, guide the collection of data, and accelerate progress of the interview and growth of the teacher. The maintenance and utilization of well-kept records are highly recommended and can represent time well spent.

Using Records

Supervisor Bixby looked at his calendar and discovered that this was the day he was to meet with Miss Noyes, the home economics teacher, who had asked him to visit her classroom last week. As a result of that visit and the ensuing conference, he had agreed to meet her again to discuss some problems she had in her classroom.

In the brief free time before Miss Noyes was due to arrive, Mr. Bixby checked through his notes on the visits he had made to her classes during the past years and the summary of each conference held at the time of the visit. He looked over the curriculum guides for the course Miss Noyes taught to familiarize himself once again with the background.

He reviewed in his mind what the home economics department seemed to be doing. He examined the teaching assignment of each teacher in the department, recalling at the same time the analyses of Mr. Frank, the principal, and Mrs. Senn, the department chairman. He had taken the time to talk to them in preparation for his conference today.

He was now ready for the meeting and would first listen, then try to help Miss Noyes reach an acceptable solution to the problem she intended to present. Was Mr. Bixby a fussbudget? Was he overprepared?

Why Some Supervisory Conferences Fail

Clues to the failure of some teacher-supervisor conferences do exist. Undoubtedly, many conferences do not achieve their purposes or their potential. In some instances the teacher is the negative factor, in others the supervisor. Or both may be at fault.

The supervisor and teacher may be jointly responsible for failure because of:

1. Lack of time — the conference seemed hurried.
2. Lack of professional ethics.
3. Improper setting — the physical surroundings were poor.
4. Emotional barriers.
5. Poor communication.
6. Lack of solutions or alternatives.
7. No real purpose.
8. Lack of understanding of the problem.
9. Little or no preparation.

The supervisor may be primarily responsible for failure because of:

1. Insecurity.
2. Autocratic attitude.
3. Laissez-faire attitude.
4. Lack of training and experience.
5. Personal involvement in the teacher's problem.
6. Lack of information.
7. Lack of preparation — the meeting was hastily called.
8. Poor follow-up or complete lack of it.
9. Few or no conferences after observations.
10. Lack of support and recognition when the teacher has made progress.
11. Use of the conference as an outlet for personal feelings.
12. Inability to assist the teacher.
13. Use of poor supervisory techniques.
14. Prevention of teacher participation.
15. Poor use of records, or complete lack of records on conferences.

16. Imposition of his own views.
17. Teacher distrust caused by supervisor's administrative background.
18. Lack of understanding of the nature of change.
19. Lack of understanding of the nature of teacher behavior.
20. Lack of understanding of the fact that the existing philosophy is inadequate for modern conditions.
21. Monopolizing the discussion.
22. Failure to focus the conference on the problem at hand.
23. Attempting too much.

The teacher may be primarily responsible for failure because of:

1. Not allowing enough time for the conference.
2. Lack of confidence.
3. Lack of preparation.
4. Lack of faith and poor attitude.
5. Resistance to change.
6. Personal dislike for the supervisor.
7. Suspicion and resentment caused by former supervisor or administrator contacts.

It may be noted that while specific reasons are here assigned to each of the parties involved in the conference, the reasons are actually quite similar. Evidently competent professionals, determined to succeed, can go a long way on the road to success by making adequate preparation. The capable supervisor should understand the reasons for possible failure of his conferences and try to overcome them when possible or to neutralize them when they do occur.

Time for Problems

Tom McCune had scheduled conferences with three different teachers for Thursday after school. In a way he dreaded these supervisory conferences — one never knew where they might lead. As the instructional supervisor for the secondary schools, he felt he must meet with the teachers whenever possible. Lately, some teachers had been asking embarrassing questions which Tom could not answer and which he really did not understand. He felt more and more on the defensive. In an attempt to counteract some of these potentially disturbing sessions, he had taken to scheduling them in a way which permitted little time. That way, he could cover what he wanted and plead lack of time for teachers' questions.

Is this a legitimate method of proceeding? Will Mr. McCune be successful in his undertaking?

Summary

Individual counseling by the supervisor is an important method of assisting teachers to change their behavior. It provides personalized assistance. The approaches are directive, nondirective, and a combination of the two. The working climate must be permissive, supportive, cooperative, and mutually helpful so that teachers will feel rewarded for the changes they make.

A study of problems reported by teachers illustrates that problems can inhibit desirable changes in behavior. Personal and economic problems were cited, as well as problems due to outside factors. Freedom to teach was often reported as lacking; many teachers feel restricted by policy, rules, or social pressures. Though teaching must be satisfying and contribute to self-realization, some teachers reported blockings. If freedom and self-realization exist, or are perceived to exist, they often act as motivational forces for improvement.

Preparation for personal assistance is necessary on the part of both teacher and supervisor. Preparation for the interview and utilization of records are necessary elements in personalized supervision.

Problems for Group Discussion

Analyze the following situations. In each, identify supervisory principles representing sound theory, if any are included. What are the basic elements which made a difference? How would you have approached the situation?

1. Mrs. Emery, a mathematics teacher, wanted to try some new grouping procedures for the next year. Since she was not sure the supervisor would approve, she went to her principal with her suggestions. As a result of discussions with the principal, she arrived for the new term expecting to implement her grouping innovation only to discover that no change had occurred. The principal had asked the supervisor for a confirming recommendation of support before making the change. The

supervisor, feeling that he had been bypassed by Mrs. Emery, had refused to support the proposal. Mrs. Emery was furious and threatened to resign on the spot.

2. Mr. Clinton was in his second year of teaching. While he was apparently an uninspired teacher, he did follow the stated curriculum, kept order in his classes, and attended the required meetings. The supervisor noted that Mr. Clinton seldom volunteered a comment and, in fact, was quite reluctant to discuss his own classroom operation. In a conference, Mr. Clinton confided that he was bored with teaching, his students were poor, and he felt generally in a rut and was seriously thinking of changing occupations. The supervisor recognized that a teacher of dubious quality was about to leave the profession and knew he must do something. What should he do?

Selected Readings

Argyris, Chris. *Personality and Organization: The Conflict Between System and the Individual.* New York: Harper & Brothers, 1957.

Berman, Louise M., and Mary Lou Usery. *Personalized Supervision: Sources and Insights.* Washington: Association for Supervision and Curriculum Development, 1966.

Coffey, Hubert S., and William J. Golden. "Psychology of Change Within an Institution," in *Inservice Education for Teachers, Supervisors, and Administrators.* Fifty-Sixth Yearbook of the National Society for the Study of Education, Part I. Chicago: University of Chicago Press, 1957.

Combs, Arthur W. "Fostering Self-Direction," *Educational Leadership,* 23:373–376 (Feb., 1966).

Gagne, Robert M. *The Conditions of Learning.* New York: Holt, Rinehart & Winston, 1967.

Getzels, J. W., and P. W. Jackson. "The Teacher's Personality and Characteristics," in N. L. Gage, ed., *Handbook of Research on Teaching.* Chicago: Rand McNally & Co., 1963, p. 506.

Hill, William M. "I-B-F Supervision," *Clearing House,* 43:539–541 (Nov., 1968).

Klopf, Gordon J. "Helping Adults Change," in *The Supervisor: New Demands/New Dimensions.* Washington: Association for Supervision and Curriculum Development, 1969, pp. 19–27.

Maslow, A. H. "Self-Actualizing People: Psychological Health," in C. Gratton Kemp, ed., *Perspectives on the Group Process.* Boston: Houghton Mifflin Company, 1964.

Medley, Donald M., and Russell A. Hill. "Dimensions of Classroom Behavior Measured by Two Systems of Interaction Analysis," *Educational Leadership*, 26:821–824 (May, 1969).

Presthus, Robert. *The Organizational Society: An Analysis and a Theory.* New York: Alfred A. Knopf, 1962.

Vergason, A. L. "Supervisory Conferences," *Bulletin of the National Association of Secondary Principals*, 34:245–251 (Dec., 1950).

eight

•

Change and Its Implications for Supervision

One of the phenomena of the modern age is change. It is characteristic of every phase of life. A philosophical debate among educators has waged unceasingly for years about whether schools
should reflect the society or should reconstruct society. Most people agree that education and the schools do change — and must if
they are to survive. Today change has touched the profession as
never before.

The supervisor must understand the relationship of education and
change if he expects to carry out his assignment satisfactorily. The
implementation of change in the schools is one of the genuine opportunities for leadership accorded the supervisor. The purpose
of the present chapter is to describe this problem in supervision and
to suggest ways of meeting it.

Changes in Society

Probably one of the most dramatic areas of change relates to concepts and knowledge of space. Continuing explorations of space,
experiments in communication via Telstar, and space travel are
affecting industries, professional practices, and just plain people in
all walks of life. Not quite so spectacular, partly because they are
less obvious to the public, are the changes that automation and the
electronic developments are bringing to business, industry, and the
various occupations. Probably the most fantastic idea reported is
one the Russians are working on which relates the entire economic
life of the Soviets to a giant computer. This computer would

control production, manufacturing of specific items, distribution, and consumption. Already the use of computers to simulate space flight and to work out problems in research which were previously almost impossible has speeded up the rate of change by many years. The implication of the service of such devices to education is only dimly seen at present. Certainly they hold a tremendous potential for improved instructional techniques, as educators learn to harness their capabilities. The whole field of cybernetics forecasts great change in everyone's life in the near future.

The number of nations admitted to the United Nations has doubled since World War II, and others are emerging from ages of slumber and colonialism. Thus the whole field of international relations has a new meaning and a new importance. As these nations mature, there are new alignments into competing power blocks, dramatically illustrated by debates in the United Nations.

Less dramatic, but very important for schools, is the shift from a rural to an urban population in America. It is related to the mechanization of the farms and to greater mobility of the people. It often brings underprivileged and culturally deprived rural pupils, including Negroes, to urban schools, creating a problem of increasing complexity and urgency to the larger cities. As the sociological composition of communities changes, schools must adapt their educational programs accordingly. Economic opportunities for workers are changing, in some cases depressing their outlook and motivation, in others bringing new hope.

Many educators interested in instructional innovation have long pointed to the debilitating effect of inflexible school construction. A school, built to last from fifty to one hundred years, stands as an impelling reason for not attempting teaching procedures which might require new uses of space. Instructional change tends to be limited to what the existing facility can easily accommodate. In the past, little thought was given to suiting spatial usage to new instructional techniques.

One of the writers visited a high school recently built along traditional lines, with square or rectangular rooms all of about the same size. A school official commented that there was not enough money to build rooms of various sizes for small- and large-group work. Visiting the classes made it obvious to the observer that this rigid design was a strong influence in the arrangement of chairs: in straight rows of exactly the same length. Both the rooms and the arrangement of the chairs seemed to affect the methods used. Hour after hour, classes were seated in alphabetical order, papers were passed out by rows, students went to the blackboard by rows, and the recitation was a traditional pupil-to-teacher action. The work appeared to be dull and uninteresting. There will be little, if any, spontaneity, class interaction, informal group work, independent study, or experimental teaching in this building without the intervention of a supervisor.

A major breakthrough in school design is now taking place. Walls are being made retractable, and classrooms of different sizes are available for specific instructional tasks. Future innovations can be accommodated in schools with movable walls. New construction emphasizes flexibility to meet whatever demands the changing instructional program of the future makes.

After Sputnik, considerable effort was made to encourage the teaching of more foreign language. One device which, although rather costly, received much attention across the land was the language laboratory, with its individual teaching stations and its complicated wiring problems. Almost as quickly as the language laboratory became generally installed in the secondary schools, a movement toward individual instruction began to appear, capable of doing the same job better and introducing more adaptability into the entire instructional program. Space needs thus changed rapidly in a manner impossible to predict. Buildings designed for flexibility took the changes in stride; others presented a greater problem.

With the help of federal funds, new interest has been shown and a good deal of rethinking has been done in the area of education for the child in his early years. Such philosophical questions as equal versus unequal educational opportunity become more concrete as experimentation is carried on increasingly with young children. Implications currently under consideration threaten to revise completely the educational pattern long followed in this country. More and earlier contacts with children in an educational setting are now probable as day care centers develop.[1]

These are only a few of the multitudinous changes taking place today. They are the source of many persistent pressures on the schools. They are also the source of many problems bearing on the

---

[1] Maya Pines, *Revolution in Learning: The Years from Birth to Six* (New York: Harper & Row, 1967).

development of objectives of education, on curriculum content, and on teaching methods. They form the background for discovery, invention, and innovation — which, in turn, are ways of making change. Schools are slow to take up new teaching techniques; they are not known for making significant and rapid modifications in curriculum. As institutions, they usually resist change, and faculties are likely to regard with suspicion suggestions calculated to "improve" education. The implementation of change in the schools represents a genuine opportunity for leadership accorded supervisors.

Don't Rock the Boat

Sy Helmer has been ensconced as secondary supervisor in the Farpoint schools for the past fifteen years. During that time many ideas have been considered for instructional improvement and have been either implemented or rejected.

The first year Sy worked diligently to change some bad practices throughout the district. For the past several years his main efforts have been directed toward maintaining the program. Teachers quickly learn not to "rock the boat" and agree to maintain the tradition of Farpoint, or to move on to other districts where they are free to try new ideas in their classrooms.

Sy is also interested in maintaining his low score on the golf course. "A man just has to get away, you know." The Farpoint District is known throughout the state as conservative and, in most respects, quite backward.

Changes in the Community

A Definition

While community may be defined in several ways, one definition concentrates on the functions it serves: protection, both police and fire, the production and distribution of goods, communication, government or the general management of its affairs, provisions for worship, and education.

A definition preferable for educational studies analyzes the nature and structure of community:

1. There is a definite geographic area with boundaries.
2. People possess a variety of traits yet some common characteristics.

3. A way of living, a way of making a living, and a pattern of work and leisure-time occupations can be identified.

4. A community history and heritage is evident; old-timers live here, and perhaps families with long histories and social status.

5. Social, private, and governmental agencies and organizations supply the basic needs of the community.

6. Individuals identify with the community; members have learned and internalized values and assimilated ways of the community.

7. Common values and community behavior, customs, class structure, prohibitions and sanctions, and ways of treating outsiders are understood and adhered to.

What happens in regard to any one of the elements happens also to the schools in the community.

Behavior Influencing Change

Each of the seven elements in the definition lends itself to study, to elaboration, and to research. However, the last will serve as illustration. In every community there are two kinds of behavior. The first is the regular, routine behavior of individuals, which is consistent and according to social expectations. It is typical of the vast majority of people and can be predicted. The second type, less predictable, is characteristic of those who do not conform to the regular expected behavior. When the number of people who behave in the expected fashion diminishes and the number who behave in a deviant manner increases, the community is undergoing change. Change in behavior patterns mirrors shifting values. As long as values and attitudes remain fixed, the community remains in a stable condition. When pressures and forces are introduced which call values and attitudes into question, life in the community is not the same.

A simple illustration may be had from old, stable communities which suddenly find themselves a part of a large suburban housing development, or of industrial expansion near a city. Before this event, minorities did not count for much, never having elected anyone to the board of education, or to the town council, and certainly never to the position of mayor. The minority accepted its lot, preferring security and known roles to the risk of inviting attacks and the application of social sanctions if its members actively attempted to achieve higher-status positions.

But with the coming of the new development, a new minority also arrives. Perhaps the minority is an aggressive, well-educated, alert group of business executives and professionals. These people, men and women alike, have no thought of sitting back and permitting the community to go its usual way. They campaign for positions on the city council, run for the school board, from pressure groups such as the Alliance for Good Government, or the Citizens' Organization for Better Schools. They join and become active members of the service clubs and other organizations. As a minority, their behavior is indeed deviant. And the old-timers are forced to react toward them differently from the way they previously behaved toward minorities. Change has come over the community because the accustomed, routinized ways of acting are replaced by conduct that was once considered unacceptable.

Instructional supervisors who feel that their business is totally with the schools and that they have no concern with community problems are unrealistic in their outlook. In addition, they are likely to be in for a surprise when new community forces turn their attention to education. The supervisor who has been comfortable in his relationships with the community power structure and has understood its educational interests and expectations may suddenly realize that different community expectations pose major threats to his program. Community unrest thus will represent a direct pressure upon the supervisor, upon the local curriculum, and upon the entire instructional program.

Effect on the Schools

At each stage of the community's evolution, whether in periods of stability, deterioration, or redevelopment, the schools are affected in nearly everything they do. Administrators and teachers who find themselves in the midst of community crises are often forced to make adjustments in their own personal lives, in their teaching, in the curriculum, and in the management of the schools. Administrators and supervisors must work hard at developing inservice education and orientation programs to minimize losses to the system in excessive faculty turnover, or to combat sinking morale and mounting frustrations.

The curriculum changes slowly and may, therefore, be somewhat inappropriate at any given stage of community development. Opposition to change in the schools is strong. Whether the community is in a stage of deterioration or redevelopment, certain influential groups will cling to the customs, traditions, and curriculum of the past. Unless the newcomers in the community are strong enough to displace such groups in the struggle for influence and power, the school staff may not be able to muster sufficient support for proposed changes. The supervisor will then find himself impotent to initiate change in the school because the social climate provides only ambivalent support.

Supervisors Plan for Increased Growth

All the supervisors in the suburban district spent a week in their own inservice program. In this once sleepy, rural district outside the big city the population was booming at an unheard-of pace, threatening to engulf the schools with problems.

The director of instruction, recognizing the signs, had arranged for some experts in urban problems to conduct a seminar on what to expect from the community as this rapid transition took place. He felt that if the supervisors realized what the various pressures were and were likely to be, they could more adequately adjust the instructional program and could assist the entire instructional staff to work better with the patrons, both old and new. A demographic study of the community was undertaken, including a section on high school dropouts and graduates.

As a result of this study, the district was able to anticipate many of the problems, to compensate for some, to bypass others, and generally to succeed in offering a continually improved level of instruction in spite of the obstacles. Well-informed, alert staff members were able to meet the challenge. One question arose: How often should this study be repeated?

The Nature of Change

Change can be thought of as having several distinct and important components, agents, foci, and implications for the supervisor. Each has been conceptualized within the system in the accompanying chart. Each will be discussed in the following pages.

Characteristics of Change

Change takes place at various rates. It may begin slowly and pick up speed, or it may begin, sputter along for a time, and then fade out, much as fads do. In the schools, change in curriculum

CHANGE SYSTEM CONCEPTUALIZED

Characteristics of Change	*Agents of Change*	*Focus of Change*
1. Rate	1. Research	1. People and
2. Direction	2. Government — laws	their behavior
3. Volume	3. University	2. Institutions
4. Quality	scholars	3. Training and
5. Levels	4. Technology	occupations
	5. Resource centers	4. Subgroups
	6. Organizations	(e.g., math)
	7. Travel	5. Attitudes
	8. The supervisor	6. Social status

Implications for Supervision

1. Initiate structures, leaders, committees, and support systems.
2. Marshal the resources.
3. Obtain and harness commitment.
4. Develop rewards and recognitions.
5. Devise feedback and input systems.
6. Recognize and develop independent thinkers.
7. Provide for unanticipated outcomes.
8. Plan to broaden experiences, enlarge horizons.
9. Demonstrate advantages of new modes; reeducate.
10. Recruit the right staff.
11. Develop appropriate support systems and maintenance organizations.

development may take years, or it may occur at a rapid tempo as it has done recently in mathematics, in the laboratory method of teaching foreign languages, and in the sciences. In the case of social and political change, a tremendously increased pace results in revolution. Change which requires a generation or more for general effect is evolutionary. In short, change may be very fast or very slow, or happen at a rate somewhere between.[2]

Rate is affected by numerous factors, some of which can be manipulated. It helps if teachers know precisely what the objectives are, and the relative advantages and practical benefits of the innovations

---

[2] Adolph Unruh and O. T. Richardson, "Counseling in an Age of Change," *Clearing House* 41:148–152 (Nov., 1966).

in question. If a proposed innovation is complex and unusually strange to the teacher, the rate of change can be increased by dividing up the task and mastering it in stages, or by involving teachers in the introductory phases of the change and giving them complete feedback services. It is also helpful if an organization to maintain teachers' morale and security can be started. Approved lines of communication, access to resources, and the opportunity to share in decision making should be parts of this organization.

Another characteristic of change is direction. Teaching may become more scientific as a result of studies of method, of learning, of testing, of interaction, and of teacher and student behavior. Some teaching is concerned with the development of tastes, sensitivity, beauty, form, and values and hence may move in the direction of aesthetics and art. When schools began admitting the mentally retarded, the blind or partially blind, and pupils with speech defects or hearing deficiencies, they instituted new programs of instruction and hence moved toward the employment of specialists and toward more complicated administrative structure. All of these represent changes in direction.

Most Americans delight in viewing and participating in change. They like to see new models of automobiles, different styles of clothing, novel forms of architecture, faster and faster travel, etc. But change for its own sake is not appropriate. The direction of change must come under scrutiny of and control by intelligence and reason. Research and creativity are employed to take into account the possible future. Then plans and programs are developed so that change takes acceptable directions. For example, many years ago a small private airplane manufacturer hired an imaginative engineer to design a plane for use ten or more years hence. All pertinent research and ideas were brought to the task. The entire establishment was affected by this approach and became dynamic, forward-looking, and planning-oriented. Of course, through the years, the original design changed many times, but the company became a leader in the industry and is today famous for its product. By seizing control of change and utilizing it correctly, the company directed its own destiny.

A third characteristic is volume. Curriculum development which begins in one subject matter area may spread to a second, then a third, and so on until change has infected the whole instructional program. The slums of a community, once confined to undesirable sections of a city and a problem mainly for the police, may grow in both size and importance and become problems for politicians, educators, legislators, churches, business, industry, and unions, and the subject of expanding educational and sociological research. Change may be insignificant, affecting only a few people, or so pervasive that its impact is felt by people in all countries of the world.

In discussing the major changes in high schools across the nation, Cawelti divided innovations into three areas: curriculum, technology, and organization.[3] There was more activity in the curriculum area than in the others. In the more populous states, schools averaged approximately seven innovations each. Suburban schools and schools in wealthy districts led the parade. From these centers, innovations spread out into smaller towns, smaller schools, and less wealthy districts.

A fourth characteristic is quality, which relates to value and judgment. Changes may be judged good or bad, acceptable or unacceptable, depending upon the point of view and the values held. Those changes upon which opinions are divided might include certain movements in art, the movement toward greater lay involvement and freedom in matters of concern to certain churches, the new militancy of teachers, sex education in schools, released time for religious instruction, and shared time which permits pupils from non-public schools to attend public schools for instruction in certain subjects. A popular axiom is that if the changes raise living standards and bring more of the "good life" to more people, they are good. To the extent that they restrict people's freedom to move about, to make choices, to be involved in decisions that affect them, to be gainfully employed, they are considered bad.

Changes occur at different levels of operation as well as at different levels of conceptualization, as has been the case in curriculum development over the years. Revision is a first-level change, requiring only some editing of units, the inclusion of more readings or activities, and perhaps a new test. At the next level is the substitution of a new unit (lesson or course) for an old one. This requires a higher degree of curriculum construction skill. Materials must be found or created, organized, and incorporated into an existing structure. On the highest level is a thorough reorganization and

---

[3] Gordon Cawelti, "Innovative Practices in High Schools: Who Does What — and Why — and How," *Nation's Schools,* 79:56–74 (Apr., 1967).

restructuring of the curriculum, starting with original sources of knowledge and attacking the original assumptions about schools and learning.

A Change Expert

Enrique Francisea, language supervisor, was a student of change. He was not merely interested but enthralled by the possibilities of change.

Because of his study of the topic, Enrique had been able to modernize the language curriculum in a relatively short period of time. Through his personal influence with both administrators and teachers he had been able to increase both the rate and the volume of change. By involving outside experts and the local community he had influenced the direction and the quality of change. Whereas the initial efforts of the district had been quite elementary and rather naive, the level of operation now was sophisticated and professional.

Enrique and the language program were developing a strong reputation throughout the entire region, and visitors from across the country arrived each week to observe the exciting things taking place in the schools. Is there danger of going too fast for the rest of the district?

Agents of Change

There are many change agents, ranging from chemical and physical to human. Those with the greatest impact upon the work of the schools are of the human variety — researchers and research organizations, for instance. Travel has a broadening effect and tends to initiate change. Professional people and managerial staff members who have the opportunity of observing firsthand practices, methods, and customs in other parts of the country generally become the innovators. The government, through legislation, brings change to the schools, as in the case of the National Defense Education Act and the Elementary and Secondary Education Act. In Title III of the latter, the government required innovations and creative approaches to education as prerequisites for funding. Consequently school people had to think beyond the present curriculum and routine day-to-day tasks. The many types of categorical federal aid are examples of pressure for change of one kind or another and represent organizational and bureaucratic influence.

University scholars are agents of change. Their constant quest for wider knowledge and for better ways of operating brings new materials and new alternatives. Developments in such areas as physics, sociology, oceanography, physiology, chemistry, biology, and anthropology force outdated knowledge out of the curriculum and replace it with more interesting, modern, and relevant data. But scholars interested in the research on learning, teaching techniques, and human behavior and interaction also contribute to our understanding. Better organization of subject matter emerges and emphasis on different methods jars schools out of traditional molds. Research has always been an irritant to the status quo and a threat to tradition.

Not the least of the change agents is the supervisor himself. He is the counterpart of the planning engineer in the airplane factory described earlier. He should be an astute student of trends and constantly concerned with imaginative projections. He cannot wait for changes to overwhelm his school; he attempts to initiate and direct them. Ever interested in the improvement of instruction, by implication he is also interested in change. He coordinates and disseminates innovations throughout his area of jurisdiction, stimulating, encouraging, and reinforcing the persons involved. The rapid progress of technology becomes a tool for his use. Various devices, such as materials resource centers located centrally or in individual buildings, aid him in facilitating change.

The authoritarian supervisor of yesterday felt that things could best be altered by administrative (supervisory) directives to teachers. The democratically oriented supervisor, capable of surviving in the world of tomorrow, is aware that interaction and direct involvement of teachers must precede consensus leading to action and accompany lasting change. Thus, while this supervisor is an agent of change he does not himself order it.

Search for a Better Way

Irene King, supervisor of English in the Fairview District, considered herself a change agent for secondary English. While she had many ideas herself and while she felt there were many ways to improve the teaching of English in the district, she refused to impose her will on the teachers. Rather, she attempted always to present suggestions for consideration, to provide alternatives for selection by teachers, to make it possible for teachers to accept or reject proposals for change. Whenever feasible, Irene used the original ideas of the teachers themselves. If nothing seemed appropriate, she would "forage far afield" and seek ideas from other sources.

Her original success as measured by overt change in instructional practice had been modest. Time proved it sound, however, and the tempo of change had gradually built until now the English departments in Fairview were considered among the best and most innovative in the state. Irene and the teachers were justifiably proud of their accomplishments and dedicated to continue their efforts to find a better way. Should this success story be used to inspire the social studies group, which has become rather stagnant?

The Focus of Change

The target of the various agents of change is, first of all, people and their behavior. There is no curriculum change unless there is a change in people. Next come institutions, represented here by the schools. (For other purposes, these could include the university, the church, a manufacturing company, and so on. Some changes or innovations have for their goal improved training of professionals, teachers, engineers, medical doctors. The period of training for a lawyer might be lengthened or reduced by a year or two; content might be tossed out and replaced with other content. The aim is to modify in some selected fashion the training of lawyers and ultimately their methods of working.)

Frequently the focus is on smaller segments of the total operation of a profession. In teacher education, there may be concentration on mathematics, or on the preparation of superintendents and supervisors, or on the teaching of English. Multiple and diverse attention of this sort eventually may change the entire school, as the efforts of specialized groups influence others in teacher training institutions. Sometimes the attitudes of teachers, staff, and administration are the target. If the proposed changes can be shown to enhance status or improve position in the small specializing group, the individual is inclined to move in the direction desired.

In each instance the change agent should first identify the target group he has to deal with to produce change. He must have his objectives clearly in mind as he interacts with the group. The means must be found to cause a behavioral change and then to support the inevitable consequences of that change. The target group will vary widely; it may include all the secondary teachers in the district or be limited to one eleventh-grade history teacher.

Supervisory Strategy

Al Burton was selected as the new supervisor largely because of his reputation for being an innovative teacher. When hired, he was told to produce as much change in the traditional secondary schools as he could.

In studying the situation while he prepared his initial strategy, Al determined to follow a logical line of progression. He was aware of the innovations recently incorporated into the elementary schools of the district. He reasoned that these modifications in the instructional program would first make an impact on the junior high teachers and therefore that he should concentrate his efforts on that group. He hoped that the students entering the junior highs would serve as the catalytic agent needed to produce the necessary concern for action. Later he could turn his attention to the senior highs. Was Al justified in ignoring the senior high teachers in this fashion?

Implications for Supervision

The supervisor who takes on the leadership in fostering and initiating change has a complicated task. He has to set up committees and get them operational. He must discover and develop leaders not only to take over these groups but to strike out in new directions themselves. Both structures and leaders need support systems, including community approval, administrative encouragement, financial backing, time to do the job, and clerical assistance.

In addition, he must marshal resources and clarify objectives. The groups have to know where they are going and must be accorded the means to reach their goals. The central actor in this drama — the teacher — is not to be taken for granted. His commitment to the process should be manifest, and it must be directed skillfully.

The supervisor must be ready with a variety of rewards. Feedback and input systems are important because they are in part the rewards and in part the incentives for continued interest in innovations. If innovations are valued, then the teacher who has a unique idea or who makes a "far-out" suggestion is to be recognized and encouraged. Industry solicits such ideas and rewards those who propose them. The public schools have seldom supported innovation in a like fashion; instead, teachers who propose new ideas are often reprimanded or even punished.

Another implication for the supervisor lies in the area of unanticipated outcomes.[4] The Supervisor's Change Control System is charted in Figure 3. Unanticipated outcomes are likely to occur at critical points in the subsystem where energy is expanded. At each of the four points indicated in the Supervisor's Change Control System, outcomes other than those desired and expected are possible. For instance, if someone in the maintenance system (1) did

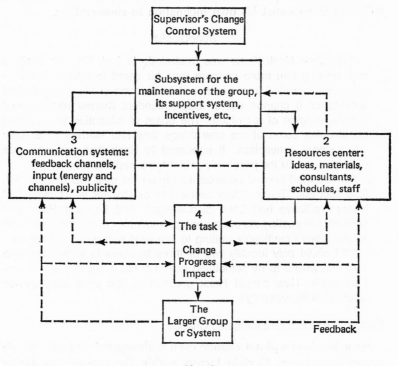

Fig. 3

A System for Change

(Solid lines indicate direct communication-action lines.)

---

[4] James G. March and Herbert A. Simon, *Organizations* (New York: John Wiley & Sons, 1959), pp. 37–47.

not perform according to the script, problems could arise in each of the succeeding subsystems. And malfunction in any subsystem can cause serious delays in the task and even prejudice the outcome.

Supervisors should concentrate on influencing the assignment of the right teachers and staff when vacancies occur. Usually those people who have had a variety of experience and who are challenged by risks will help his cause.

New curricula and methods should be observed in person by the supervisor. Different social customs and economic patterns or various industrial and political organizations, when viewed at firsthand, will help him combat his own inclination to conservatism.

Roadblocks

Supervisor Hank Kerns was frustrated. In fact, his new position was causing him more concern than he cared to admit. True, he had been recruited from another state because of his demonstrated success as a change agent. Superintendent Kramer had assured him the support of his office. The board of education was excited about doing some of the new things they had learned of at their last national convention. It appeared to Hank that everyone was enthusiastic over the possibility of change except the teachers.

He had tried several approaches during the past two months with little success. The problem seemed to be that for years individual teacher initiative had been discouraged. Not knowing Hank and certainly not trusting his open approach to instructional problems, the teachers were cautiously waiting to see what was going to happen.

"If I could only identify two or three teachers in a building who might be willing to try something new, I could make a start," grumbled Hank. How should Hank proceed at this point to convince teachers of his sincerity?

Factors and Conditions Inhibiting Change

Some teachers will not change even with support systems operating in their favor. Certain factors within the person may be as important as any outside stimuli. One of these personal factors is insecurity. If techniques or curricula are unfamiliar or not understood, problems and frustrations will arise. Insecurity begets fear, which may result in severe emotional strain, which practically ensures failure.

Conservatism and the conviction that the old ways bring the most satisfaction may cause a reluctance to try new things. Attitude is important — some teachers are sure that the new ways will fail. There is also the disposition toward indolence; like everyone else, teachers can be lazy and indifferent and therefore will not attempt to make changes.[5]

Conditions over which the teacher has little control may modify or cause delays in the plans for innovation or even result in post-ponement or complete cancellation. Some of these are the bureaucratic structure with its policies, red tape, and administrative caution, community indifference, and lack of funds and staff.[6] Inadequate communication and bureaucratic intrusion can render many an action invalid. To offset such conditions, the establishment of a good support system becomes very important.

Most writers in supervision place fear and insecurity high on the list of innovation inhibitors. One reason for teacher insecurity is the general shift in methods and curriculum development from content to process.[7] Much emphasis is being placed on the methods of inquiry and discovery and on the processes of problem solving, independent studies, and creative thinking.[8] Many teachers apparently lack the communicative skills, the ability to ask questions, the ability to teach critical thinking or scientific modes of thought. Yet these are the modern requirements that are laid down by changes in curriculum and methods.

A Challenge

When Mr. Ernest was hired as the new supervisor, the superintendent went to great lengths to explain what was expected of him. He learned that the board of education wanted some of the instructional innovations they had been reading about in the journals to take place here. The superintendent had convinced the board that such innovations, on a large scale, could be instituted if he were permitted to add a supervisor to his staff, and Mr. Ernest was selected.

---

[5] Richard I. Miller, "An Overview of Educational Change," in Richard I. Miller, ed., *Perspectives on Educational Change* (New York: Appleton-Century-Crofts, 1967), p. 8.

[6] Glen Heathers, "Influencing Change at the Elementary Level," in Richard I. Miller, ed., *Perspectives on Educational Change* (New York: Appleton-Century-Crofts, 1967), p. 24.

[7] J. Cecil Parker and Louis J. Rubin, *Process as Content: Curriculum Design and the Application of Knowledge* (Chicago: Rand McNally & Co., 1966), p. 2.

[8] Jerome S. Bruner, *The Process of Education* (Cambridge, Mass.: Harvard University Press, 1960), p. 13.

The new supervisor realized that healthy, enduring change was not easily accomplished. He set about to get acquainted with teachers of the district, hoping to ascertain where change was possible or where new things were already occurring. He reasoned that these spots were the logical places to begin. Later he would have time to push for his own programs. He must first gain the confidence and support of the teachers and their administrators.

While he was eager to move as the board wanted, he felt he must proceed with extreme caution at the outset. He asked himself, "How can I identify the teacher who is inclined toward change and not afraid of risks?"

There are other deterrents to change, some of which can be eliminated or considerably reduced. One is the nebulous, ephemeral nature of the objectives of education as usually stated. They are nonbehavioral, and the outcomes they are supposed to generate are amorphous and unmeasurable. Teachers seldom know whether the objectives have been accomplished.

Long-term program planning with built-in support systems and evaluation and feedback is a process few people master. In the case of teachers, they have neither the time, nor the requisite skills, nor even the knowledge to develop long-term strategies for change. Besides, teachers have been punished, have been separated from their jobs, or have suffered embarrassing transfers for instructional or curricular deviations. In many institutions their freedom to experiment is severely restricted by the bureaucracy. Obviously, then, they are reticent to plan for the long haul and fear to take risks, for they are still vulnerable to the whims of the hierarchy.

The problem of dissemination of data is ever present. Lack of information or misinformation about changes and their effects or about pertinent research can be serious. There are assumptions, such as "If changes were good, we would hear about them," which are false. Assumptions that say "Changes cost money" inhibit action; the opponent of change need only refer to the automobile industry's very expensive changeover to prove his point. This is sometimes enough to stop the discussion of innovations.

Supervision for Change

Supervisors, administrators, and staff members can easily become lost in a maze of daily details. Time spent taking care of them is not available for the consideration of new problems. The fact that this is an age of change often has little effect on decisions relative to priorities. Today is not only a period of change; it is a period of revolution. In the second Charles W. Hunt Lecture, Lindley Stiles took for his topic "Revolution — In Instruction" and offered the following as characteristics of the revolution:[9]

1. Demand for excellence in teaching.
2. New designs for instruction.
3. Electronic aids to teaching.
4. Self-direction in learning.
5. Reorganization of content.
6. Research: the instrument of improvement.

It is in this climate that the supervisor must work and prove his worth. Obviously he must keep abreast of the changes in society and in the world, for these do affect the American scene. One need only recall the furor over education that the advent of Sputnik created in this country, or problems of "cold wars" suddenly turning hot as in Korea, Vietnam, and the Middle East. Likewise, the supervisor has to be alert to the innovations in education itself. They come from a variety of sources, and difficult though the job is, keeping up with them is a necessary self-assignment.

Origin of Change

The wise supervisor will seize upon every turn of events which will strengthen his hand in making needed changes in the curriculum and in the techniques of instruction. The advent of a new leader in the school system, especially a superintendent or principal, may represent a propitious time to begin new projects. Generally speaking, leaders who have grown old on the job or who are approaching retirement are not so inclined to start new long-term activities. Young and mobile leaders often bring new ideas with them, are willing to commit more of themselves to major tasks, and thus become change agents.

External pressures, such as those created by the Ford Foundation projects in the use of teachers aides and television, the new federal education acts, or the impact of the university scholars in a subject matter area, present useful bases for initiating change. Formal learning experiences such as institutes, workshops, summer schools, con-

---

[9] Lindley J. Stiles, "Revolution — In Instruction" (Washington: American Association for Colleges of Teacher Education, 1961).

ventions, or visits with the purpose of observing a project are excellent under certain conditions. There must be prior preparation
and those who visit other schools and projects, for example, should
engage in extensive reading and discussion relating to the purpose
of their visit. Many observations have produced nothing simply
because the observers were not alert to what could be seen.

Most supervisors will first turn to the teachers themselves. Those
creative individuals who are not content with the status quo are
readily identifiable. By deliberately working with them a supervisor can usually form the nucleus for change. Perhaps several
teachers want to find new ways to give students a more active role
in the classroom; they can become the starting point for a completely different approach to teaching.

The supervisor tries to develop in the teacher a perception of
the present state of the art of teaching and an awareness of his
possible inadequacy. Seeing where he is with reference to where
he might be, realizing that the profession has moved ahead and
that he could become a straggler, may be incentive enough for the
teacher to change his ways.

A Plan for Change

Supervisor Cal Partridge was determined to do all in his power
to completely revise the secondary science program. The instruction,
he felt, was not only dry and tedious but in too many instances unrealistic, inaccurate, or lacking altogether.

He mounted a several-pronged attack. First, he tried to arrange
for as many of the senior high teachers as possible to get into
summer institutes around the country. Second, he established committees to select new textbooks for the junior high. Third, he looked
for individuals who seemed creative and attempted to stimulate
them toward some well-planned and broadly organized curriculum
innovations. He was able to obtain the services of specialists from
two universities to assist him with a local summer institute for
teachers able to attend. What else might Cal have done in this early
stage of development?

Initiating Change

New people in the system, often the younger people, have po-
tentiality for becoming change agents. And so does the creative,
perceptive teacher, the one who is bored with detail, routine, and

repetitiveness. The supervisor needs only to capitalize upon the energy being generated by the situation to develop conditions which will release power and creativity. Not only can these people be found; they can be developed.

Some supervisors begin by importing ideas from other schools and, with the aid of the local faculty, adapting them to the local situation. There must be ways, then, of discovering and identifying appropriate material in other schools, after which the desired change may be introduced on a tryout basis and eventually may stimulate system-wide emulation. Of course, all support systems must read "go." Whatever the innovation, it must be given every chance for success.

Constant evaluation and feedback are essential. At the end of the experimental period, there must also be a rigorous evaluation as a basis for further decision making. All this experimentation and evaluation must be widely reported so that interested groups and individuals are made aware of what is taking place. Results should be presented many times so they can permeate the social structure: to selected segments of the faculty, to the PTA, to parent groups, and on and on until the community is thoroughly familiar with the pilot project.

The final phase in instituting change is to repeat the cycle by putting the new activity into effect in the entire system. New structures are created; new and comprehensive support systems are established. The pilot project becomes a model for the development of a system-wide innovation, a guide and a criterion against which to evaluate the total attempt.

Change need not envelop the schools as if in a surprise raid. Good leadership anticipates moves and deploys forces and resources in attack, rather than defense. In supervision there are various kinds of forces and resources, most potent of which is research. Basic research will probably come from the universities and elsewhere outside the school. Action research, however, can be conducted within the schools. It may include projects aimed at answering classroom questions, finding new methods, or solving problems related to materials, facilities, etc.

One writer on supervision proposes that the amount of action research in the school system should be proportional to the number of departments in the high school. An arbitrary index for schools would be based on the number of schools and the number of sections in each school and reduced by a constant to make the index practical. For example, District R-2 is a system with five secondary schools containing fifty sections each. Fifty percent of the teachers have been in the system five years or less and are getting started on their careers; 20 percent are busily and happily perfecting their teaching and probably should not be disturbed; and 20 percent are not really experimentally minded. Initially, 10 percent represents the minimum number of sections which should be concerned with action research. The formula for ascertaining the anticipated number of projects reads: $\dfrac{5 \times 50}{10} = 25$, or 25 action research projects which can give direction to change.[10]

Change in schools immediately raises the problem of finances, a part of the support system. Education in the future will certainly cost more than it has in the past. Supervisors must help educate the public to accept the idea that quality in education costs money, just as does quality in defense or in industry. Supervisors must work for some "risk capital" in the district's budget. Change involves risk because the projects may not result in anything worth incorporating into instructional or other phases of the school program. Change also often involves expenditures for equipment. For example, Lumsden reported that English teachers can reduce the time spent in reading and criticizing compositions by 50 percent with the use of dictation machines.[11] This statement was proved by teachers in the Evanston Township High School, Illinois, and others. But dictating machines cost money. The public and the budget makers must be among the supervisor's pupils if the needed support is to be provided.

Action Research

Supervisor Eldon was able to get most of the secondary social science teachers to agree to search actively for better ways to involve students in the learning process. Mr. Eldon served as the project leader, and several volunteers acted as subcommittee chairmen. Plans were drawn up outlining appropriate activities and acceptable steps to follow.

---

[10] Lawrence W. Downey, "Direction Amid Change," *Phi Delta Kappan*, 42:186–191 (Feb., 1961).

[11] Robert Lumsden, "Dictation Machines for Theme Correction," *Chicago Schools Journal*, 43:17–19 (Oct., 1961).

Many of the teachers were involved directly, as were many students also. One subcommittee was charged with making certain that adequate evaluation devices were included and that the necessary data could be obtained at the proper time. Considerable publicity was accorded this action research project throughout the entire district and the community. At every opportunity Mr. Eldon saw to it that the participants were given as much recognition as possible. What did Supervisor Eldon neglect to do in this project?

Working with the Faculty

Ultimately, all changes in education — in instruction or in improvement of learning — take place in the classroom and are carried out by teachers.[12] The teacher, then, is the crucial person in the situation, the base on which all programs are built. Therefore, the supervisor's first consideration is to develop a climate in which teachers accept the concept that better ways can be found and should be sought. If teachers and school systems over the country improve their programs, and if a trend develops toward better methods, surely obsolescence shall overtake the hindmost. Support can come from the supervisor in the form of suggestions, assistance, compliments, and the provision of materials, opportunities, etc. From the administration, moral and financial support are necessary.

The supervisor should attempt to allay the fears, doubts, anxiety, and feelings of insecurity that teachers have when embarking on new projects. Teachers should know that regardless of the outcome they will have contributed to the total knowledge and experience of the staff. An important way to show support for teachers is to get the people in the community, parents and others, to compliment teachers for their bravery, their initiative. Rewards from both staff and community are important to teachers.

Some of the ways — techniques, change agents, or inservice education projects — of stimulating teachers to improve instruction may be effective with certain teachers and not with others. Some are designed to complement and supplement the teachers' education, some to explore new fields of knowledge. The enterprising supervisor will have a stock of possible techniques in mind so that he will not be found wanting when teachers come to him for sugges-

---

[12] See Chapter Seven for a more complete discussion on changing teacher behavior.

tions. A model for changing behavior has been included here to help conceptualize this complex process.

MODEL FOR CHANGING BEHAVIOR

Input A

1. Questions, information
2. Results from observations and studies (intellectual setting)
3. Understanding and support
4. Assistance and reinforcement
5. Material provisions and physical conditions (physical setting)
6. Group support, peer approbation (social setting)
7. Sense of safety in the undertaking[13]
8. Consistency in relationships with others, and in expectations[14]
9. Establishment of the value of change (philosophical setting)
10. Input B: Feedback from output. See Output 8.

Processes

1. Generation of dissatisfaction
2. Inquiry and study
3. Discussion
4. Analysis and comparison
5. Reflective thinking
6. Decision making
7. Evaluation
8. Confrontation

Output

1. Acceptance of open-ended situations
2. Experimental attitude
3. Setting up of alternative actions
4. Better motivation
5. New directions for energy release
6. Identification with change as a change agent
7. Occupational dissatisfaction[15]
8. (All elements in this list enter the feedback system.)

---

[13] Glen G. Eye and Lanore A. Netzer, *Supervision of Instruction: A Phase of Administration* (New York: Harper & Row, 1965), p. 169.
[14] *Ibid.*
[15] Anne Roe, *The Psychology of Occupations* (New York: John Wiley & Sons, 1956), p. 33. A. S. Thompson, "Personality Dynamics and Vocational Counseling," *Personnel and Guidance Journal*, 38:350–357 (Jan., 1960).

Supervisory Leadership

Supervisor Hayward had several major projects he wanted to try somewhere in the district. Each would require strategically placed master teachers in the key slots and additional teachers for the remainder of the experimental group. All the proposed projects were sufficiently complex so that a great amount of teacher cooperation would be needed to make them work. He had been waiting for a favorable opportunity to initiate them.

At the last board meeting, a group of high school teachers had complained that there was not enough opportunity for teachers to innovate curriculum change within the district. The teachers asserted that many of their number were master teachers, well qualified in their profession and capable of much more significant output than monitoring cafeterias and unloading buses. The superintendent had agreed to consider their suggestions and the board encouraged some future report of any resulting activity. How could Supervisor Hayward make use of this situation?

In a meeting called by the director of instruction, spokesmen for the teachers met with the central instructional staff to consider possible projects. While the teachers were eager to do something, they had few tangible suggestions. Mr. Hayward explained to the group the plans he had been considering. This was just what the teachers had meant and a lively discussion ensued. They agreed to try one of Mr. Hayward's proposals, somewhat modified by the group. Plans were begun to recruit teacher volunteers to join the project.

Very soon the necessary number of qualified teachers were identified. The superintendent gave his support to the project and helped obtain sufficient funds and released time to carry it along. The teachers felt, and rightly, that they had a direct involvement from the initial planning stage. They also felt a strong commitment to help the plan succeed. Mr. Hayward felt that his objectives were being met and that change was taking place in an orderly way. Members of the board were interested and as a result became much more familiar with parts of the instructional program and with many staff members. What other consequences might be expected?

Appropriate Supervisory Activities

A sampling of appropriate supervisory activities is presented here:

1. Provide opportunities for the discussion and investigation of research and support local studies.

2. Encourage discussions in small groups, conferences, and meetings, in which new methods, changes, and trends in education and problems in education are the center of attention.

3. Provide opportunities for teachers to observe the techniques under consideration in some actual school situations. In one school system, the money to be spent on summer workshops for foreign language teachers was used to send them to the country of the language to be taught.

4. Devote some meetings of the faculty to a dramatic description of change in the profession, in the various businesses and industries, and in the community.

5. Organize skill sessions for those who are interested in making tapes, transparencies, overlays, 3" × 5" slides, simple teaching machines, and other teaching devices.

6. Establish skill sessions in the use of the group process for training, practice, and assistance as needed.

7. Provide for demonstrations of machines and the skills needed to operate them.

8. Bring in state agencies, including experts on new curricula from the state department of education. Much help can be had in most states from this quarter.

9. Construct hypothetical models of the department itself which would include all the latest equipment, techniques, facilities, housing requirements, staff, and projected changes.

10. Experiment with television, closed-circuit or otherwise. Obtain equipment on rental or loan basis.

11. Discuss with teachers methods of teacher growth and continued education. How can sabbaticals, travel, and year-long institutes serve this need?

12. Utilize institutes and workshops on specific problems such as methods for initiating change.

13. Obtain clerical help, aids, and facilities which are flexible and available for teachers.

14. Convince school boards and administrators that these items are crucial for successful innovation.

Summary

The supervisor who is implementing educational change is providing educational leadership. The phenomenon of change must be understood by the supervisor, as must ways of meeting the challenge presented by it. Changing behavior patterns in the community influence the schools. Change in today's society is inescapable. Characteristics of change are rate, direction, volume, and quality. Among agents of change one finds supervisors. The focus of change is first in people, then in institutions. Factors and conditions inhibiting change are powerful.

Supervisory applications of the principles of change should be based on an understanding of the origins of change and on the ability to reshape structure. The supervisor must ever work with the faculty so that the eventual changes in instruction or in the curriculum occur within the classroom.

Problems for Group Discussion

Analyze the following situations. In each, identify supervisory principles representing sound theory, if any are included. What are the basic elements which made a difference? How would you have approached the situation?

1. The superintendent has established the first full-time instructional supervisor in the district. There is little if any coordination within the instructional program at present. The new supervisor is charged with making some rapid changes throughout the district.

2. The supervisor was working very closely with the fifteen teachers in the innovation program. He knew that the decision to continue or to drop the program would be made at the end of the year, largely upon the results of current research. One of his primary concerns was to assist the teachers to become more adequate persons so they could in turn transfer this feeling of adequacy to their pupils.

3. The supervisor considered himself the change agent in the district and made it a point to tell everyone so. Furthermore, whenever possible he attempted to upset existing patterns, on the premise that little change would occur if present practices were allowed to continue undisturbed.

Selected Readings

Association for Supervision and Curriculum Development. *Educational Leadership,* Vol. 17, No. 5 (Feb., 1960).

Bruner, Jerome S. *The Process of Education,* Cambridge, Mass.: Harvard University Press, 1960.

Cawelti, Gordon. "Innovative Practices in High Schools: Who Does What — and Why — and How," *Nation's Schools,* 79:56–74 (Apr., 1967).

Downey, Lawrence W. "Direction Amid Change," *Phi Delta Kappan,* 42:186–191 (Feb., 1961).

Eye, Glen G., and Lanore A. Netzer. *Supervision of Instruction: A Phase of Administration.* New York: Harper & Row, 1965.

Fischer, John H. "Our Changing Conception of Education," *Phi Delta Kappan,* 42:16–19 (Oct., 1960).

Guba, E. G. "Diffusion of Innovations," *Educational Leadership,* 25:292–295 (Jan., 1968).

Heathers, Glen. "Influencing Change at the Elementary Level," in Richard I. Miller, ed., *Perspectives on Educational Change.* New York: Appleton-Century-Crofts, 1967.

Lippitt, R. "Role and Processes in Curriculum Development and Change," in *Strategy for Curriculum Change.* Washington: Association for Supervision and Curriculum Development, 1965, pp. 11–28.

Lumsden, Robert. "Dictation Machines for Theme Correction," *Chicago Schools Journal,* 43:17–19 (Oct., 1961).

March, James G., and Herbert A. Simon. *Organizations.* New York: John Wiley & Sons, 1959.

Miles, M. B., ed. *Innovation in Education.* New York: Bureau of Publications, Teachers College, Columbia University, 1964.

Miller, Richard I. "An Overview of Educational Change," in Richard I. Miller, ed., *Perspectives on Educational Change.* New York: Appleton-Century-Crofts, 1967.

Morse, Arthur D. *Schools of Tomorrow — Today.* Garden City, N.Y.: Doubleday & Company, 1960.

National Association of Secondary School Principals. *The Bulletin,* Vol. 46, No. 270 (Jan., 1962).

Parker, J. Cecil, and Louis J. Rubin. *Process as Content: Curriculum Design and the Application of Knowledge.* Chicago: Rand McNally & Co., 1966.

Pines, Maya. *Revolution in Learning: The Years from Birth to Six.* New York: Harper & Row, 1967.

Pressey, Sidney L. "Unresolved Teaching-Machine Problems," *Educational Digest,* 27:1–3 (May, 1962).

Roe, Anne. *The Psychology of Occupations.* New York: John Wiley & Sons, 1956.

Rogers, E. M. "The Communication of Innovations in a Complex Institution," *Educational Record,* 49:67–77 (Winter, 1968).

State Education Department. *Commissioner's 1961 Catalog of Educational Change.* Albany: The State Department, New York, 1961.

Stiles, Lindley J. "Revolution — In Instruction." Washington: American Association for Colleges of Teacher Education, 1961.

Thompson, A. S. "Personality Dynamics and Vocational Counseling," *Personnel and Guidance Journal,* 38:350–357 (Jan., 1960).

Trump, J. Lloyd, and Dorsey Baynham. *Focus on Change, Guide to Better Schools.* New York: Rand McNally & Co., 1961.

Unruh, Adolph, and O. T. Richardson. "Counseling in an Age of Change," *Clearing House,* 41:148–152 (Nov., 1966).

nine

•

Supervision Through the Use of Group Techniques

A well-planned program of supervision will utilize many approaches to the improvement of instruction and the growth of personnel. One approach which has been found to be effective and in keeping with the principles of democracy is group process. The modern supervisor must constantly deal with groups, and he must know how to become a part of many and varied groups.

Group process may be described as a stream of experiences rising from the interactions of people and culminating in more satisfying relationships among them, or in cooperatively finding more adequate solutions to problems.[1] This stream of experiences is affected by interstimulation, circular reaction, and social facilitation. It has direction, rate of flow, quality, and quantity. The individual has a feeling of accomplishment when the process moves forward — a feeling that can be a source of satisfaction and a factor in achieving good work.

The objectives of group process in the present context are the improvement of teaching, the improvement of the curriculum, and the making of certain behavioral changes in individuals. The approach is not meant for use in analyzing individual personalities or undertaking psychotherapy. The group techniques described have been tried many times and are known to be effective. They foster progress and growth of all members involved and are applicable in the classroom as well as in staff meetings.[2]

---

[1] Donald Thomas, "T-Grouping, the White Collar Hippie Movement," *Phi Delta Kappan,* 49:458–460 (Apr., 1968).
[2] Arthur Blumberg and Edmund Amidon, "Teacher Perceptions of Supervisor-Teacher Interaction," *Administrator's Notebook,* 14:1–4 (Sept., 1965).

Studying the Group

Definition of a Group

The supervisor should know that a collection of people — such as the staff and teachers who make up the faculty — has the potential for becoming a group. But a collection of persons is not actually a group. (Many people have said that teaching is not a profession; what they mean is that teachers often seem to be a collection of people, not a group. Teachers tend to be individualistic, discipline-oriented, much like their college professors, who are not known especially for cooperation!)

A group is two or more people who have common objectives and perceptions. They have common interests (type of client or service) and tools with which to ply their operations. They have in common certain types of skills and concepts, and therefore a common language. The environment in which they work contains shared elements such as resources (public or private), and the agencies (legal and voluntary) and organizations (professional and legal) through which their work is carried on.

The group exerts an effect on its members. Individuals reinforce each other and provide assistance where needed. They support one another in their resistance to the hierarchy and the bureaucracy; they orient new members and build morale. The group becomes a nucleus in the communication system, receiving and disseminating information. It contains opinion leaders — opinion seekers and givers — who alert members to threats to their morale or safety, emphasize certain items in the official bulletins or unofficial news, and provide direction for group thinking. On a more formal and larger scale, this phenomenon may be observed at conventions at which speakers analyze and interpret events and their implications for the future of the group.

There have been many efforts throughout the years to bring all teachers into one group so that in total they might develop appropriate objectives, obtain competence with professional tools, and become self-starting and self-directive, thus acquiring more of the characteristics of a profession. One of these efforts is represented in the AFT; another in the NEA.

Also encouraging teachers to work in groups are state departments of education, honorary educational fraternities, and professional

organizations. The supervisor too, with his inservice education program, attempts to create groups — composed of individualists, persons new to the profession, and raw recruits — that will carry on the
work of the schools efficiently. They must be able to undertake
problem solving, project development, and curriculum change with
a minimum of static, diversion, and loss of time, using skillful leadership and group process.

Classifications of collective behavior provide insights into group
behaviors. At the bottom are such elementary behaviors as hysteria,
panic, and mob action, which develop when routines are disturbed
or forcibly altered, when social and emotional drives have been
thwarted, or when there has been a major shift in expectations and
perceptions. Next comes the behavior of the casual crowd, a collection of people in the street observing an accident or a fire, or listening to a soapbox orator. Above the casual crowd is the conventional
crowd, such as spectators at a football game or at the cinema. These
people have more in common, and one can expect "conventional"
behavior. At the top is the group of individuals, pulled together for
a common purpose, actively attempting to reach accepted goals.
An investment club of teachers who meet in different members'
homes regularly to identify and then purchase stocks represents this
group.

Certain traditions, codes, folkways, and customs are operative in
these collectivities. A preschool meeting of the faculty in September,
when all the teachers and staff are brought together in an auditorium
or via television for the first time, represents a conventional crowd.
Out of this crowd the supervisor must fashion both formal and informal groups to carry forward the work of education.

Characteristics of Groups

The term *group*, then, is here applied to two or more teachers
working cooperatively on the improvement of instruction. Of
course, all teachers may be involved, the large group being composed of many smaller groups. However, it is the transfer of power
and control from smaller groups to the whole that makes work in a
school system go forward and the democratic achieving of system-
wide goals possible. In the literature of group dynamics this is
called *locomotion*.

Bartky has pointed out that teacher groups, even as other groups, are at times subject to fads.[3] Ability grouping, the platoon system, activity units, and many others originally started as innovations in certain districts and spread in a cursory, superficial manner to many parts of the country, but often were short-lived. Bartky's view is probably an oversimplification of the actual conditions because a fad that sweeps a profession — teaching, medicine, the clergy — has much more substance than a new design in clothing, a new car style, new dance steps, etc. Most so-called professional fads, have strong elements of planning, objectivity, and evaluation. Instead of decrying fads, critics would do well to analyze them. Often they can be used to enrich the profession.

There is genuine danger that group process might become a fad. Teachers and supervisors who give only lip service to group process will never really comprehend it. Some will superficially mimic it. Some will actually believe they are using it when in reality they are simply retailing information to a captive audience. Nevertheless, those who seriously desire to do so can learn the process. Skills in group leadership can also be learned. Once group process functions properly, the individuals involved in it often make considerable personal growth. They may never be the same after an encounter of this sort. Thus, for those who have had a genuine experience with it group process can never be merely a fad or a fashion. It will permanently add something to their techniques, philosophy, and personal and professional stature.

In successful group process, groups are characterized by a quality of cohesiveness, described variously as belonging, groupness, weness and identified by use of *we, us, ours,* as opposed to *I, me,* and *mine.* It is reflected in behavior: regular attendance at meetings, working and sacrificing for the group, praising the group, mutual admiration, and a rather close identification with the group.

Teacher groups likewise have cohesiveness. However, its level may be high or low, and too often it is low. It becomes the task of the supervisor to raise this quality when it is low or to maintain it if high. Cartwright and Zander have shown that a factor in cohesiveness is *valence,* or the attraction a group has for its members.[4]

---

[3] John A. Bartky, *Supervision as Human Relations* (Boston: D. C. Heath & Company, 1953), p. 182.
[4] Dorwin Cartwright and Alvin Zander, eds., *Group Dynamics: Research and Theory,* 2nd ed. (New York: Harper & Row, 1960), pp. 76–82.

Valence depends upon the objectives, programs, activities, organization, and status of the group, and upon the nature and strength of
the individual's needs. When these can be closely related, the
cohesiveness of the group will be high. Educational leaders have
long been trying to build "high cohesiveness" groups. The best
way to do so is to relate the group to the individual through effective group processes.

A Basic Ingredient

Every group is made up of individuals, and each individual must
be accorded dignity and worth by all the other members. His contribution should be actively sought. When this contribution is at its
maximum, group process is proceeding effectively. When all the
suggestions of all the members of the group are collected, winnowed,
and evaluated, the resulting decisions and actions are likely to be of
a high order, less susceptible to criticism or outright opposition.
The fact that every person in the group has had a share in the
decisions and will feel he has a personal stake and responsibility in
their administration is of great importance to the success of the
process.

Every leader must have faith and confidence in every member of
his organization. If he feels otherwise, he will consciously or unconsciously convey his attitude to the group. Individuals will feel
slighted and misunderstood at first, then annoyed, and finally suspicious of the leadership. The morale of the individual may drop
and the attactiveness of the group for him be reduced. The resulting lowered efficiency on the part of one person could impair the
total efficiency of the group.

Basis for Growth

Both individual growth and group growth are influenced by the
contribution of the individual. Ideas never expressed become blocks
to growth. When someone has tossed his idea into the discussion,
one of two things happens to him. If the idea is a good one and is
accepted by the group, he takes pride in his contribution; his search
for more ideas to offer inevitably leads to growth. If his idea is rejected by the group, he can relieve himself of the burden of enter-
taining it and turn to other, more worthwhile ideas. The group,
meanwhile, is enriched because it has, in the first instance, a contribution it can use. In the latter instance, even though it refused

the idea, the group experiences the opportunity of examining it and the group's present position is the stronger for having made a choice from various alternatives.

Progress is related to the advancement of the group, not the advancement of one or two individuals. Scientists and scholars are concerned with finding the truth rather than with the consequences of their discoveries. The fact remains, however, that the excellence of any way of living, or of any civilization, depends upon the general diffusion of what is known, what is believed, and the common practice of what is considered to be good, true, and beautiful. The same may be said of the educational profession.

Shaping the teaching profession into a cohesive group has been an objective of educational leadership for years. One way to develop esprit de corps is to control the membership rigidly, regulating the means of entrance, to indoctrinate, and to build prestige through the use of law (licensing, and legislating conditions surrounding practice). Education has pursued this path. Also, it has chosen to educate its members and then to educate the general public. This is a slow process but, until recently, acceptable to the profession, and one in which the effort of generations of interested persons has been spent.

Lethargic Teachers?

Mrs. Lena Gibson, secondary supervisor in the North City schools, was well known to educators throughout the state. She was always present at the state or regional meetings. At national conferences she was to be found conversing freely with leaders from all over the country. Mrs. Gibson was generally considered a very knowledgeable supervisor, familiar with the latest trends in secondary education.

The secondary curriculum in North City, however, was conservative, traditional, and described by many as dull and uninspiring. Lena had given up on the teachers in the district some time before. She used to try to interest them in experimenting with the new practices she found elsewhere, but there was little response. For a time she sent out information sheets telling about innovations she found of interest. No one had come forward wanting to try them, so she finally gave that up, too.

Lena is now convinced that all the teachers are lethargic and unimaginative practitioners. What understanding of working with people has she evidenced?

Building the Group Processes

The Association for Supervision and Curriculum Development presented a formula for building group process in 1948 in *Group Processes in Supervision.*[5] The elements of the formula were (1) group thinking, (2) group discussion, (3) group planning, (4) group decision, (5) group action, and (6) group evaluation. The 1949 yearbook, *Toward Better Teaching,* described a related approach to building group processes: (1) establishing rapport, (2) setting up goals, (3) planning experiences, (4) group decisions, (5) division of responsibilities, (6) opportunities to gather and distribute materials, (7) cooperative learning extending beyond the classroom, and (8) group evaluation.[6]

Gibb, Platts, and Miller arrived at eight principles which govern the dynamics of group process: (1) atmosphere (physical setting), (2) threat reduction, (3) distributive leadership, (4) goal formulation, (5) flexibility, (6) consensus, (7) process awareness, and (8) continual evaluation.[7] Cartwright and Zander presented a documented study of how the group operates; they were concerned with (1) group cohesiveness, (2) group pressures, (3) group standards, (4) group goals, (5) group locomotion, (6) group properties, and (7) leadership.[8]

From these and a number of other approaches to group work, we offer the following list as being particularly pertinent to supervision:

1. Group objectives
2. Group discussion
3. Group decision
4. Group action
5. Group evaluation
6. New objectives

This list has been arranged into a flow chart to depict graphically what happens as the group decision-making process develops. Two

[5] Association for Supervision and Curriculum Development, *Group Processes in Supervision,* 1948 Yearbook (Washington: The Association, 1948), pp. 1–38.
[6] Association for Supervision and Curriculum Development, *Toward Better Teaching,* 1949 Yearbook (Washington: The Association, 1949), p. 51.
[7] J. R. Gibb, Grace N. Platts, and Lorraine F. Miller, *Dynamics of Participative Groups* (Boulder, Colo.: J. R. Gibb, 1951), pp. 4–50.
[8] Cartwright and Zander, *loc. cit.*

systems of roles supporting the group process have been added to the flow chart to demonstrate the relationship of roles to the process. One system specifies the group task roles, or content-bearing roles. The other system specifies the group and process maintenance roles which keep the group alert and moving toward an objective.

Group Decision-Making Process

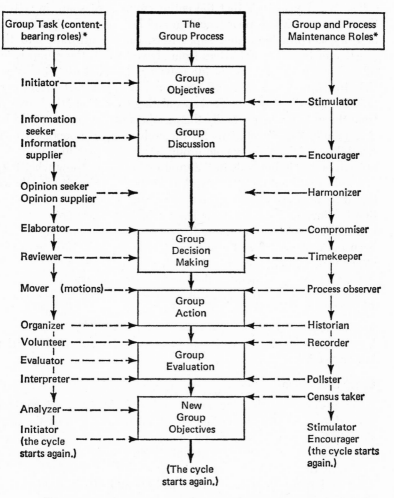

Note: These roles are explained more fully later in this chapter.

Group Objectives

Objectives are all-important. The individual's life is governed by his objectives. Societies are geared to objectives. Institutions are founded because of objectives. Every lesson serves one or more objectives. Modern methods of appraisal of students are in terms of objectives. All of this may be succinctly stated: "All behavior is goal oriented."

The key, however, is that the entire group must share in setting the objectives. Much poor teaching, and lack of professionalization of teachers, principals, and supervisors, can be attributed to the practice of imposing objectives from above. When the group is inhibited by direction from outside (above), it cannot meet its potential. Initiative, creativity, and even commitment to action are curtailed. Valuable time is wasted speculating over what "they" expect from the group, when actually the members of the group should be determining the expectations for themselves based upon their own capabilities. When the whole group has had a part in setting the objectives, the individuals in the group will clearly know what they are and so will not feel their work is aimless. Earlier it was shown that objectives are closely related to morale. One source of frustration is eliminated when people know where they are going.

Broadly speaking, programs for curriculum reorganization have been most successful in those communities in which a cooperative attack was made first upon objectives. Such a development usually proceeds from the general to the specific. Unless a course or subject articulates with the objectives of education, it becomes tangential. Finally, each lesson, cooperatively set up with students, must serve specific objectives within the overall framework. Thus, objectives become guidelines upon which all involved in the subsequent action have agreed.

Group Discussion

Discussion and planning are everybody's business. Sometimes organizations grow so large that not all members are in on the decisions in the initial planning and instead have a voice through their representatives. One of the basics of the group approach to problem solving is that all persons share in the development of all policies and regulations under which they will operate. If this principle is literally followed, almost any enterprise becomes an exciting adventure for everyone concerned.

Often supervisors and others in an administrative capacity fail to give members in the organization opportunities to help in planning. The reason, it is said, is that involvement of all members slows down the procedures and delays decision making. Or, since there is a division of labor, it is assumed that teachers are not interested in budgets, or public relations, or zoning, or state aid. Or, the argument continues, the more people that are involved, the more answers are forthcoming, most of them utterly useless. In this connection, Parker and Kleemeier cite the principles on which the International Harvester Company built its communications program.[9] One is that employees have a right to any information which management has. A second principle, complementing the first, is that employees are intelligent and capable of reasoning; provided they had all the information available to management, they would probably come to similar conclusions.

If the group has set as its objective the improvement of instruction, it will set about implementing this objective. The supervisor will be kept busy stimulating, directing, coordinating, supporting the efforts of the group. He need not worry about finding worthwhile projects. Instead, he will make available to the group every useful type of materials, resources, aids, facts, and understandings. His role will be one of leadership and provision of services.

Working with the Group

Today Henry Freeland was a busy supervisor. The Ad Hoc English Committee was scheduled to meet tomorrow afternoon and there were many things Henry needed to do in preparation for the meeting. The committee had requested certain data which Henry had agreed to procure. The computer center had not yet made its run for him. He must stop by and get that material later in the day. He also had to visit the professional library and pick up the books the librarian was selecting for him. Those, with the materials Henry had in his own office, should provide the basis of study for the meeting.

Now that the committee had taken his initial suggestion and developed some objectives, they were able to plan their activities in an orderly, productive fashion. Most of the group seemed to feel that they were moving in the right direction — and so did Henry. It did

---

[9] Willard E. Parker and Robert W. Kleemeier, *Human Relations in Supervision* (New York: McGraw-Hill Book Company, 1951), pp. 30–33.

keep him busy just providing the items they needed to function properly. He was rather glad there were not a dozen such dynamic groups in operation all at once.

Has Henry exhibited leadership or is he merely serving as an "errand boy"?

Group Decisions

All teachers have a vital interest in what their school does because it affects their personal welfare and professional status. All teachers, directly or indirectly through their duly elected representatives, should have a voice in any decision made by the school as such.

Participation in decisions brings participation in responsibilities. It means shared leadership. It means sharing the prestige and praise attendant upon achievement. If decisions are made by the group, cohesiveness is increased. As long as others make the decisions, execute them, and merely call staff meetings to announce what they have done, the group reaction will range from indifference and boredom to suspicion and hostility.

There are several devices that can be used in approaching decisions. First, it is necessary to decide what the problem or issue is, and to fix upon operational definitions to be used. Certain other rules for discussion may be cooperatively set, e.g., the amount of time to be devoted to the problem, the order of events, speakers, subtopics, etc., and whether action will be necessary. In trying to obtain decisions by the group, the leaders will do well to use the straw vote method. This is the method of predecision, or finding out whether agreement is possible. It also permits the group to phrase and rephrase the final statement of action (motion) without creating tensions or precipitating a new outbreak of polarization (grouping for or against).

Few decisions in life are so important as to make unanimity imperative. Whatever happens to be under consideration, there may be reasons for not achieving a unanimous view. In most groups there are personality clashes of more or less intensity, though these will be minimized if a good human relations program has been followed. Tension reduction may be one of the outcomes of the group process.

Sometimes information is lacking. Intelligent people will be loath to make decisions or to take action on very limited knowledge except when further data are simply not available. A unanimous judgment is sometimes impossible because of varying points of view. People have different prejudices or biases, and their backgrounds represent different experiences which may result in different interpretations of the same set of facts. It then becomes necessary for all members in the group to practice tolerance. Patience and a variety of approaches, along with elaboration and illustration of points, will bring dividends. Perhaps total consensus cannot be reached because of the immaturity and naiveté of some in the group, who simply cannot disassociate a person from the idea he has presented. They have not learned to be objective. If they do not like the person, they cannot like the idea. If they do not like the idea, they will learn not to like the person, and any subsequent contribution he makes will be suspect in their eyes. The supervisor should be aware that he will have in his groups mature-looking people with many years of schooling who will continue to exhibit this weakness.

Lacking consensus, groups are sometimes content to operate on the basis of a majority. Perhaps even a majority cannot be reached. Then the situation may be saved by obtaining an agreement to continue the study of the problem. Thus a delaying strategy may be used. It is possible for a group to move too rapidly in a given direction, the implications of their action not being completely understood by all. A straw vote would indicate this and might be used to protect the group from itself.

Group Action

Decisions lead to action. The inevitable question after a decision has been reached is "Who will do this?" Several methods may be utilized to carry out the group's will. Perhaps at the highest level of action is the voluntary shouldering of responsibility. One or more persons agree to carry out the decision and the group agrees to let them do it. Hence, the requisite amount of authority commensurate with the obligation is granted by the group.

Or the usual democratic processes may be put in motion. Nominations are accepted and those present are requested to make selections. In smaller groups, or groups with selected membership, agreement in the form of "unanimous ballots" is common. However, many persons consider themselves fortunate indeed when they have been able to obtain a simple majority.

Another type of action, often used in the past by administrators and supervisors, is at the appointment level. It may or may not

carry group approval. In a mature group, the trivia of administration are often of little moment. Yet the filling of any position, or the
taking of any action, each or both of which are vital to the welfare
of the group, should be made with the "advice and consent" of the
group. Too many appointments made by supervisors and administrators have the veneer of democracy but not its essence. Cooperation in such instances becomes a unilateral relationship; it is necessary only to review the levels of possibilities loosely described as
"cooperation," namely, compulsion, exploitation, compromise, bargaining, leadership, and democratic cooperation to recognize that
there are as many one-way as two-way processes.

Good Rapport

Michele Warren was recognized as one of the best supervisors
ever to work in the city schools. She had been for years a careful
student of group process and she made good use of it in her daily
work. Most teachers in the district were more than happy to work
with her on a committee because they knew that their ideas would
receive a proper hearing. She could be relied upon to lead and
encourage the committee in such a manner that the best thinking of
the various members would result in a genuine contribution of which
all could be proud.

Because Michele had developed this reputation with the teachers,
her task was made easier in many ways. She did not have to take
valuable committee time to "prove herself" but could work with the
members to select appropriate courses of action, reflecting sound
group decisions. How might the other supervisors gain from her
experience?

Group Evaluation

Evaluation starts with objectives. The first question to be asked
is "What did we set out to do?" The second is "Did we accomplish
our mission?" Answers to these questions raise other questions. If
success was complete, and the objectives were achieved, the group
should be disbanded. New groups should be created around new
objectives. If only partial success was achieved, the group might
reexamine the whole procedure, beginning with the appropriateness
of the objectives, and search for alternatives.

If the objectives are found to be appropriate, well stated, and still
acceptable, attention might next turn to the planning phase. In
what respects did the planning go awry? Was it a matter of insuffi-

cient data? The decisions can be reexamined for possible flaws. The action of all responsible parties could come under the close scrutiny of a more critical group.

Frequently the only evaluation made of any group project is in terms of quantity: the amount of money raised, the number of books read, the daily attendance, the number in attendance. The outline of the evaluation should give attention also to the quality of the group action. Did the individuals grow in skills, abilities, and understanding during the group process? Was leadership willingly shared and assumed? What has happened to morale? Have the interpersonal relations of the members improved? Are individuals better able to communicate with each other?

New Group Objectives

Often group enterprises end with evaluation. Units of learning begin nobly with objectives and end with evaluation. Evaluation closes the course, the workshop, or the school year. Yet there are very often — almost always — next steps to be taken, and evaluation should lead to them. There is little point in giving intelligence tests and then filing the scores in the counselor's office. Their value is in the information they reveal as to what should be done.

Evaluation is for the purpose of learning whether and to what extent the objectives have been achieved. If achievement was 100 percent, then obviously, as an opportunity arrives, the same project could be repeated in the same way. That would become the new objective. If achievement was less than 100 percent, the new objectives should vary from the original ones. The stage of considering differing objectives precedes a new cycle: objectives, planning, decisions, action, evaluation, new objectives.

A Tale of Two Committees

Supervisor Jones was chairing a meeting of all social studies teachers in the district. The announced purpose of the meeting was to look at the secondary curriculum in social studies and to identify parts needing change. Mr. Jones had carefully arranged for the meeting to be held on school time, not teacher time, and he had provided comfortable accommodations, including the customary cup of coffee.

Much to his distress, however, Mr. Jones found himself in the center of a discussion of fluctuating intensity which strayed far afield from his recommended agenda. The teachers, it seemed, had little interest in the topic. Some discussed behavior of certain students; some lamented their small salaries; some even complained because they had been asked to leave their classrooms!

Meanwhile, in another building across town, Supervisor Janowitz was chairing a similar meeting with the English teachers. The group working with Miss Janowitz, however, was vigorously discussing the items on their agenda, many eagerly awaiting their turn for the floor. The reason for this enthusiastic interaction was that Miss Janowitz had prepared the English teachers for the meeting and in so doing she had helped to establish a group which the members accepted. In fact, the agenda items had come largely from previous suggestions of the teachers themselves as to topics they wanted studied. An advance agenda with suggestions for pre-preparation had reached all teachers well in advance of the meeting. Miss Janowitz's group had cohesiveness, a sense of direction acceptable to the members, and a commitment to accomplish something considered significant and necessary.

It is quite obvious that the English teachers represent a group while Mr. Jones's social studies teachers are merely a collection of individuals with no formulated aim or purpose in being. Until he can get the teachers to accept some recognizable objective for meeting, Mr. Jones and his people will flounder. The longer it takes to reach a starting point, the more difficult it will be to do so. In contrast, Miss Janowitz is well along, and shortly her group will be ready to move to new objectives. What should Mr. Jones do?

Group Interaction

Sensitivity Training

Both education and industry have shown much interest in the working of groups, especially small groups, for a number of years. The results are embodied in such specialized taining programs as laboratory education or sensitivity training as developed by the National Training Laboratories at Bethel, Maine, and elsewhere.[10] This is a direct outgrowth of the studies cited above and the work of the behavioral scientists. It is also a recognition of the principle of human worth and dignity described earlier. The supervisor

---

[10] For information regarding training laboratories, one may write to Dr. Leland P. Bradford, National Training Laboratories, National Education Association, 1201 16th Street, N.W., Washington, D.C.

should be familiar with the T- (for training) group. Briefly, this intensive training activity attempts to provide individuals a clear understanding of effective group operation. Learning takes place through the participants' diagnoses of their own behavior and their attempts to find new, acceptable behavior. Major learning results from the interaction of the group members themselves.

The purposes of sensitivity training, of which T-groups are one form, are:

1. To improve a situation, the relationships between and among people, and to improve interaction, hence to be therapeutic.
2. To train for leadership in group situations.
3. To develop understanding and insights into oneself, the roles and expectations of others, and one's own role in the group.
4. To improve skills in communication.
5. To provide experience in the use of group methods for management, in making functional analyses, and in playing missing roles for the group.

The assumptions underlying this technique are that it gives meaning to the philosophical ideal of human worth and dignity; it sets the stage for higher production with higher morale and greater satisfaction on the part of the members; it builds insight and affords practice in developing better human relations and human interactions, thereby lowering interpersonal tensions; it reduces role and personality conflicts and provides for a better adjustment of the conflict between members and bureaucracy alluded to earlier.

Sensitivity training is an excellent technique for educating administrators at all levels — school, college, and university. Results reported by training laboratories indicate that supervisors who have had sensitivity training become more effective group leaders. They have clearer perceptions of the behavior of others and are able to identify significant changes in the lives of others. Supervisors should be cautioned, however, not to use this intensive, in-depth experience for all teachers. Some individuals do not profit from the tactics used in such groups. One of the outcomes of sensitivity training is that it permits participants to learn about the impact they have on the group. Certain concepts described in this chapter, such as cohesion, group maturity, climate, and group structure, can be studied in sensitivity training settings. The small group can be used to stimulate the informal group in a bureaucracy. Obviously this type of training has many possibilities.

Making Use of Available Resources

Supervisor Kleinschmidt was convinced that there must be more group process throughout the district if substantial improvement was to take place in the instructional program of the secondary schools. He recognized that he could not accomplish everything by himself, that he must obtain help from others in the district.

After some months he got the superintendent to agree to send a team of three people from the largest high school to a summer session of the National Training Laboratories in Bethel, Maine. The principal, an assistant principal, and a department chairman would go. Mr. Kleinschmidt began to speculate about the many possible types of group participation which could be initiated in that school next year. He could hardly wait to get started! Was the supervisor being realistic in his enthusiasm for group work?

Membership Types

Much significant work has been directed to finding out how people behave in groups. One approach is to analyze the role types they play, especially those necessary to keep a productive group in action.[11] Task roles (necessary for carrying out the work of the group) are taken by the initiator, the recorder, the information seeker, the information giver, the opinion seeker, the opinion giver, the elaborator, and the critic. These are group-oriented roles, rather than individual roles played for individual benefit. Group maintenance roles have the purpose of keeping the group functioning, preventing it from splitting into splinter groups, and moving the attitude and the will of the group toward a decision as expeditiously as possible. Playing these roles are the encourager, the stimulator, the harmonizer, the compromiser, the gatekeeper, the clock watcher, the expediter, the standard setter, the process observer, and the follower.

A more negative type consists of individual roles which tend to be more self-centered than were the previous categories. In these roles are the aggressor, the blocker, the recognition seeker, the self-

---

[11] K. D. Benne and P. Sheats, "Functional Roles of Group Members," *Journal of Social Issues*, 4:42–49 (Spring, 1948). Leland P. Bradford, ed., *Group Development* (Washington: National Education Association, 1961).

confessor, the playboy, the group dominator, the help seeker, and the special interest pleader. The list is not meant to be all inclusive; any supervisor could add to it from his observations of faculty meetings.

The Study of Process

Group interaction can be quite revealing to the knowledgeable observer. The process of interaction is the means of arriving at consensus on a program of action. Presumably, if the process is correctly utilized, the program will be a better one, and more likely to be implemented.

In studying group interaction, the purpose is to sensitize the individuals to the group and its work, to eliminate the dominators and the self-seekers, to avoid imposed decisions in favor of group action and group consciousness. The ideal is something like a well-organized, well-coordinated, highly motivated, and conscientiously developed teamwork of a professional basketball club. The members are all driving toward a shared goal.

The process itself may move briskly or it may meander among random ideas and contributions of the members. Sometimes all will be clamoring eagerly for the floor; sometimes the interchange may degenerate to a dialogue or be replaced by a monologue or lecture. The participation may be very uneven over a period of time.

The writers have evolved a form (see Fig. 4) on which the participation of the group can be evaluated, on three dimensions: the number of times an individual contributes to the discussion, the quality of the contribution (group or individually oriented, negatively or positively directed), the length of the contribution. The time element is built into the form so that the process of change can be described. Symbols are provided for recording the contributions.

The individually oriented responses are recorded by means of five symbols:

Symbol	*Meaning of Responses*
0 (zero)	No value. Someone may interject a word into the discussion: "Oh, come on!" or some frivolous comment.
/ (tally)	Custodial value. "Let's get started." "I'll open the window." It may also have simple procedural value — obtaining supplies.

Symbol	Meaning of Responses
+ (plus)	Positive value. "I believe this is a good idea." "I can see the value of this." "I think we should set up a study group."
− (minus)	Negative value. "I am opposed to this." "I don't think this will work out."
? (question)	"How can this be?" "Will someone tell me . . . ?"

The group-oriented responses (symbols enclosed in a circle or parentheses are shown by three symbols:

Symbol	Meaning of Responses
(+) (plus)	Someone might say, "We can do this if each of us will take a part." Or, "I move we sell the building to the highest bidder."
(−) (minus)	"We don't have the manpower for this project and shouldn't even be discussing it."
(?) (question)	"If we purchase this book, will we then have time to rewrite the units?"

Such a system of recording gives a simple but clear description of participation and changes in group attitudes over time. Some of the results which might be identified are: the development of cohesion within the group, identification of the troublemakers during the discussion, the shift from a collection of individuals to a group, and an increase in the ability of the group to successfully handle discussion problems. The supervisor who uses this technique will know much more about what happened than is revealed in the minutes of the group meeting.

The procedure not only will permit careful analysis of the particular discussion but, when used several times in succession, may indicate some of the inner tensions of members. It can also point to relationships of people in the group. Such analysis might assist the supervisor in the selection of leaders for committees and faculty groups. It can surely assist him to identify the shy and backward teachers who need special attention. It could also give him an indication of the faculty's readiness for independent studies and self-direction.

When group process is utilized regularly, a large variety of statistical manipulations becomes possible. Correlations with outside

Symbols — Type of Response			
+	Individual Positive	(+)	Group Positive
–	Individual Negative	(–)	Group Negative

Symbols — Type of Response			
?	Individual Question	0	No Contribution
(?)	Group Question	/	Custodial

Names	Intervals of Time in Minutes						Totals								
	5	10	15	20	25	30	+	–	(+)	(–)	?	(?)	0	/	Totals
1. Fran	+? ?	? (?) (?)	(+) (–)	(–) (+)			1		2	2	3	2			10
2. Jerry	(+) (+)	(+)		(+) (+)	(+)	(+) (+)			8						8
3. Ron		?	? ?	?	– –	–		3			4				7
4. Randy	– –	(–) (?)	(?)	+	(+) (+)	(+)	1	2	3	1		2			9
5. Leddy	(+)								2						2
Totals	8	7	5	6	6	4	2	5	15	3	7	4			36

Fig. 4

Group Process — Chart of Participation

criteria can be made. Rank-order correlations using successive applications of the chart may reveal that interesting changes are taking
place within the faculty. Curves can be plotted; the data from a
number of applications usually have the characteristics of a learning
curve. When the group has matured and can cope with its problems effectively and efficiently, the curve recording changes has a
tendency to flatten out, approaching a straight line; the group can
be expected to handle a difficult problem well.

Figure 4 represents a hypothetical committee meeting, charted
by supervisor Jones. Many interesting facts emerge. Fran raised
questions at first, took a negative attitude, and finally gave in to the
group. Jerry was group oriented all the way. Ron was never convinced. Randy was convinced after he had a chance to raise some
questions and get something off his mind. Leddy was with the
group all the way but did not make any contributions. Participation
started high, then dwindled to half of the starting level. Almost 70
percent of the contributions were group oriented while only 30 percent were individually oriented. Also, 47 percent of the contributions were positive in attitude, and only 22 percent were negative.
These people would soon settle down to a high level of operation.

Since Mr. Jones is interested in whether the members of the group
are making any progress toward modifying their group behavior, he
should keep a record of several meetings. By studying the charts,
he can determine the number of responses of an individual nature
and of a group nature made by the various participants.

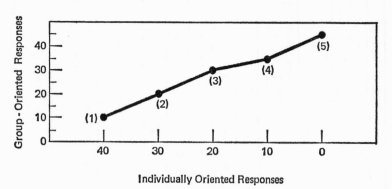

Fig. 5

Types of Responses per Trial for Five Trials

The similarity of the curve in Figure 5 to a learning curve is apparent. It is possible that after a series of attempts at group solutions to problems a group will reach a plateau of performance. Having thus learned to work together as a team, the group will exhibit few individually oriented responses and many group-oriented responses as it pursues its goals through group discussion, group decisions, group actions, and group evaluation. The behavior of members of the group can then be described as mature.

The Life Cycle of a Group — Biological Model

A useful concept for supervisors taking the group approach to problems in supervision is that of a life cycle. Groups (committees) come into being, live and work, deteriorate, and die. Recognition of these stages makes it possible to conceive of groups as if they were single human beings; in actuality, groups are social organisms. Knowing the life cycle stages, the supervisor knows how to approach the group and what to expect of it at each level of development.

Infancy

Some groups and committees begin by exhibiting the traits of an infant — random movements, babbling sounds, inability to care for their own needs, unawareness of problems or conditions, distraction by light, motion, or sound. Action is uncoordinated, aimless, and useless. Individuals have nothing in common. There is no group goal and therefore no orienting, directing force. Committees at this level of development have nothing to do and therefore accomplish nothing. The members wander about the room visiting with each other, looking at pictures, and in other ways amusing themselves.

In such a group leadership is the key. Leadership draws from the group common concerns or goals, or points them out clearly for consideration. The leader presents problems and issues as such. He stimulates interest and discussion and encourages the emergence of other leadership. He starts the processes of social integration, both individual and group, and of differentiation. Random behavior is eliminated and goal-oriented behavior takes over.

A New Group

Supervisor Davis has appointed one teacher from each of the secondary schools of the district to a new Committee on Articulation.

As members of the committee gather for their first meeting, all are uncertain about what they are supposed to do. Some are willing to do what is asked of them. Some are definitely waiting to be convinced that they should work for this cause. Some resent being asked to appear at all and have a decidedly negative feeling. Until Mr. Davis, the status leader in this instance, can get the committee to accept the obligation and to start thinking constructively about the problem, the group remains in the infant stage.

Adolescence

The adolescent stage may be characterized by a diversity of opinions, goals, and ideas for action. The individuals in the group exhibit a temporary interest in many ideas and activities, seldom settling on any one. Vigor and enthusiasm are shown, but there is difficulty in channeling them in constructive directions. A committee at this period of development has great potential for work and leadership but has not matured to the point of working together on a specific task.

Adolescence is a step on the way to "groupness," and spontaneous contributions are typical of it. Unsophisticated statements, naive questions, unsolicited comments are brought out by the individuals involved. If there is a leader (chairman, sponsor, etc.), the contributions are usually directed to him. This is one method of seeking status. Individuals are competitive in their relationships within the group, subjective in their reactions. This is the stage of growing up — the teen age.

Sometimes, as with some professional persons who have a common orientation, training, and goal, the group begins at this point rather than at infancy. There is much goodwill and a desire to accomplish something. Projects, ideas, and actions are suggested. The committee may dash headlong in some direction, making decisions and preparing for action before the discussion of alternatives has been completed. After experiencing the frustration of arriving at a blind alley, the group settles back to a more discriminating, intelligent, and potentially productive discussion.

A Short Time Later

After a period of time, Supervisor Davis has been able to outline the problem facing the Committee on Articulation to the satisfaction of the members. As various persons begin to get "carried away" by the spirit of the group, many suggestions and proposals for action are given Mr. Davis. Most are quite superficial, representing no great thought by the originators. The group is now beginning to function, although at a very low level. It is in the adolescent stage of growth.

Maturity

Emotional stability, a high degree of motivation to work at worthwhile tasks, and an attitude of patience toward others who are in the process of growing up mentally, socially, or professionally are the marks of maturity. The mature person feels secure and does not need to be a playboy, a "blocker," or a usurper of the time of the committee in order to build his ego. He values people, ideas, and processes. He is oriented toward the goal and the group. He can entertain an idea regardless of who suggested it.

The group can be considered mature when its members gather on time at the appointed location and begin immediately to set up goals, plan programs, make decisions, take action, evaluate their work, and set up new directions, with or without the aid of leaders selected beforehand and with or without a previously arranged agenda. Leadership may and does change hands, and there is no jealousy, envy, or competition for status position. The level of participation is high. The constructive group and individual roles far outnumber the negative roles played by members. The action is constantly goal oriented and moves rapidly, with relatively few diversionary, splintering, or fragmentary maneuvering.

Success!

Supervisor Davis continues to work with the Committee on Articulation. He gradually turns the remarks directed to him back to the group itself for consideration. As the members begin to realize that it is truly *their* committee and that its productivity will be limited only by its own efforts and capabilities, a new atmosphere develops. Interaction between members of the group replaces the individual dialogues with Mr. Davis. Meetings are held without Mr. Davis, and various members take responsibility for performing the tasks of the group. Not only is the committee becoming self-sufficient; it is becoming a productive unit. Each member understands the others; a general consensus has been reached of what needs doing. Sophisticated progress results. The group has reached maturity.

Senility

The mind of a senile person no longer functions well. Relationships cannot be identified, sequential occurrence of chronological events becomes confused, and there are complete lapses of memory. Some senile persons have lost their sense of direction; some, their concept of distance. They may spend a good bit of the day in sleeping. Communication is often interrupted by failure to maintain continuity of thought, by wandering into irrelevant areas of experience, or by falling asleep.

Committees and groups grow old, too. They rarely meet for working purposes, and when they do, they seldom accomplish anything. Members find themselves variously occupied. There is much yawning and shuffling about. Impatience is obvious, as is clock watching. The women fiddle with their gloves, adjust their hats, retouch their makeup. The men are deployed about the room in a way that indicates individual interests.

One of the authors once happened upon a senile committee. It was in Room 231, Jefferson School, at 4:00 P.M., on a Wednesday in spring. There were seven committeemen and a chairman. Two persons were carrying on a private conversation near the back of the room. One person was seated at the right side of the room, near the windows, writing a letter, while another, two rows back, was slumped down in the chair taking a nap. Seated in the front row were two individuals engaged in conversation with a third person. The latter sat facing the room, and it was not clear whether he was the chairman or simply wanted a good view of everyone present. The remaining person stood gazing out of the window. The group process as a working arrangement for social purposes had died out.

The committee had been appointed the year before to select a history textbook and done so well that the principal decided to make it a standing committee to consider any and all new texts in the subject. This was a mistake, for, having reached its objective (making the selection), the committee's new objective was to disband! It was continued in office needlessly. So the committee per se became old and tired. Malfunction and dysfunction set in. It is obvious that this committee should have been dismissed with praise and recognition the day its task was done.

Other groups, even faculties, may go through these stages. In one metropolitan area a new housing development went up quickly, and it was necessary to build school buildings and employ a new staff. The new staff was told to develop a new and unique program of education. Highly educated and ambitious teachers were recruited, and when they met for the first time in September, randomness was evident in their movements and conversations. Most of the teachers present had no understanding of what they were supposed to do. After the first day of orientation and much "buzzing," they were all highly charged and ready to go. But what to do? How to start? With what materials and supplies? The group was now at the adolescent stage. After a semester for some, a year for others, the faculty settled down to what they had come for, the development of a distinctive program. The members were maturing rapidly. However, after a few years, and with a very fine program in operation, progress stopped. Slowly, at first one by one and then department by department, the faculty slipped into a routine, slowed to a walk, and gradually aged. They felt that history would prove the excellence of their program, and it certainly was easier to reminisce than to be creative. Vested interests and lines of succession were established so that the protection of these interests and the opposition to change came from the same sources — the erstwhile leaders of a unique program. One cycle of infancy, adolescence, maturity, and senility had been completed.

Termination

Supervisor Davis worked with the Committee on Articulation for the entire year. He actually spent a limited amount of time with it during the second half of the year, being occupied with other pressing matters and recognizing the ability of the group to function satisfactorily without him. During the summer the committee recommendations were completed and submitted to the superintendent.

As the group was disbanded, Mr. Davis made a point of giving each member special recognition and credit for the success of the project. The superintendent also commended each member for the fine work accomplished. As the Committee on Articulation was dissolved, all participants had the satisfaction of having done a good job and having their efforts recognized by others. This group was not permitted to become senile.

Leadership in Supervision

If group techniques are to be utilized, some people will become concerned about leadership. Who is the leader in the group process? What will happen to the supervisor's control of the group? Research on this topic is beginning to accumulate. There is little reason to fear that the leadership will go astray unless, of course, there is real incompetence at one of the levels of building the group. If the supervisor is himself inept in managing people, the group may flounder.

Leadership may be defined as *the discovering, exploring, releasing, and stimulating of the talents, abilities, and skills of the staff, and their coordination and direction.* This does not say that the supervisor, the principal, or the superintendent must be the one who is constantly striding in seven-league boots from one leadership promontory to another. Modern educational systems and programs are so complex that it is entirely unreasonable to expect one person to be the leader in many fields. Leadership may fall to anyone in the group; it is *the opening of doors for others.* Parents, teachers, coaches, and guidance workers know the meaning of this statement. But sometimes people in authority or with responsibility misuse the role of leadership. Opening doors for others does not mean that the porter must precede his charge. In fact, he may never go through that door! Presenting opportunities for staff members to be of greater service is good supervision.

There are two general types of leadership: status and emerging. Status leadership is enjoyed by those who are employed to fill certain positions in the hierarchy: principals, supervisors, superintendents, managers, foremen, mayors, etc. These positions depend heavily on delegated authority. The board delegates to the superintendent, who delegates to the principals, who delegate to the teachers. Almost universally, the salaries attached to these positions are commensurate with rank or position in the hierarchy; status is reinforced with economic rewards. Basically, status leadership often has originated with the experience of a group which preferred the leadership of one individual who had the competence, the special skills, or the right answers to solve the group's problems. Yet these characteristics may or may not be evident in the board's next appointee. In any event, he is given the position, responsibility, authority, and salary. Ability is presumed.

The second type, emerging leadership, has also been termed shared leadership.[12] It is impossible for any one person to have all the answers or appopriate plans of action for whatever problems confront the group. It is quite likely, if he is a good leader, that the status leader will recognize the value of the talents, abilities, and skills of the people in the group. He will seek alternative solutions. During the discussion, an individual may emerge who sees the problem in its various dimensions more clearly than others. He perceives what must be done and makes astute, positive suggestions. He is able to implement his suggestions and propose a course of action. For the moment, this person has become the leader. For the moment, and perhaps longer, he has leadership status. His status is not delegated in the sense used above; it is, rather, earned or derived — it has emerged.

The genuine leader is not fearful of losing his status. By properly utilizing the talents, abilities, and skills possessed by members of his staff, he is in reality making his position more secure. The conductor of the orchestra does not play all the instruments himself in order to bring forth beautiful music. He does use the instrumental sections in their appropriate places, providing opportunities for leadership in various quarters. He is not worried about his position. The more effective he is at discovering, exploring, releasing, and stimulating the talents of his musicians, and in coordinating and directing these talents, the more assured is his position.

Yet some common errors are committed by supervisors. Any manipulations of persons merely for the individual gain of the leader are improper. Nor is it right to compare the shop teacher who never seems to have any discipline problems with the English teacher who always seems to have more than her share. This is the same type of mistake teachers make when they compare siblings in order to motivate one of them.

Another error is the appeal to loyalty. The leader points out that he is the leader and therefore he should be followed. "Pulling rank" is a well-known ploy. In the presence of one of the writers, a supervisor once said, "As long as I am the supervisor here, this is the way we will do it." Pulling rank irritates people and stops any frank appraisal of the problem, with the result that the best solutions may never be applied to the situation.

---

[12] Association for Supervision and Curriculum Development, *Group Processes in Supervision, op. cit.,* pp. 1–30.

One other faulty practice is the appeal to certain known prejudices within the group in an attempt to gain support for a project from indifferent segments of the group. The key here becomes the emotions of the individuals rather than the merits of the proposal itself. In any discussion group, the leader should be concerned with obtaining expressions from the members and not with delivering his own speeches or playing on their emotions.

In an analysis of a departmental curriculum meeting, it was observed that the discussion lasted for ninety minutes, of which the leader used fifty-four minutes to explain his position and the position he thought the department ought to take. Thus there were no objectives established by the group, very little time was given to group planning, no group decisions were reached, and no group action was proposed. In addition, no evaluation was made and no one knew what was to be done next. This type of staff meeting does not represent satisfactory group work.

The leader must develop the habit of and skill in asking questions: "Would someone explain . . .?" "Who has some information on this problem?" In this type of questioning, some words call for a higher type of contribution than others. For example, questions requiring a yes or no answer leave the discussion rather flat, but those that make use of words like *analyze, apply, classify, illustrate, introduce, list, outline, predict, prove, recapitulate, screen, summarize,* and *trace,* often elicit a process-building and -maintenance contribution. All these words should be directed toward the group and individuals in the group: "Who will analyze . . .?" "Mr. Brown, how can you apply this proposal . . .?" "Miss Smith, would you illustrate . . .?" Note that the group is sharing the burden.

Some of the leader's duties can be listed here, but it must be remembered that each group will be different from every other. The roles of the leader will change. However, if discussion has not begun, he might stimulate it by asking the group to establish objectives. He should see that group officials are elected, such as recorders, observers, and others as needed. He should use the recorder to establish continuity, the historian to trace certain developments, the critic to keep standards up, and in general should try to keep contributions coming in. The leader should not get into the discussion per se unless he has pertinent data, facts, or research the group lacks.

By use of discussion and preliminary voting, and by the use of majorities, the leader should establish where the points of trouble are, where the minorities are, what the points of agreement are, and which hypotheses are acceptable. He should drive, gently but persuasively, toward group decisions and action. He should watch the time (better still, have someone keep track of it) and call for summaries. He should try to play various roles as they are needed: contributor, encourager, summarizer, and others. He should spend most of his time, however, in encouraging others to play these roles.[13]

"I'll Do It Myself"

Alex Machek is a dynamic individual, self-assured, poised, and always with a ready answer. When he is assigned to a task, everyone knows it will be completed in a fashion that is acceptable and within the allotted time. These are desirable attributes, but they do sometimes lower his efficiency as a supervisor. His natural tendency toward meeting challenges with speed and dispatch causes him to become impatient with members of a group and with group process in general. He knows that he can do a better job himself and often in less time. The teachers in his district have learned what to anticipate when Alex is a member of the committee, and they usually capitulate early and let Alex have his way.

As a result of this pattern, over a period of time Alex has become physically exhausted almost to the point of having a breakdown. Only his stubborn determination keeps him going. Many matters need attention, but he simply does not have the time to deal with more. The reports and studies he has completed are still as good as ever. The teachers who are concerned with various instructional problems have learned to bypass Alex and either solve the problems themselves or, when help is necessary, go to another supervisor who will take the time to help them.

If Alex were more flexible, more understanding, and had more faith in his fellow man, he could become an outstanding supervisor. Until he learns to work with, for, and through groups, however, he will never be as effective as he should be, especially in this day when the ratio of teachers to supervisors is so great that the supervisor must use ingenuity to extend his influence. Is Alex hopeless as a supervisor?

---

[13] Robert F. Bales, *Interaction Process Analysis* (Reading, Mass.: Addison-Wesley Publishing Co., 1950), p. 9.

Summary

Group process is a complicated procedure involving as many persons as possible in the development of decisions, policies, and programs of action which are of concern to the group. Supervision committed to group process demands a higher type of educational statesmanship than that utilizing a status leader to make decisions and promulgate rules. Interaction of group members is an important aspect of the process.

Groups have certain characteristics not well understood by many supervisors. Group growth depends on individual growth. Each group and/or committee experiences the life cycle of a human organism: infancy, adolescence, maturity, and senility.

In the group process, the supervisor must learn to play various roles and induce others to play them also. He should recognize and encourage emerging leadership and individual growth of staff members.

Problems for Group Discussion

Analyze the following situations. In each, identify supervisory principles representing sound theory, if any are included. What are the basic elements which made a difference? How would you have approached the situation?

1. The supervisor of the junior high school senses a lack of commitment on the part of many teachers. He decides to attack this problem indirectly. He schedules a meeting of all teachers. First, however, he discreetly identifies the leaders and potential leaders and asks them to serve as small-group discussion leaders to identify problem areas in the junior high instructional program. The groups represent a cross section of the various cliques, subject areas, and buildings throughout the district. All teachers will eventually be asked to select topics for further study based on decisions reached in their small-group discussions.

2. The supervisor agrees that group process is important to successful instructional improvement. He has worked out a pattern which he likes very much. Each year he gets all teachers together and assigns them topics to discuss in small groups. In fact, he has a well-used set of topics that he pulls out each year. He knows they are good because the discussion level is always loud when he employs them. He also knows his group process is successful because many teachers want to talk when he calls his meetings. Yes, he believes in group process.

Selected Readings

Association for Supervision and Curriculum Development. *Group Processes in Supervision.* Washington: The Association, 1948.

Association for Supervision and Curriculum Development. *Toward Better Teaching.* Washington: The Association, 1949.

Bales, Robert F. *Interaction Process Analysis.* Reading, Mass.: Addison-Wesley Publishing Co., 1950.

Bartky, John A. *Supervision as Human Relations.* Boston: D. C. Heath & Company, 1953.

Benne, Kenneth D., and Bozidar Muntyan, eds. *Human Relations in Curriculum Change.* New York: Holt, Rinehart & Winston, 1951.

Benne, K. D., and P. Sheats. "Functional Roles of Group Members," *Journal of Social Issues,* 4:42–49 (Spring, 1948).

Bennis, Warren G., Kenneth D. Benne, and Robert Chin. *The Planning of Change: Readings in the Applied Behavioral Sciences.* New York: Holt, Rinehart & Winston, 1961.

Blumberg, Arthur, and Edmund Amidon. "Teacher Perceptions of Supervisor-Teacher Interaction," *Administrator's Notebook,* 14:1–4 (Sept., 1965).

Bradford, Leland P., ed. *Group Development.* Washington: National Education Association, 1961.

Bradford, Leland, Kenneth Benne, and Jack Gibb. *T-Group Theory and Laboratory Method: Innovation in Education.* New York: John Wiley & Sons, 1964.

Cartwright, Dorwin, and Alvin Zander, eds. *Group Dynamics: Research and Theory,* 2nd ed. New York: Harper & Row, 1960.

Craig, Robert L., and Lester R. Bittel. *Training and Development Handbook.* New York: McGraw-Hill Book Company, 1967.

Gibb, J. R., Grace N. Platts, and Lorraine F. Miller. *Dynamics of Participative Groups.* Boulder, Colo.: J. R. Gibb, 1951.

Paris, Norman M. "T-Grouping: A Helping Movement," *Phi Delta Kappan,* 49:460–463 (Apr., 1968).

Parker, Willard E., and Robert W. Kleemeier. *Human Relations in Supervision.* New York: McGraw-Hill Book Company, 1951.

Thelen, Herbert A. *Dynamics of Groups at Work.* Chicago: University of Chicago Press, 1954.

Thomas, Donald. "T-Grouping, the White Collar Hippie Movement," *Phi Delta Kappan,* 49:458–460 (Apr., 1968).

ten

•

Controlling and Directing Curriculum Change

Curriculum work at the local level is often a patchwork of assorted projects and sometimes no more than mere tinkering. Any inherent value of such work is usually diminished or lost because there is little understanding of how the individual project is supposed to fit into the total scheme of things. Often there *is* no total scheme or rationale for curriculum development.

A rationale is needed, however, for it supplies direction and consistency — a framework into which all the necessary pieces will fit so that a pattern can emerge. Curriculum work, of whatever type, then can become meaningful, and the results can make a difference in the way the school operates. A rationale considers the relationships of parts to parts, and of any part to the whole of curriculum development. It provides guidelines for producing new instructional materials or establishing a better learning environment.

Implementation of curriculum work often proceeds on illogical assumptions, erratic patterns, and faulty methodology. It need not be so, but people are often unwilling to give the funds, energy, materials, time, and personnel to do the job right.

Curriculum development is discussed in this chapter with reference to two levels of operation. The first level deals with general problems of design and strategy, and with the involvement of people. The second level concerns organization for curriculum development in action and the function of the coordinating curriculum council. Finally, someone eventually must write needed curriculum descriptions; the resource center serves as the laboratory in which this production can be accomplished.

Building a Rationale

The first task in building a rationale for curriculum development is to identify the elements needed to produce the total picture. If curriculum is regarded as a process, it should be possible to differentiate a number of subprocesses involved in it. When all of these are functioning and properly aligned so that the tasks being carried on are correctly articulated, curriculum development should become more efficient and effective. Elements needed to construct a reasonable rationale include:

Analysis of society
Decisions relating to the function of schools
Philosophy of education
Analysis of learner and learning
Sources of knowledge
Educational objectives
Criteria for content selection

Each individual element should be examined in terms of its relationship to the others.

Analysis of Society

A clear description of society, with its problems and needs, is essential in curriculum development. It provides guidelines for establishing the main objectives of education by illuminating current undesirable conditions such as the ugly ghettos, crime in the streets, excessive accident tolls, malfunctioning institutions (the electoral college), the pollution problem (air, water), and the school dropout problem. Analyses of society may be made by the school staff and members themselves. For instance, a department of distributive education might analyze the community to help provide the basis for the school program. Pupil personnel services might conduct a neighborhood study seeking data to support the initiation of a new program. Often analyses made by other agencies can be utilized by school authorities to start curriculum improvement.

Decisions Relating to the Function of Schools

There are at least three ways of looking at the school's function. One approach maintains that schools should train the intellect by means of the various disciplines. Some disciplines are thought to be better adapted to the task because they are "tough" and have more logical internal structure. For many years Latin was considered the most prestigious discipline. Recently, this honor has been transferred to the sciences and mathematics.

A second position, characterized as utilitarian, holds that education should lead to something worthwhile and useful. It should provide a social and economic ladder to a better life. An argument to convince students to stay in school is that their earning power rises in direct proportion to the amount of education they have. Courses developed to serve this function include industrial arts, home economics, vocational and technical curricula.

The third line of thought regards general education as the right of every American youth, while recognizing at the same time that there must be provision for individual differences. Not all students will choose to pursue an academic career, and it is therefore illogical to force all students into the curriculum designed solely for the college bound. The non-college-bound youth needs a curriculum which meets his special needs; it will be different from that provided the academically oriented student. An illustration of the third approach, continuing general education and education for diversity, is the comprehensive high school, which offers a curriculum for the academically inclined and college bound, for the vocational-technical student, and for the student who simply wants and needs a good terminal secondary education.

Developing a Philosophy of Education

The supervisor should develop a philosophy of his own and assist teachers in developing theirs. In curriculum work a philosophy of education serves several purposes. It provides an orientation for the curriculum and for the school system; it establishes direction for the setting up of educational objectives; it is a source of criteria for content selection and offers guidelines for curriculum organization and evaluation. Faculties which start the curriculum process at some later point, such as unit construction, often find it necessary to postpone activity until they have developed a philosophy. Other elements in the rationale are dependent on the completion of this task.

Analysis of the Learner and of Learning

An analysis of the learner complements an analysis of society. Curriculum workers need to know as much as possible about students — their social and cultural backgrounds, their problems, frustrations, and motivations.[1] Studies of ghetto and inner-city children, delinquents, and dropouts have amply proved the importance of such understanding. For some students, the traditional curriculum has little if any relevance. For some it is too advanced; for others, too elementary. Such factors must be taken into account if learning is to be most effective.

Recent studies have added to our information about learning. Learning in school is affected by the student's social and cultural background. Learning is an active, individualized process.

Readiness becomes an important concept. If students lack the background of experiences needed to undertake the new task, they will not accomplish the task.[2] It is now recognized that readiness can be stimulated and achieved sooner in some cases than was once thought possible. Modern culture has influenced many children to want to read and write at a much earlier age.

More is known today than formerly about concept development, about the cognitive process, and about creativity. Creativity and high intelligence, as measured by IQ tests, are no longer thought to be synonymous. Additional attention is being paid to learning theory as a vehicle to accomplish instruction.[3] More emphasis is being placed on newer methods of teaching and learning which use discovery, inquiry, inductive thinking, and adventuring. In an inquiry-oriented school this approach is accompanied by a reduction of telling or exhortation by the teacher and of the traditional reward and punishment system.

Sources of Knowledge

There are at least two ways to analyze the sources of knowledge. One is to reassess the disciplines to determine whether some important content has been omitted or whether there is newer and perhaps more relevant content available. Scholars can be helpful in this exploration. Another is to examine the basic groupings of knowledge. The latter approach was demonstrated recently by a group of thirty supervisors in a university-sponsored workshop and is described here in some detail.

---

[1] Association for Supervision and Curriculum Development, *Youth Education: Problems/Perspectives/Promises* (Washington: The Association, 1968).
[2] Association for Supervision and Curriculum Development, *Learning and the Teacher* (Washington: The Association, 1959), p. 66.
[3] John E. Searles, *A System for Instruction* (Scranton, Pa.: International Textbook Company, 1967).

A Class Project

After considerable discussion, the supervisors decided there were three basic sources of knowledge. The first they termed the non-human universe (nature), in which the physical and biological sciences are the sources of knowledge. The studies of physics, chemistry, earth science, and part of biology as now taught in the schools have their roots in these sciences. With the addition of man, more disciplines come into view: anthropology, sociology, psychology, political science, history, and economics. A third source of knowledge was called the "contrived universe" by the group, meaning those areas of study and knowledge which man has constructed: the fine arts, language, religion, philosophy, mathematics, the practical arts, and the knowledge of the professions.

Such speculation led to a second major matter of concern. Perhaps at the elementary and secondary levels curriculum workers should strive for as much integration of knowledge as possible. A better balance of the three areas seemed desirable to the group.

The supervisors examined the current literature. Bruner reported that the various disciplines could be taught advantageously according to their structures.[4] In this type of teaching the learner is presented with concepts, principles, information, and data, and perhaps some hint of their applicability. Benefits attributed to this plan are that bits of information are not learned in isolation, and the study of any discipline can be begun at a very early age. The structural approach provides an organization for the development of scope and sequence.

The supervisors' workshop participants accepted the concept of structure but looked for a way of using the classifications of knowledge. After further discussion, they decided that the most important concept was process. Such words as *growing, aging, transforming, changing,* are indicative of processes around which knowledge could be organized. The group decided to use processes as the focus for a curriculum. The following is a partial list of the processes identified:

a. Processes involving the nonhuman environment
   (1) Creation, mutation, reproduction
   (2) Aging, decaying, decomposing, degenerating

---

[4] Jerome S. Bruner, *The Process of Education* (Cambridge, Mass.: Harvard University Press, 1960). See also Stanley Elam, ed., *Education and the Structure of Knowledge,* Fifth Annual Symposium of Educational Research (Chicago: Rand McNally & Co., 1954).

(3) Evolution
(4) Growth, physical and chemical change
(5) Conservation

b. Processes involving society — the human environment
   (1) Social, political, and economic competition, accommodation, cooperation, interaction
   (2) Creation: new social and political groups, institutions, states
   (3) Social change
   (4) Revolution
   (5) Differentiation: developing separate and distinctive functions or roles for individuals and groups; specialization and the development of professions
   (6) Communications
   (7) Controlling, administering, governing, decision making
   (8) Distributing, disseminating, consuming
   (9) Degeneration and deterioration of groups, communities, institutions; social, political, and cultural disintegration
   (10) Integration: developing a group, assimilation, acculturation

c. Processes relating to the individual
   (1) Psychological: growth, development, maturation, motivation, perception, personality development, integration and differentiation; the processes of learning, thinking, and deciding
   (2) Biological: life processes, physiological processes, heredity
   (3) Social processes: development of personality, the genesis and operation of groups, alienation, assimilation, socially acquired drives

The workshop participants felt that a curriculum based on the concept of process would have certain advantages, such as accelerated learning, a functional, meaningful content, improved methods of teaching, and a greater possibility of understanding the unity of knowledge.

Development of Objectives of Education

There are two types of educational objectives. General objectives relate all the foregoing — analyses of society, functions of schools, philosophy, the learner, knowledge — to the work of the school.[5] They provide general guidelines for the educational program. Derived from the general objectives are the specific ones, first for

---

[5] Benjamin S. Bloom, ed., *Taxonomy of Educational Objectives, Handbook I, The Cognitive Domain* (New York: David McKay Co., 1956).

courses and finally for learning activities. Examples of the two kinds of objectives may be taken from the social studies. A general objective states that the student is to learn the meaning of citizenship. A specific objective speaks of student behavior as demonstrated in these statements: "The student can plan for and direct group discussion"[6] or "The student can demonstrate the use of appropriate research tools whether he is undertaking a library research study or an independent field study." In the latter case, he would need to know how to make surveys, take polls, and use statistics at least in an elementary way.[7]

Criteria for Content Selection

According to Benjamin Franklin, it would be good if everything useful and everything ornamental could be taught, but, since that is impossible, only those things which are most useful and most ornamental must be selected. Criteria for content selection should bring together all the work that has gone before to provide a process by which the final selection of learning activities and methods is made. The criteria for content might well draw upon the analyses of society, functions of schools, philosophy, the learner, knowledge, and objectives described in this chapter.

Figure 6 illustrates one possible application of a rationale for content selection. Stressed in this model are philosophy of community, educational philosophy, objectives, and the learner and learning process, chosen as important among the several elements contributing to a curriculum rationale.

The supervisor who is concerned with organizing his efforts and planning discrete steps in the curriculum development process will find it profitable to build for himself some such rationale as described here. As he gives particular attention to the various components, he can also begin to shape his role as the instructional supervisor. Chosen elements can then serve as guidelines for curriculum activity, be it at the building or district level. Failure to consider carefully some of the components has caused unhappy situations to arise in more than one district.

---

[6] Robert F. Mager, *Preparing Instructional Objectives* (Palo Alto, Calif.: Fearon Publishers, 1962).

[7] Association for Supervision and Curriculum Development, *A Look at Continuity in the School Program* (Washington: The Association, 1958), pp. 128–135.

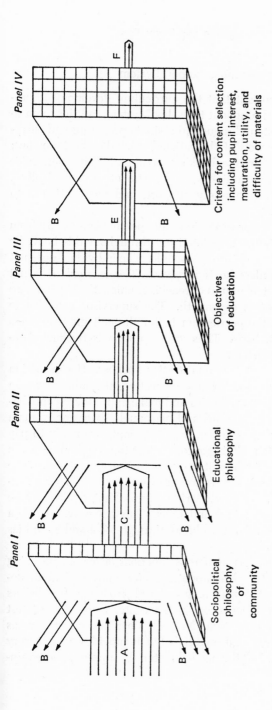

Fig. 6

Demonstration of a Rationale in Use

Selection process for content: In each succeeding panel the process becomes more critical. Less and less useless or inappropriate material is allowed to pass. *A* represents all the possible concepts, principles, ideas, data, etc., available. *B* represents the portion that was not permitted to pass through the panels. *C, D, E,* and *F,* represent increasingly appropriate curriculum materials.

Developing a Support System

It is extremely important that the curriculum development program receive support throughout the school system and the community. A supporting system designed to assist in preparing and carrying out the various aspects of the rationale includes the following: group process, administrative backing, resources center, inservice program, business office, audio-visual department, personnel office, guidance department, community support, and cooperation with the nearest university.

No curriculum worker or supervisor can operate alone, away from the total school situation. As pointed out throughout this book, he must work with people and through people. The individual does not grow professionally unless he is involved. The curriculum is not improved, nor are the techniques of teaching, unless the teachers are committed to the process of growth. The supervisor can change both individuals and the curriculum better through group process than on an individual basis. Thus *group process* is the first component in the support system.

The second component is *administrative backing*. If supervision and instruction are to become more effective, the administration must be aware of its responsibilities and make appropriate contributions in the form of money, time, and personnel. Everyone wants a quality education for his children, but few people are ready to pay the full costs. Too often administrators reflect the community or the "efficiency" bias and thus inhibit progress in instruction and in the curriculum. Much recent innovation has been carried on with supportive components heavily underwritten by the United States Office of Education and by certain foundations. This has proved to be a most effective way for schools to break through local and state bias which resists change.

The *resources center* has numerous functions, a major one being the generation of better ideas about teaching and curriculum development. A constant flow of new materials from both publishers and other schools will keep users of the center alert to the latest ideas and practices in education. Not only does the center serve as a repository for instructional materials but it provides a laboratory in which work groups find the needed materials, supplies, and equipment at hand.

The *inservice program* needs to include offerings designed to ensure that curriculum development is improved instruction in the schools. Offerings can range in depth from topics which might be treated in two or three sessions, including laboratory experiences, to those which might well consume twelve to fifteen meetings or one full semester. The inservice work lends itself to independent studies, small-group study, and large-group instruction.

The *business office* of the school district presumably exists for the purpose of making possible and facilitating teaching and learning. It must observe the specifications for materials and supplies prescribed by the curriculum department. If it alters them, as was done in one school, the teaching-learning process will suffer. In this instance the supervisor, in collaboration with the instructors, selected a particular book. The business office ordered a cheaper edition. When the copies arived, the instructors found to their consternation that the introduction, editorial comments, and glossary were completely missing! The edition could not serve the original purpose. Time, money, and human energy were wasted because someone in the business office made a curricular decision.

The *audio-visual department* is very much involved in support for curriculum development. How can teachers hope to utilize a multimedia approach unless the audio-visual department is attuned to what is going on? This department can order and supply the films, slides, tapes, models, dioramas, video tapes, and other media; it also can create new ones expressly for particular purposes. It can help design classroom learning situations making use of decor, displays, and exhibits. It is imperative that this department be brought into curriculum planning because of the contributions it can make to increased learning.

The *personnel office* works the year round. The officers go to professional meetings and conventions; they are constantly looking for people with outstanding talent in the various phases of curriculum development, such as specialized staff or consultants, as well as locating prospective teachers. If the administration makes budgetary provisions for specialized assistance, and if the supervisor avails himself of it, a vigorous thrust can be provided by the personnel department.

The *department of guidance* can conduct continuing studies of students' needs, capacities, interests, and achievements. The information gathered can be fed back into the curriculum process to supply additional direction in the refinement of objectives and the selection of content. The department can also assist in the inservice program by providing the leadership and materials for workshops in such areas as improving teaching styles and preparing teachers for individual and group educational counseling of their students. Schools which use the results of studies of the guidance department in curriculum planning and administration are often among the first to make appropriate changes.

The ninth component in this system is *community support.* If the administration and everyone on the faculty have done their professional duty, the community will have been completely informed, its opinions and attitudes studied, and a special program of continuous public relations in depth initiated. It is necessary that the supervisor and the public relations office work closely together because the supervisor's knowledge of the curriculum becomes the raw data for use by the public relations staff.

As a final suggestion, the supervisor might develop some ties with the nearest up-to-date teacher education institution. Much good can come from interaction between such an institution and a progressive school system. Each stimulates the other. A large variety of specialists should be available from the teacher education institution, as well as help from its service bureaus.

The supervisor must constantly strive for means of providing better coordination between these diverse elements of the support system. His statesmanship and educational leadership can do much to involve others in important phases of the implementation process.

Energizing the System

Supervisor Hochmeyer has been working diligently with most of the teachers in the Lincoln School for the past several years. As summer arrives, Mr. Hochmeyer looks back on their activities and tries to recall just how they decided to establish a new approach to the instructional program which is scheduled to start next fall. He is well aware that the new program was not his idea. In fact, he had no intention of getting into anything so detailed and elaborate when he first asked to meet with the teachers.

As nearly as he can remember, he merely wanted to "talk through" with the faculty some of their concerns and problems with the existing curriculum in the belief that he might be of some assistance.

Before Mr. Hochmeyer knew it, however, two or three young teachers began raising serious and basic questions which led to further increasingly excited discussion by more and more teachers as time went on.

Being a prudent individual, Supervisor Hochmeyer gave the reins to the interested teachers and played the role of consultant, coordinator, and especially "provider of needed information." The initial onslaught of enthusiastic discussion gradually settled into a steady pattern of work. Weak spots in the curriculum were identified, and eventually it was determined that the only solution was to revise, drastically, the whole approach to the curriculum.

Mr. Hochmeyer paved the way with the administration to ensure its support. At his suggestion the resources center and the audio-visual department collaborated on some well-prepared materials and visual aids. He also found some university and state department people who encouraged his teachers to clarify their thinking and suggested alternatives to consider as remedies for the existing situation.

Now an exciting professional experience awaits Supervisor Hochmeyer, who is ready to move into a new phase, that of implementation. So far as he can tell, everything has been done in the planning stage that could be done. What develops next year will show whether the preplanning was adequate and the basic premises were sound.

The Implementation Process

The supervisor must concentrate upon the implementation of curriculum whenever and wherever applicable and to the extent that it is feasible to do so. He must have a clear understanding of curriculum design patterns. He must understand people and how to bring out the best in others. He must understand the learning process and what approach is acceptable with students of various ages and at various stages of development. He should be a competent writer of satisfactory curriculum publications.

The Dynamics of Implementation: Level One

There are two kinds of implementation. The first is the continuous search for minor improvements in the present curriculum. The curriculum changes very slowly but steadily. Its original structure tends to endure. An analogy here is that a minor engine tune-up, and perhaps a new set of spark plugs, will make the educational machine run more efficiently.

In contrast to this gradual approach is revolutionizing everything at once. The revolutionary change agent wants no engine tune-up; he advocates moving to a completely different machine, perhaps a jet-powered one rather than the six-cylinder job he has now. He will accept nothing less than a major revision. The history of such traumatic changes indicates, however, that, while they command much initial attention, they often shortly disappear.

Fortunately, most supervisors are not forced to commit themselves solely to either of these positions. The pragmatic view demands that the daily quest for improvement of instruction must constantly be taking place. At the same time, the increasing amount of educational research suggests many new and often revolutionary practices for the supervisor to consider as he searches for the best "mix" of old and new. The behavioral sciences allow him to choose from alternatives never before available.

Curriculum specialists generally agree that changing the curriculum requires the changing of people. While to some extent this has become a cliché, the premise it is based on was never more true than it is today. And here lie the supervisor's opportunity and obligation. As he works with the groups involved in curriculum implementation, he himself must provide positive leadership. At the same time, he must identify leaders among the faculty, both actual and potential, and encourage them to become productive agents of change.

In addition, the supervisor should recognize that he has to concern himself with another category of the implementation process: materials. The finest curriculum theory imaginable will be of little consequence unless it can be translated into something productive in the classroom. Invariably, this must revolve around the materials of instruction — the production of newer types, the revised use of standard items, the replacement or supplementation of those currently in use.

Assimilating New Instructional Materials

One instructional supervisor recently set out to implement a revised mathematics curriculum for his district. He knew that the proposed change had not come from all the mathematics teachers and suspected that many would resist.

His approach was to work with the teachers, providing various types of aid to make the transition easier. Key teachers who were competent in the new programs were asked to conduct demonstration sessions which could be observed and appraised by the rest. Teachers were relieved from their own classes for a day to watch certain other teachers at work under the new conditions. Materials workshops were held in which teachers were assisted in making instructional aids useful for conveying mathematical concepts. The supervisor was also developing an evaluation process to compare instructional strengths of the old and new curricula.

The teachers were becoming interested as they found themselves involved in the various activities and became comfortable with the new program. They waited for the evaluation results with anticipation, coupled with some good-natured banter as to what the results would actually be.

Who Is Involved?

Diverse groups and individuals, both lay and professional, should and often do become actively engaged in the implementation of curriculum. The supervisor should be aware of them and the impact which they might be able to make. More and more, as the supervisor plays the role of the politician to effect enduring implementation, he must be capable of functioning successfully with these people. Community analysis provides information about leaders and community power groups.

Unquestionably, an improvement in the instructional program directly involves the teacher. Opinions differ as to whether the most effective implementation comes about through doing things *to* the teacher or *with* the teacher. The former, by implication, considers the teacher unnecessary in the decision-making portion of the process. The latter assumes that the end result will be strengthened by the early and continued inclusion of the teacher. The contention of the authors is that the teacher must, from the outset, understand what is being considered and feel free to raise questions, suggest alternatives, and experiment with possible solutions as the study and eventual implementation proceed. Only through such involvement can teachers be expected to support the outcome strongly.

The supervisor must be aware of the important part the administrator plays in curriculum development. A multitude of line decisions may accelerate or retard progress or wreak havoc upon the entire project. Since the administration usually controls the resources, the budget, and the time of the personnel, the needs in these areas must be carefully and accurately portrayed. It is vital, therefore, that administrators both understand and approve of the implementation process.

Boards of education, as elected representatives of the public, have to be considered a basic part of the implementation team. As they wrestle with policy matters and pursue the never-ending quest for funds, they give general direction to and support for various curriculum undertakings. Most parts of the curriculum are eventually translated into figures on the budget sheet which receives board approval. Hence, it becomes very necessary for the board members to know what is proposed and to be sufficiently committed to finance the implementation. The wise supervisor will not leave this to chance; he will do all in his power to ensure proper understanding by the board.

In many ways implementation will depend on the support of parents and students. The best supervisory practice will include parent and student groups in the deliberations. The results will be less effective and of shorter duration if these groups are not in agreement with the intent of the implementation. Actually, if they are in opposition, change is not likely to occur in the first place, as some unsuspecting supervisors have learned to their chagrin.

Today, outside agencies are playing a larger role in curriculum development than heretofore. State and federal activity has been inceasing through manipulation of purse strings or the placing of controls upon acceptable practices at the individual district level. In this respect, state and federal agencies vie with the local district for the power to influence the curriculum. The publishers of textbooks have long had a direct impact on the curriculum and the efforts of the supervisor. Lately they have been joined by other industrial leviathans which are providing both "hardware" and "software" for use in classrooms. Sometimes these products ease the supervisor's task. Sometimes they obstruct or retard the specific curriculum being attempted. It is doubtful that "canned" (commercially prepared) programs are effective at the local level; usually these are packages to be used without teacher modification in classrooms.

A recent entry into curriculum activity is the academic scholar, who is now recognizing that what is included in or omitted from the curriculum is of tremendous consequence. Since he is primarily interested in his own scholarly discipline, rather than the gamut of available offerings, he tends to operate from an ego-involvement which fails to put all parts of the curriculum into proper perspective. He would add to the school program more of his discipline at the expense of almost any other because he recognizes his own familiar field as the most important. The activity of scholars, both as national critics and as developers of national curriculum packages, has had a profound influence upon secondary education and upon the work of the secondary supervisor.

The supervisor should be familiar with potential allies and should plan to use them to strengthen his own endeavors. The preceding discussion has related primarily to activity at the individual building and the district levels, where most curiculum implementation of concern to supervisors takes place. Curricular discussions occur in other areas, however. The supervisor not only needs an understanding of the potential of these levels but should set up the best communication lines with each that it is possible to initiate and maintain.

Increasing attention is being given to the establishment of a regional unit, larger than the county, which can operate at a level somewhere between district and state. By providing a broader base for both revenue and research purposes it could strengthen curriculum projects and be of assistance to the supervisor in many ways. Such a unit should be staffed by well-trained professionals ready to add their expertise to that of the supervisor. Regional centers usually can provide electronic equipment to help the supervisor in his research.

The present momentum of many state departments of education would indicate a more active role for them in the future. Although the state is often regarded as having a mainly regulatory function, the successful supervisor will recognize for his purpose an even more important part for it to play. He, too, is seeking more than minimum standards. He can turn to the specialized knowledge available within the state department of education as one more element to reinforce his proposed program revisions.

With the advent of massive computers and other electronic marvels and with renewed interest in educational research, it seems likely that another significant move will be toward cooperative arrangements among neighboring states. Already state departments of education, often operating like ad hoc committees, are coming together to solve common problems. The massing of their capabilities for confronting the complex issues of education will certainly have a tremendous impact upon the instructional program. The supervisor should recognize this potential and seek to utilize the assistance represented by such organizations.

Renewed and strengthened relationships with the universities must become a part of the supervisor's strategy. The competent instructional supervisor knows his own limitations, while at the same time he is very much aware of the specialized support available from experts at the university.

A combination of these available strengths from diverse sources will be most appropriate for his purposes. For example, he might choose to use several educational experts in the pre-school orientation meetings, other outside experts to assist in upgrading some faculty group which is in difficulty, and still others for research and evaluation aid to accomplish what his own staff and faculty cannot.

Involving Teachers

Some boards of education from time to time hear groups of teachers discussing curriculum development. Sometimes the comments indicate that the teachers themselves are perfectly capable of doing their own curriculum work without interference from supervisors and others. Sometimes the comments indicate a strong teacher disapproval of curriculum development activities. In the case of the former, the teachers recognize the importance of curriculum but are not effectively communicating with the supervisory staff. In the case of the latter, not only are the two groups not communicating, but the teachers are revealing their naiveté about the importance of curriculum.

Most districts, fortunately, are not concerned with such problems if their supervisory staffs have been able to maintain a good working relationship with the teachers. Today, with the increasing unrest throughout the profession, this working relationship is doubly important. Those districts lacking this advantage are now finding themselves in deep trouble as they attempt to identify and clarify acceptable relationships with adamant teacher groups.

Many supervisors have worked closely with teachers for a long time. One district familiar to the authors has regularly included teachers in all aspects of curriculum development. The stated educational philosophy of the district makes specific reference to teacher involvement. Supervisors, as a matter of course, not only bring teachers in at the initial planning stage of a proposed innovation but actively seek teacher suggestions for worthwhile projects to consider. Through the years, these professionals have, working together, become quite sophisticated in their procedures, especially in the way their curriculum projects employ specific objectives. A careful evaluation process is linked to the objectives in such a manner that it becomes possible for the experimenters to determine the degree of success being realized.

Attacking the Problem of Design

The instructional supervisor, general or specialized, is uniquely equipped, both by training and by professional qualifications, to be aware of the total educational program throughout the district. His focus must not be narrowed by nor limited to the work in one building, as is the case with most teachers. Being sufficiently removed from the exigencies of the classroom to be objective in his analysis of the whole instructional program, he is in a favorable position to see the problem of obtaining and maintaining satisfactory curriculum design. He should recognize that, regardless of the curricular emphasis at any particular time, careful attention must be given to the overall scope and sequence. Provision must be made to include those necessary experiences which will provide optimum learning for students in an organized sequence so that new skills and broader knowledge logically build upon previously acquired skills and knowledge.

A Good Working Relationship

An instructional supervisor known to one of the authors has for several years been perfecting a strategy of curriculum implementation. He has established a good rapport and a favorable working relationship with both teachers and administrators throughout his district. There is general consensus that he knows what he is doing and that he is always interested in involving all interested individuals in his projects. Thus, the suspicion and mistrust which surround some supervisors' efforts are minimal.

This supervisor attempts to provide the staff with all available facts related to a project. While he does assist the staff members in reaching a conclusion, he does not predetermine or prejudge that conclusion. Teachers have learned that they can be candid in their deliberations with him. A "solid front" has developed more often than not. Since all individuals working on a particular implementation project understand what is involved, it becomes possible to direct the attention and energies of the participants toward the pertinent questions.

This supervisor has a sufficient grasp of curriculum design so that he can, on the one hand, suggest alternatives for the consideration of teachers and, on the other, provide some leadership in effecting a balance in the total program. He can, therefore, encourage improvements in the curriculum and at the same time be a stabilizing influence toward retaining the best of the existing program.

Pressure is constantly being put on the curriculum worker to include new courses with exotic titles. The supervisor, therefore, must constantly resist the temptation to add "just one more important course" until and unless it can be demonstrated that the resultant learnings cannot be obtained in any other manner. Perhaps a three- or four-week unit in an established course would be sufficient to cover an important topic instead.

Just as he resists novelty for the sake of novelty, the supervisor must resist an overly formal curriculum. Traditionally, the design of the curriculum has followed a subject organization with discrete pieces identified, labeled, and boxed in measurable portions.[8] This method of curriculum development has been criticized lately for overcompartmentalization and a resulting inhibition of originality and creativity.

In recent curriculum implementation the instructional supervisor has received much assistance from outside agencies and experts. Increasingly boards of education are accepting responsibility for the continuing education of teachers and are appropriating funds for this purpose. Also innovative programs supported by federal and state funds have permitted the use of consultants and specialists.

In some states the supervisor has the benefit of guidelines prepared by professionals and emanating from the state department of education. Often representative supervisors and administrators, together with specially selected authorities and educators and teachers from throughout the state, make up the committee which prepares the guidelines. One example of this procedure comes from the California State Department of Education and its Social Studies Framework. Broad spiraling themes were identified and locked into

---

[8] Rudyard K. Bent and Adolph Unruh, *Secondary School Curriculum* (Boston: D. C. Heath & Company, 1969), p. 79.

the curriculum at various grade levels, kindergarten through Grade 12. Thus a somewhat uniform, sequential curriculum was constructed for the entire state, giving local districts direction in the field of social studies. Each district was left to prepare the specific content and experiences necessary to interpret at the local level the themes decided on at the state level. Under such an arrangement, the supervisor need not spend his energies selecting the themes to be employed but can concentrate on preparing the instructional experiences and the content to develop them. The design is partially laid out, and his task is to complete it.

Designs in the mathematics and science fields have recently received much attention. In these areas scholars have prepared a total curriculum for a given subject, in some instances with all of the content and necessary teaching experiences restructured and included. The classroom instructor then has only to find out what is in the program and how he is to carry out the teaching process. It is almost as if he were expected to memorize the steps, procedures, etc., and automatically apply them without much selectivity.

With the advent of curriculum projects funded and operated on a massive scale, almost overnight a great change took place in the subjects involved. Never before in the history of American public education had such an impact been felt so deeply. Curriculum directors had not experienced the type of support that accompanied these efforts or been presented with such a common agreement upon content. Institutes throughout the country reimbursed teachers for attendance during the summer to learn the new curriculum, with the expectation that they would return to the home school as devoted missionaries. Many teachers and supervisors took advantage of this inservice education; at home they then helped implement newly evolved curricula.

For various reasons, even massive curriculum development has failed to produce all the changes of an enduring nature which the scholars originally hoped for. Sometimes local funds were insufficient to continue the new programs. Often inservice efforts were unable to reinforce the institute experience and teachers fell back into the old pattern. At this writing, there is substantial concern over the lack of lasting effects generated by these total curriculum programs.

Now the focus is on local production of curriculum packages for use in a given course. Here the intent is to provide short specific activities that are complete within themselves. The packages sometimes enable teachers to individualize instruction as they cannot when relying on a textbook as the primary teaching tool. Groups of teachers, working with a team leader or the supervisor, can quickly become proficient in writing such curriculum packages. The supervisor should make certain that the objectives for the packages complement and supplement the overall design of the curriculum of the district.

Unavoidable Delays

Supervisor French was having more than his share of problems this year. Last spring, the decision had been reached to examine and update the secondary social studies curriculum. The work was to have been accomplished during the current academic year.

The curriculum council had designated the necessary teacher committees under one central committee chaired by Mr. French. Two committees had quickly decided that their problem was outdated texts and had begun to search for better ones. Mr. French had had a difficult time getting the concept through to these teachers that the design must be clearly established before they examined texts.

Then two different groups of local citizens became interested in the committee activities and volunteered some advice as to what the community felt should be included in the courses. Mr. French took the position that, while the emphasis suggested by the citizens satisfied their own interests, it would be inappropriate for a course designed for all students. At times, the resulting discussions became quite emotional.

Eventually, Mr. French's position was upheld by the board of education and the committees were permitted to continue their original deliberations. But the school year was almost gone and the original timetable had long since been abandoned. Mr. French would need at least another full year to complete his task. Should he have been expected to keep on schedule?

Developing a Strategy

The curriculum is constantly in flux. From time to time it alters its direction. As the resistance to change lessens or grows, the rate of movement is modified accordingly. Only rarely will it remain stationary for long.

There are currently pressures from many sides. Were the supervisor to accede to all of them, chaos would probably engulf the instructional program. Instead, he must carefully examine the demands and suggestions and support those which seem likely to further the objectives of the curriculum as accepted by the district. The original design can then become a reality, and the total curriculum can be strengthened rather than aborted through misdirection.

Not only is the supervisor an active advocate of sound curriculum development; he more than anyone must clearly understand that process and its strengths and weaknesses. He should be familiar with the latest research and experiments throughout the country which might modify, support, and reinforce it. Furthermore, he should be able to evaluate innovations, both implemented and proposed, in light of the total curriculum development program in order to determine whether they are likely to be constructive or destructive to an optimum progam. Most people agree that change merely for the sake of change is not justified; few feel qualified to decide which change should be supported. The supervisor must take a leadership role in reaching such decisions.

To the extent that the supervisor can influence the direction and the rate, he can play a primary role in curriculum development. He will find a more enduring pattern emerging if he can operate through staff-type persuasion rather than line-type coercion. When individuals are convinced that a move is correct, they become more committed to the venture. Consciously or unconsciously they tend to work a little harder to make it succeed. And herein lies a strong ally of the supervisor as he encourages curriculum implementation.

The Dynamics of Implementation: Level Two

As the educational ferment intensifies and staff members find it easier to ask themselves the thorny questions which must be asked — and answered — the supervisor can plan to move into the second phase of implementation. Now a central curricular policy-making body should be utilized. Whether it be labeled a steering committee or a policy committee, an advisory committee or a curriculum council is not as important as the fact that it exists and functions, for it is through this body that the supervisor can best work.

Rare is the individual blessed with knowing exactly what is needed at any given point in a curriculum deliberation. Better decisions result from group deliberations, as a rule. The curriculum council can serve as the arena in which to examine issues, study suggestions and theories, and eventually recommend action. Ideas, wherever they originate, can proceed along a clearly established line to the curriculum council so that anyone, lay or professional, interested in the curriculum of the district may make his suggestion knowing that it will receive consideration.

An active curriculum council (see Figure 7) eliminates the necessity of the supervisor's always making the decisions by himself. It provides him ready access to the thinking of a representative group of the professional staff. Such an amalgam of thinking should produce a stronger, better designed attack on the problems of the curriculum. If a curriculum council is not available in his district, the supervisor would do well to establish one at the earliest date possible, making sure that the membership represents all portions of the instructional and administrative staff.

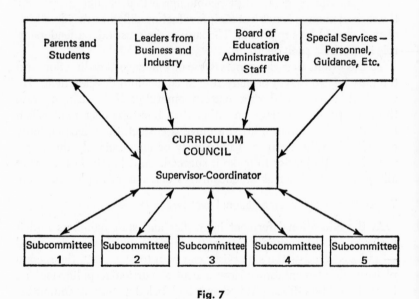

Fig. 7

*Organization for Developing Community Support
and Feedback in the Curriculum Process*

It is crucial that the supervisor be able to involve not only a large proportion of the professional staff but individuals outside the professional staff in the deliberations and subsequent action. The lay members should include students, parents, and others interested in good education who are able and willing to provide expertise. The supervisor will immediately learn that he now has another task: coordination of the efforts of the various committees which eventually emerge, thus helping keep all groups on course. Often lay committee members in particular become very enthusiastic and want to redo the entire educational program at once; they may provide more confusion than actual assistance.

The supervisor who can get all groups to work together can bring considerable benefit to his district. Sometimes a teacher feels he cannot discuss professional problems with someone outside education. He is certain the lay person would not understand, and he is loath to admit concern and uncertainty lest they be misconstrued as weakness. The lay person sometimes hesitates to enter the discussion because he is impressed by the learning the teacher has and his own obvious or imagined lack. He may feel it presumptuous to make a suggestion to the "expert." The successful supervisor is able to get both groups to realize that only by working cooperatively can they create the best curriculum for the students.

It is at this point that the skills of group process pay off. The supervisor must be able to operate smoothly in groups, eliciting the best contribution possible from all members. He must be able to function unobtrusively as the facilitator or the summarizer and in the other roles a leader in the group process is expected to play. Above all, he must be able to make each individual feel that not only his contribution but he, himself, is important. Anything less will produce inferior results in the complicated work of curriculum development. He will also need to train others in the use of group process.

The supervisor has the most directed contact with the individuals and groups interested in and involved with the instructional program of his district. He must be cognizant of the power groups both within and without the professional staff. Successful supervisors are able to identify accurately the key individuals and to decide either how to gain their support for a new venture or how to bypass them to achieve the desired goal. Long is the list, however, of those who misjudged a situation or who tried to ignore the power structure and experienced bitter failure.

The pilot program is the device most supervisors employ for curriculum change — an experimental program involving a small number of people. The supervisor should work very closely with the pilot group throughout the various stages of the experiment. He can help develop the original design, making certain that sufficient planning precedes implementation. He should see that evaluative devices are included from the start. At the earliest possible point those who eventually will be implementing the proposal should have the opportunity to contribute to development of the final plan. It is not good to spring a pilot program on either faculty or parents. Everyone concerned should be aware of the planning.

Another important part of the change strategy is disseminating information about an innovation to those not directly involved. The supervisor should make specific provisions for this communication to occur. If it does not, misinformation, rumor, or speculation could result in a negative attitude which might hinder or completely stop an otherwise successful innovation.

Routine of a Curriculum Council

One curriculum council in a large district was composed of representatives of administration, teachers, curriculum supervisors, and other supporting staff groups. The council met regularly and conducted business in an orderly fashion, receiving suggestions on curriculum from all sources — the general public, the board of education, classroom teachers, administrators, and supervisors. A written response concerning the disposition of each suggestion was sent to the originator. Action of a major nature was approved by the council prior to its implementation in the schools.

This method of operation ensured a cooperative and coordinated curriculum action throughout the district and made it possible for all recommendations to be heard. A communication channel was thus established which was known by and available to everyone. What might be done to speed up the process?

Writing Curriculum

As the supervisor attempts to implement curriculum, he finds himself deeply involved with the production of curriculum materials: memoranda, in-house curriculum newsletters, bulletins, courses of study, curriculum packages, resource units, innovative designs, and the like. In some districts he is expected to do the actual writing; in some he coordinates the writing efforts of others.

Supervisors should recognize that words on paper, no matter how well written, cannot guarantee curriculum development. They merely reflect actions of individuals and provide guidelines for future actions. They cannot replace personal interactions.

Regardless of whether he writes the items himself or has the writing done by others, the supervisor must take the necessary precautions to ensure satisfactory publication. One crucial consideration is the formulation of clear, intelligible goals. Poor curriculum writing is partly due to misunderstood objectives. Most statements of objectives are broad, vague, and so general as to be worse than useless. They confuse the person who is trying to create a unit. Since the objectives are meaningless, it is impossible to evaluate what has been accomplished because performance cannot be measured against nonspecific expectations.

Recently, through the work of the behavioral scientists, new importance has been attached to definition of objectives in curriculum publications. Not only must the goals and objectives be put in understandable terms; the behavioral scientist demands that they also be stated in behavioral terms. If teachers can readily identify what specifically is being sought, they can measure progress toward it. Preparation of objectives becomes much more exact than it has been in the past, and more specific behavioral definitions open new approaches to better evaluation.

Probably Mager's criteria for objectives are as well put as any:

1. An instructional objective describes an intended outcome rather than a description of summary of content.
2. One characteristic of a usefully stated objective is that it is stated in behavioral or performance terms that describe what the learner will be *doing* when demonstrating his achievement of the objective.
3. The statement of objectives for an entire program of instruction will consist of several specific objectives.
4. The objective which is most usefully stated is one which best communicates the instructional intent of the person selecting the objective.[9]

With such directions in mind, the supervisor can do much to help teachers meet reasonable objectives in their teaching. It then becomes possible to understand what is to be accomplished, when it has been accomplished, and to what degree. Communication with the teaching staff through the written word is at last meaningful, and much individualized conference time can be saved — no small consideration for the supervisor working with a large number of teachers.

[9] Mager, *op. cit.*, p. 24.

Clear Objectives Are Important

One supervisor recently made an all-out effort to update and re-write the district's curriculum guides. He established several committees of master teachers who were willing to assist in the project. Before any writing took place, however, he conducted two sessions with all involved in the project to acquaint them with recent thinking on instructional objectives.

The group practiced writing clear, concise behavioral objectives. This orientation enabled them to structure the eventual guides so each teacher making use of them could easily direct his teaching and evaluate his progress.

Organizing a Unit

Most educators recognize the necessity of organizing curriculum into manageable parts, and many supervisors and teachers believe in organizing content into units. Presumably, one starts with a master or resource unit which contains more content and a greater variety of learning activities than one needs or can cover. However, this abundance of suggestions provides leads for working with students of differing abilities and interests. The teacher then develops his teaching unit using as reference the larger resource unit or some other previously prepared material.

A problem in such organization is that there is no one structure for all curriculum workers to follow. Taba advocated an eight-step model.[10] The authors propose a simplified structure of four steps:

Steps in Preparation
of a Unit — Simplified Model
1. Establish behavioral objectives.
2. Select and organize learning activities.
3. Select and organize methods and media.
4. Test and evaluate.

The shorter version has the advantage of simplicity, flexibility, and specificity. Any point in the model may be expanded as needed.

Unit teaching requires planning. The units for a semester, and in many cases for a school year, may be planned tentatively at the

[10] Hilda Taba and Elizabeth Noel, *Action Research: A Case Study* (Washington: Association for Supervision and Curriculum Development, 1957), pp. 343–379.

same time. Flexibility must be built into the programs so that individual differences are taken into consideration. Teachers know that differences among students range at least two years above and below grade level. The learning activities planned and the content selected should reflect the variety among learners.

College graduates usually have had little training in developing units. Most of their preparation has been in the form of observation or developing lessons — daily encounters with students. However, such short-term planning is not particularly helpful to the student. It does not utilize much of what is known of the learning process. It is actually a piecemeal approach to both teaching and learning. The broader view involved in teaching units must be learned and practiced on the job. The following is an elaboration of the four-point unit structure.

Unit Title

1. Establishment of behavioral objectives
   a. Disciplinary and philosophical objectives: systems of thought
   b. General objectives relating to concepts, principles, and understanding
   c. Specific objectives relating to skills, information, attitudes, and appreciations
2. Selection of learning activities and/or content
   a. Learning activities, instructional materials, selected according to the criteria for content selection (see Fig. 6, p. 243)
   b. Range of materials
   c. Materials classified and ordered according to
      (1) the logical organization of the materials (structure of the discipline)
      (2) the abilities, maturation, and motivational levels of students
3. Selection of teaching methods and media
   a. Pretest
   b. Selection of activities and/or projects
      (1) lectures, discussions, demonstrations
      (2) multimedia approaches (including both techniques and materials)
      (3) computer-assisted instruction, programmed materials, machine learning
      (4) independent study and group work
      (5) research techniques unique to the particular discipline
   c. Continued diagnosis, appraising, teaching

4. Evaluation
  a. A variety of tests, measurements, observations of pupil behavior
  b. Interpretations and elaborations of the findings
  c. Feedback to change
    (1) methods of data gathering on learning and achievement
    (2) methods of instruction
    (3) materials of instruction (content)
    (4) objectives (relevance)
  d. Initiation of change
    (1) modify teaching procedures
    (2) move on to a new unit or new objectives

The unit organization and method are admirably suited to independent study. When students are given greater freedom to pursue their studies in the library, laboratory, classroom, and elsewhere, a well-prepared unit provides the necessary organizational framework which ties together both time and place for them. The regular daily schedule then becomes less important. Many innovative schools have given up the class bell and regular recitation periods for more flexibility of instruction as they have refined their unit approach to curriculum development.

The teacher who utilizes the unit approach finds that he is cast in a new role. No longer does he hear recitations one by one or listen to a class of thirty repeat a textbook page by page. He becomes a diagnostician of learning problems, a coordinator of instructional services, a previewer and collator of materials, and finally a guide for learning activities. In such an environment the supervisor's role also changes, in relation to what the teacher does, whether he is supporting or encouraging innovative teaching.

Working Through a Curriculum Council

Early in the school year the Curriculum Council determined to make a careful study of the total secondary curriculum, with particular attention to sequence of course offerings in the various high schools of the district. Much preliminary work, such as a study of the success of the graduates and the problems of the dropouts, and a community survey, had been completed in preparation for an accreditation visitation. Now expressions of dissatisfaction with alleged duplication, overlapping, and, in some instances, voids in secondary curriculum had brought the problem of the entire secondary school curriculum to the attention of the council.

Supervisor Green had been appointed chairman of a subcommittee to investigate possible curriculum revisions and make recommendations to the council. This, it turned out, had become a formidable undertaking, to say the least. The subcommittee had held innumerable meetings, had heard from many groups, had sampled offerings in other districts, and had even visited two districts which had recently gone through a similar experience. Mr. Green had involved as many different individuals and groups as possible in the various stages of the study.

It came as no great surprise to anyone, then, when the subcommittee report to the Curriculum Council recommended a major revision of the secondary curriculum. The proposal seemed so logical that many wondered why the change had not taken place long before. The reason for the wide acceptance of the report, Mr. Green realized, was the fact that what had been transpiring throughout the subcommittee deliberations was well known and that most of the eventual proposals had originated with the suggestions of individuals throughout the district.

The Curriculum Resource Center

As indicated throughout this chapter, one useful adjunct to curriculum research, planning, and writing is a well-stocked and -staffed curriculum resource center. The supervisor who embarks upon a curriculum improvement program must face three important problems: personnel, materials, and space. Progress in his program will be in direct proportion to the extent to which he has solved them.

The most significant of these requirements is personnel, and a critical problem for personnel is time. If supervision cannot stimulate the staff to study curriculum problems — if it is unable to find, or to make, time for them to do so — progress will be slow at best. The second requirement, materials, means textbooks, magazines, monographs, bulletins, pamphlets, outlines, sources of study, films, tapes, exhibits, etc. Excellent free or inexpensive materials, compilations of community resources, and numerous recent bibliographies should be provided. The third requirement is space in which to work. There is a need for meeting rooms to hold small and large groups. Work space is necessary to prepare curriculum publications. Storage facilities are needed to house the audio-visual equipment and materials, the central professional library holdings, and the specialty items of instruction not kept in individual buildings.

The district supervisory staff will sooner or later, as curriculum implementation proceeds, find a curriculum resource center essential as a support facility. Many districts have for years been maintaining one of sorts. Other districts have recently recognized the necessity and have been carefully staffing and outfitting such a center.

In those districts which were able to obtain grants under Title III of the Elementary and Secondary Education Act, supplemental education centers have been more easily organized. The hard work of convincing the community, the school board, and the administration that a resource center should be given a high priority in the budget was unnecessary. Recent federal funds available for both materials and manpower have been a boon to curriculum development and in the process of innovation. In some instances they have shifted the supervisory role from one of mounting a battle for the establishment of a center to one of making creative use of it.

If the faculty is convinced that a resource center is important to their work, they may demand it, and call on the supervisor to demonstrate to the board how it is to be used. Indeed, if the center is not forthcoming, it might be forced by negotiation procedures. Such action would represent one more example of teacher responsibility for professional growth. The beginning of a materials center is described in the notes of a curriculum committee:

Curriculum Implementation

Several people in our school system have felt that a materials center of a central curriculum laboratory would be of great benefit to curriculum improvement. About a year ago, the superintendent appointed a committee composed of three principals, two coordinators, and one resource teacher to study the possibilities.

Letters were written to schools throughout the United States known to have such centers. Periodicals and other printed materials were combed for ideas. Empty rooms in one building were discovered and rough drawings were made of potential layouts.

Then a detailed report was written and presented to the entire leadership group for consideration. Debate and discussion ensued, and two significant questions emerged. (1) Can our district afford a materials center? (2) How will we use the center?

These questions came back to the original committee for study. Firstly, the matter of financing the center was admittedly crucial as our district is bracing for a tax election with a substantial increase in amount re-requested. Secondly, the committee had been aware all along that people and ideas would be more important than materials in the success of the center.

How will we use the center? The committee suggested some specific ideas for a nucleus of the plan so that a picture of successful operation could be presented to all staff members concerned with the problem.

If money is not forthcoming for extensive resource materials, we can still go ahead with what we have now. We can put tables and chairs in an empty room and begin with one area of curriculum improvement such as elementary science.

Many elementary teachers hesitate to do much in science except assign reading in the textbook because they feel unsure of themselves in developing science units and projects.

We can begin with a series of "how-to-do-it" sessions. Mr. B., a sixth grade teacher, is an "expert" on aquariums. We can ask him to plan three or four sessions on aquariums; bring one in to demonstrate, and then show what to do, explain what supplies are needed, and where to obtain them. He will discuss the place of aquariums in the science curriculum.

Example: One of our principals is an authority on the development and use of bulletin boards. He has accumulated 35 mm slides with which he can illustrate good and poor bulletin board procedures. We can display printed materials on methods of using bulletin boards, and we can involve everyone in a project by dividing teachers into teams which would compete with each other in making up specimen bulletin boards at our inservice meetings.

Example: Miss H., a primary teacher, made a detailed study of how to teach about magnets. She could share her knowledge and techniques with us.

How to use the microscope, how to locate chemistry all around us, how to use photography in teaching about light — these are all topics on which some teacher in our system is well versed and could work up an interesting series of lessons.

Bulletins could be prepared on these various topics, and schedules listed could show which projects are being featured at the center. Since the demonstrations and workshop sessions would be on schedule, teachers who were interested could attend those meetings which filled a need.

The empty room in Building X could be used for wall displays, books, and materials brought in to implement these suggestions. The materials center would not only be a by-product of curriculum development, it would be the heart of it. Written guides would be developed during summer projects in which teachers would par-

ticipate on a voluntary and interest basis. In the winter, or the
regular term, teachers and principals would take these guides and
expand them into units which would be supplied at the center.

Example: Some teachers and principals are enriching the curriculum by organizing "listening centers" in some small room, alcove,
library, or carrel. One problem has been the procurement of tapes.
If permission to copy a tape has been secured, or tapes were made
locally, then those tapes can be reproduced very inexpensively in
almost unlimited numbers. The materials center could become the
facility for programming and reproducing tapes for school listening
centers.

Example: Many schools will not be able to afford machines of
various kinds. Our materials center would purchase at least one
machine of each kind and begin an orientation and instruction
program. When machines do become available to us, we will have
trained personnel ready to utilize them to advantage. The following list is simply illustrative, and is not intended as a recommendation:

> projectors of various kinds
> laminators
> controlled reader
> teaching machines.

A school survey team reported to the board and administration of
the Edwardsville Community Schools, Madison County, Illinois, as
follows:

> A curriculum laboratory would need to house at least the follow-
> ing functions:
> 1. General business
>   Telephones
>   Mail service — in and out, U.S. and internal
>   Secretarial services — including additional stations when pro-
>   duction schedules are stepped up
>   Administrative — desks, files, etc.
> 2. Receiving and dispatching
>   Mail, requisitions
>   Shipments and samples
>   Memos — bulletins, guides, courses of study
>   Books, magazines, research studies
> 3. Cataloguing, classifying
>   Supplementary texts and other books
>   Audio-visual aids
>   Resources: general and community

4. Displays and storage (racks, tables, shelving, wall space)
   Curriculum materials, guides
   Books, magazines
   Dioramas, models
   Records of various kinds
   Vault for expensive and hard to obtain items
5. Demonstration area
   Teaching machines
   Reading pacers
   Laminators
   Recording devices
   Communication media
   Desks, tables, screens
   Adequate provision for utilities
   Micro readers
   Projectors
   Controlled readers
   Copying machines
6. Production and service area
   Typing and duplication of materials
   Materials for sorting, collating, and assembling functions
   Binding and letter folding for mailing
   Materials collection area
   Area and materials for preparing graphics
7. Meetings and conferences
   Adequate space for several committees to meet
   Larger (departmental and interdepartmental) conferences
   Administration-supervision conferences

The previous quotation is included to illustrate the fact that a materials center, or a curriculum resource center, has many functions to perform. The seven just mentioned are essential to all centers, although some schools may find it expedient to begin a center on a more modest basis. In this case several functions can be combined. A center must be given considerable use if the advantages are to accrue to the system and if its expansion is to be justified.

A curriculum resource center can do several things for the instructional program: (1) It makes for greater satisfaction in curriculum work and provides a basic laboratory setting. (2) It physically indicates the importance placed on curriculum improvement by the community and the administration. (3) It houses and protects files, materials, records, equipment. (4) It makes possible the collection at one central point of various facilities for assisting professional personnel with curriculum problems; it houses the curriculum personnel operating as "staff." (5) It enables publishers, colleges and universities, and school suppliers to contact the appropriate persons when problems of curriculum are involved. (6) It minimizes communication difficulties, stalled requisitions, duplicate requisitions, and irresponsible curriculum ventures and serves as a clearinghouse for information related to the curriculum. (7) It may attract a higher type of professional person to the school system; the opportunity to do creative work, to effect progress, and to do research is a factor in drawing the best minds to public school work. (8) It awakens and sustains motivation for professional improvement. (9) It is a constant source of new ideas and innovation and, when properly used, keeps the faculty alert to trends and changes. (10) It is the center of a communications network for the school system where professional dialogue can take place.

The Curriculum Resource Center

The curriculum resource center which is functioning satisfactorily will become the hub of district curriculum and instruction activity. One of the authors is familiar with such a center in which a wide variety of activities regularly took place. A conference room plus two rooms suitable for average-sized groups were constantly used for planning meetings, inservice sessions, preview and examination of special equipment, text and library book displays, and many other purposes. The audio-visual department for the district housed district-owned films, filmstrips, models, collections, and the like. It also loaned some equipment to the schools for short-term needs and provided a repair service for the district.

The professional library contained a large number of professional and technical volumes for the district. Many were titles which were in limited demand and were too expensive for the individual buildings to provide. A comprehensive sample of textbooks was also housed here. Bookmen regularly provided their newest books so that any staff member in the district could quickly examine everything available in a given discipline.

The instructional supervisors provided curriculum leadership and coordination throughout the district and maintained their offices at the center. All curriculum publications for the district were edited and published from this location. In short, this curriculum resource center was maintained to serve the instructional program of the district and did so in a variety of ways. It was a center for things as well as for ideas.

Summary

The first section of the chapter is concerned with helping the supervisor devise a rationale for curriculum development. Such a framework is the best means for providing direction, order, and consistency in the process. A useful rationale includes the analysis of society, prior decisions about the function of the schools, the building of a philosophy of education, the analysis of the learner and the learning process, the sources and classifications of knowledge, the development of objectives of education, and the use of criteria for content selection.

The chapter also discusses the dynamics of implementation and directions for creating action programs. Implementation has two levels: On the first are general problems, such as the comprehensive versus the piecemeal approach, the involving of lay and professional persons in the processes, the setting of designs and strategies for curriculum work. On the second are the organization for curriculum work, the curriculum council, the utilizing of assistance from outside groups, the writing of curriculum and units, and finally, the organization, development, and use of the curriculum resource center.

Problems for Group Discussion

Analyze the following situations. In each, identify supervisory principles representing sound theory, if any are included. What are the basic elements which made a difference? How would you have approached the situation?

1. Assume that you have just come to your position as supervisor of instruction and curriculum. One of the high schools with which you will work has had a reputation for being "difficult." Yet it is about as "good" as any in your area. Money has not been a problem as your district spends more per student than any of the neighboring districts.

The teachers have planned the curriculum for college-bound students. Teachers sit at their desk most of the time and lecture. Tests are over content; they are designed to tax the memory and are difficult. All teachers follow a tough grading policy. They give out only a few B's and almost no A's; the assumption is that the students must learn what college is like. This teaching-grading system is well entrenched, and many parents think it is good. The only people raising questions about the system are the principals and the superintendent.

What are the problems in this situation? How should a supervisor go about attacking them?

2. In a certain well-to-do community parents and residents are all business people or professionals. The median income is high. The school is judged "good" by the community as evidenced by the fact that a number of seniors are always admitted to the best private universities in the country. Also, a number of students always make high scores on achievement tests.

In general, however, teachers are easygoing. Students have unlimited makeup privileges and are permitted to do assignments over as often as the teacher thinks it necessary. The philosophy calls for a balanced education including extracurricular activities for everyone. Each student is scheduled for some club activity. The academic factors are not overemphasized. The "ideal student" is one who can earn an average of C and participate in clubs and athletics. The justification advanced is that the well-rounded student is best fitted for life in both the community and college.

How adequate do you think this philosophy is? Should it be changed? How would you go about changing it?

3. The supervisor worked for some months with teachers in his district to prepare a comprehensive social science curriculum. Detailed guides had been produced for and with the help of teachers. The new program was implemented in the fall and the supervisor was pleased with the smooth progress being made. Then the superintendent's telephone began to ring all day, and it became evident that the new curriculum was in difficulty. Several controversial items had been included and were being approached very frankly by the teachers. The parents, however, had been unaware of the impending changes and were upset with what they heard was taking place. What problems had been generated by this procedure?

4. The teachers of the district leaned heavily upon the text; they were content to stay with their broad ideas of what should be taught. The supervisor attacked this problem on the departmental level and sought to assist departments to develop specific instructional objectives so stated that both the behavioral changes sought in the learners and the knowledge level associated with the behavior could be identified readily. Much initial objection was raised because the teachers felt they were

being restricted in their teaching activities. As they became familiar with the process and experienced some of the results, they began to realize the help such objectives actually could be to their teaching. Is this a desirable approach to curriculum implementation?

5. In the past, either the principal or the department chairman was expected to select new textbooks for the district. The new supervisor disagreed with this practice and set out to modify it. He established textbook committees composed of teachers and administrators who were to examine available titles and prepare recommendations for adoption. Many committees quickly discovered a need for prior study to establish acceptable goals and objectives for the courses. Yet in the end a stronger, better articulated program than had existed before emerged. Should the supervisor feel dissatisfied with delays encountered in selection?

6. During the summer the science supervisor prepared materials, ordered new equipment, and began to obtain information on new materials and new programs. In addition, he started a file of resource persons and field trip locations throughout the community. When school opened, all science teachers were invited to visit his office and explore the "resource center" and were shown how the available material, information, etc., could best be used by each teacher.

Whose resource center was it? How did it come about? What would you do if no science teacher showed up?

Selected Readings

Association for Supervision and Curriculum Development. *Learning and the Teacher.* Washington: The Association, 1959.

Association for Supervision and Curriculum Development. *A Look at Continuity in the School Program.* Washington: The Association, 1958.

Association for Supervision and Curriculum Development. *Role of Supervisor and Curriculum Director in a Climate of Change.* Washington: The Association, 1965.

Association for Supervision and Curriculum Development. *Youth Education Problems / Perspectives / Promises.* Washington: The Association, 1968.

Bennis, Warren G., Kenneth D. Benne, and Robert Chin. *The Planning of Change: Readings in the Applied Behavioral Sciences.* New York: Holt, Rinehart & Winston, 1961.

Bent, Rudyard K., and Adolph Unruh. *Secondary School Curriculum.* Boston: D. C. Heath & Company, 1969.

Berman, Louise M. *New Priorities in the Curriculum.* Columbus, Ohio: Charles E. Merrill Books, 1968.

Bloom, Benjamin S., ed. *Taxonomy of Educational Objectives. Handbook I, The Cognitive Domain.* New York: David McKay Co., 1956.

Brickell, Henry M. *Organizing New York State for Educational Change.* Albany: New York State Department of Education, 1961.

Bruner, Jerome S. *The Process of Education.* Cambridge, Mass.: Harvard University Press, 1960.

Burnham, Reba M., and Martha L. King. *Supervision in Action.* Washington: Association for Supervision and Curriculum Development, 1961.

Doll, Ronald C. *Curriculum Improvement: Decision Making and Process.* Boston: Allyn & Bacon, 1964.

Elam Stanley, ed. *Education and the Structure of Knowledge.* Chicago: Rand McNally & Co., 1968.

Hott, Leland, and Manford Sonstegard. "Relating Self-Conception to Curriculum Development," *Journal of Educational Research,* 58:348–351 (Apr., 1965).

Leeper, Robert R., ed. *Curriculum Change: Direction and Process.* Washington: Association for Supervision and Curriculum Development, 1966.

Lippitt, Ronald, Jeanne Watson, and Bruce Westley. *The Dynamics of Planned Change.* New York: Harcourt, Brace & World, 1958.

Lucio, William H., ed. *Supervision: Perspectives and Propositions.* Washington: Association for Supervision and Curriculum Development, 1967.

Mager, Robert F. *Preparing Instructional Objectives.* Palo Alto, Calif.: Fearon Publishers, 1962.

Morphet, Edgar L., and David L. Jesser. *Cooperative Planning for Education in 1980.* New York: Citation Press, 1968.

National Education Association. *NEA Research Bulletin,* Vol. 4, No. 4 (Dec., 1966).

Raths, James, and Robert R. Leeper, eds. *The Supervisor: Agent for Change in Teaching.* Washington: Association for Supervision and Curriculum Development, 1966.

Richardson, Don H. "Independent Study: What Difference Does It Make?" *Bulletin of the National Association of Secondary School Principals,* 51:53–62 (Sept., 1967).

Searles, John E. *A System for Instruction.* Scranton, Pa.: International Textbook Co., 1967.

Taba, Hilda, and Elizabeth Noel. *Action Research: A Case Study.* Washington: Association for Supervision and Curriculum Development, 1957.

Thomas, R. Murray, Lester B. Sands, and Dale L. Brubaker. *Strategies For Curriculum Change: Cases from 13 Nations.* Scranton, Pa.: International Textbook Co., 1968.

Unruh, Glenys G., and Robert R. Leeper, eds. *Influences in Curriculum Change.* Washington: Association for Supervision and Curriculum Development, 1968.

Wiles, Kimball, and Robert R. Leeper, eds. *Strategy for Curriculum Change.* Washington: Association for Supervision and Curriculum Development, 1965.

eleven

•

Evaluation in an Era of Change and Innovation

The decade of the sixties ushered in many changes in education, which have increased the pressure for improved evaluation. New methods and concepts are required in order to test the innovations and chart the next moves. It is in the field of evaluation that the profession may be most vulnerable. This chapter recognizes the new pressures and is concerned with evaluation of teaching, of the inservice program, and of curriculum development itself.

Forces Influencing Instruction

New power groups are emerging which will influence evaluation of the instructional program. Their impact will have implications for the supervisor's new role. One, within the profession, is the militant teacher's organization, whether it be the local NEA affiliate or an AFT group. Increasingly, teacher groups are insisting upon participation in decision making on both policy and administration levels. They take the position that past performance of administrators has proved ineffective and inadequate. Where well-developed negotiation agreements are in effect, certain specific subjects for negotiation are spelled out: the number, time and place, and type of professional meetings, their substance and the leadership to be used, for example.

Consequently, much new and different evaluative information about the instructional program will be needed. Supervision may be expected to provide such data by means of a sophisticated program of evaluation. Participants on either side of the negotiation table may call for details on appraisal of the English curriculum or a better picture of the tenth-grade achievement test results. Perhaps the negotiators want to see the long-range plans for replacing and updating the junior high textbooks. In each instance, the supervisor may be on call and expected to provide the necessary information.

Another pressure group is made up of the manufacturers of the instructional "hardware," and the "software" to go with it. Increasingly, these producers are developing a total approach, providing the machines, packaging the curriculum, and supplying the necessary inservice education programs to prepare teachers to utilize them. Institutes and short courses for teachers are made available in which the new curricula are studied and the methods needed to teach them are practiced. Supervisors should be familiar with all aspects of this activity if they are to learn how to evaluate properly materials which may be used in their districts. Lack of such evaluation may result in the bringing into the schools of an element of supervision from the outside.

What will be the new role of the supervisor? Should he attend institutes in order to be able to carry on his function? Should be schedule short courses for the teachers? Or should he strongly resist the outside pressures?

A third force already making itself felt in the local district through aid programs is the federal government. The effectiveness of the aid programs must be evaluated — and by the school. In numerous cases administrators have had to call in consultants to help devise an evaluation program because no one in the district could do it. Again supervision must play a key part, either in developing the evaluation design or in explaining the instructional program and its stated goals to the outside consultant.

Fourth, more use is being made of computers. They have proved efficient in recording, collecting, retrieving, collating, and arranging data and in supplying various combinations of data for a multitude of uses. It is difficult to foresee the impact that full utilization of computers will have on evaluation, but their contribution is expected to be large. Certainly, district-wide data can be made available in a manner never before possible for use in analyzing the total instructional program. Too often in the past supervisors had to play hunches and make broad generalizations for lack of "hard data." Now the electronic marvels can readily provide even item analysis of specific test results. Scope and sequence difficulties can be examined and articulation of the curriculum thereby improved. Machines could necessitate more sophisticated methods of documenting observations and quantifying them, make possible the development of school profiles, improve the quality of action research, and enhance the supervisor's ability to analyze learning situations and to explain to teachers and principals objectively the teaching-learning phenomenon. It is likely that computer-assisted instruction will also materially change teaching styles. Old methods of analysis and evaluation may become inappropriate.

Lastly, instructional innovations might be mentioned. Team teaching, in either the vertical or the horizontal organization, may serve as an example of the changed conditions under which the supervisor must work with the teachers. Many teachers do not alter their methods of evaluation when they change from teaching small groups to teaching large ones although evaluation has to be adjusted to be appropriate for each group. In team teaching, teachers must learn new procedures such as proper diagnosing accompanied by improved evaluation techniques.

As new forces influence instruction, supervision will need to establish evaluative techniques more sophisticated and better designed than ever before. Often the supervisor will be the only individual with sufficient evaluative know-how to perform this task. He will be called upon in any event and if he is prudent will sharpen his evaluative skills in order to function most effectively.

Collect Data!

Supervisor Ebring had been working with Principal Gomez and the teachers at Lincoln School all semester. They were deeply engrossed in some experimental devices to provide better for individualized instruction.

During the early planning and from time to time during the semester Mr. Ebring had cautioned the group to keep good records of what was being done. He knew from past experience that written information often proved to be more useful than human memory. As a result of his urging, most of the teachers had kept a diary of sorts, recording the major activities and their reactions to them at the time.

Today Principal Gomez came to see Supervisor Ebring, greatly concerned over a telephone call from the superintendent's office. The funding agency supporting the experimental work had written a letter outlining what would be necessary to obtain further financing for the ensuing year. High on the list was adequate evaluative proof that the project was actually succeeding in what it had set out to do originally. *Evaluative data* was the term used. Mr. Gomez needed help and wanted Supervisor Ebring to provide the data to satisfy the agency.

Can adequate evaluation ever occur after the project has been completed?

Evaluating the Instructional Program

One of the supervisor's major concerns is the evaluation of the instructional program. The scope of an inservice program has been described earlier. Such a detailed program should be matched with a design for evaluation.

The entire program should be evaluated constantly against established criteria. One criterion is the appropriateness of the curriculum and of the instructional materials.[1] Materials should be the best available. They must fit the philosophy of education and the objectives of instruction accepted in the school system. They must be representative of the latest knowledge and organized sequentially to meet students' needs and interests.

A second criterion is adequacy and relevance for national, community, and individual needs. Adequacy and relevance are related to utility, for obviously useless exercises become boring and reduce motivation for learning. Benjamin Franklin pointed out that only what is *most* useful should be taught since lack of time prevents the teaching of *everything* useful. Never was this idea more appropriate than today.

A third criterion against which the curriculum may be evaluated is variety. Here the first consideration is the wide range of student interests. Students' interests range across the whole spectrum of human endeavor and activity. They include current issues and problems. The second consideration is the provision of a range of difficulty. Students may progress from high interest–low difficulty materials to high interest–high difficulty materials. Difficulty varies in respect to vocabulary, style of writing, and development of concepts, principles, and relationships. In other words, materials should

---

[1] Arno A. Bellack, "What Knowledge Is of Most Worth?" in William M. Alexander, ed., *The Changing Secondary School Curriculum, Readings* (New York: Holt, Rinehart & Winston, 1967), p. 221.

be carefully graded before they are used, and teachers should know the students' intellectual level.

Fourth, programs should be evaluated against the criterion of balance in the curriculum. In some schools, for example, science is slighted, or mathematics, or the fine arts. Sometimes the subject matter content does not adequately represent the concepts inherent in the discipline. Even the inservice program for teachers may be unbalanced — perhaps loaded with techniques but lacking sufficient content, or having plenty of content without adequate treatment of techniques. Balance is also involved in integration of the disciplines. As subject matter experts work on curriculum, they frequently forget that most modern problems are not solved by the use of only one discipline. For example, social problems are related to economic problems and political problems and cannot be solved by the sociologists alone. The supervisor and the teacher must work together toward a balanced curriculum which includes interdisciplinary studies.

Outside Pressure

Officials of one school district recently found themselves in an embarrassing position with the board of education. The junior high school staffs had been exploring ways of providing more flexibility for students by expanding the number of electives in foreign languages and sciences and thus widening the students' choice. After deliberating for the entire year, they seemed to have reached a solution which was an improvement, but admittedly there were still some problems for a few subject areas — the arts in particular.

The district administration accepted the proposed changes submitted by the junior high principals and took the matter to the board for formal (and routine) approval. To everyone's surprise, a large group of influential citizens was on hand to defend vigorously the old program and to fight the new one, which could hinder the arts. As might be expected, the board refused to accept the change.

In this instance supervision had not been used properly in the decision-making process. Not enough concern had been shown for providing a balanced program. An overemphasis on variety of instructional offerings in foreign languages and sciences had threatened to reduce education in the arts.

What can be done to make certain this process is not repeated? Or should it be permitted?

Evaluating Teaching — Not Teachers

For years teachers have had the uncomfortable feeling, too often justified by actions, that supervisors were really "snoopervisors." They have come to expect supervisors to "report" to the superintendent the good and the bad teachers within the district. They have come to anticipate that such reporting will lead to promotion for some and possibly dismissal for others. In consequence, some teachers are reticent about confiding fully in their supervisors but attempt instead, in every way possible, to convince them of their strong capabilities.

This is the situation when the supervisor is functioning as a line administrator. The trouble with "reporting" on teachers is that the supervisor tends to coerce and the teacher to resist. Classroom visitations produce long checklists, dutifully filled out and signed. Such evaluations remind teachers of their attention or inattention to details of classroom management and other similar insignificant aspects of classroom behavior. Yet these evaluations seldom get at the heart of the teaching act. In addition, they serve as threats, as inhibitors to creative teaching, and often as deterrents to instructional improvement. Too often teachers wait to see what is expected of them rather than searching, on their own initiative, for better ways of working with students.

In the final analysis, some system of recording an evaluation of the teacher is probably justifiable and desirable, but only when used by the line administrator — the principal or the superintendent. Evaluation for promotion purposes should not be conducted by the supervisor, who must remain distinctly in a staff capacity, apart from this kind of appraisal, if he is to maintain his own effectiveness within the instructional program.

To become and remain an instructional leader, the supervisor must develop a candid rapport with teachers. To really evoke creative teaching, to produce realistic and lasting change, supervisor and teacher must accept each other's strengths and contributions to the instructional program. This acceptance will not be forthcoming if the supervisor is writing an evaluation of the teacher which the teacher feels might be used against him by his principal.

Supervisors are reaching the conclusion that they and their teachers must jointly evaluate *the teaching act*. Hence the supervisor and the teacher plan together, as a team, what should be done, and later evaluate what was accomplished. This analysis then becomes the basis for further planning, revision of techniques, and general teaching strategies. Here the supervisor is the expert resource person, the stimulator, the supporter, but not the suppressor, the inhibitor, or the deterrent to improved teaching. The teacher is challenged to make changes and is supported in that effort by the supervisor. It is at this point of sharing evaluation of the teaching performance that the supervisor truly becomes the instructional leader.

The inexperienced supervisor may doubt that he can make this type of instructional evaluation. He will need to give serious thought to his future strategies. Not enough is known about the logic of methods, the structure of styles, the elements of classroom interaction, and the process of learning itself to make such evaluation a science. Yet it may be undertaken through a clinical approach.[2] How well has the teacher conceptualized the teaching process?[3] Has he clarified his goals in relation to the cognitive abilities, the skills, and the appreciations his students are expected to master? Are his goals stated in terms of behavioral objectives? Do teacher-made tests investigate more than simply the accumulation of information? How does the teacher evaluate and interpret test results? Does he see clearly that the results have relevance for evaluating methods, content, and the testing procedure itself?

Supervisor-Teacher Interaction

Supervisor Hurd and Miss Hinkle, high school biology teacher, are working together on the biology teaching which is taking place in Miss Hinkle's classroom. First they met and planned their strategies. Mr. Hurd reviewed with her Miss Hinkle's goals and objectives for the course and in particular the specific objectives for the lesson he was to observe.

After visiting two successive classes, Mr. Hurd again met with Miss Hinkle, this time to discuss each person's analysis of what had transpired. They agreed on the strong points of the class and iden-

---

[2] Louise M. Berman and Mary Lou Usery, *Personalized Supervision: Sources and Insights* (Washington: Association for Supervision and Curriculum Development, 1966), p. 25.
[3] Melvin M. Tumin, "Teaching — A New Diagnosis," *The B.C. Teacher,* 47:93–99 (Dec., 1967). British Columbia Teachers' Federation.

tified some other points which both felt could be improved upon. During this conference Mr. Hurd kept reminding Miss Hinkle of good learning practices.

After they had evaluated the teaching, they made plans for Miss Hinkle to try several other techniques the next day and to develop an entirely new approach for her next unit.

Throughout the entire process the emphasis has been placed upon evaluation of instruction, not on the evaluation of Miss Hinkle. She understands this, feels no threat to exposing her inadequacies, actively seeks ways of improving her teaching. At times Mr. Hurd provides support, at times he stimulates and encourages her, at times he provides a sounding board for her ideas.

Can Mr. Hurd really justify this expenditure of time?

Perhaps the teaching styles can be analyzed as to the use of either an open or a closed system.[4] Recent curriculum innovations and accompanying techniques generally stress an open system approach. Teaching patterns might be analyzed by using a polarized scheme such as the following: Is the teacher

Open System		Closed System
democratic	or	autocratic
sympathetic, responsive	or	reserved, aloof, rigid
imaginative, creative	or	traditional
change oriented	or	dependent on texts
supportive of interaction	or	a constant talker
in favor of divergent thinking	or	given to rewarding set answers

It is possible also to observe whether teachers are developing and adapting to the new roles necessitated by the introduction of innovations. More and more, the teacher is becoming an instructional specialist. He learns, it is hoped, to employ the techniques of diagnosis, to coordinate the work of teacher aides, to use the new media efficiently, to work harmoniously as a member of a team, and to employ positively the subtle pressure of the peer group in his room. Excellent results have been obtained by teachers who have organized their classes into small groups for independent study and have combined interests and abilities among students. In such classrooms students are working constructively, discussing their projects, crit-

---

[4] American Association of School Administrators, *A Climate for Individuality* (Washington: The Association, 1965), pp. 29–40.

ically, developing new projects, testing ideas. They raise questions, set their own assignments, and evaluate the outcomes. They are adventuring, exploring, and coming up with hypotheses. The curriculum has relevance to the present, and experiences are built around interests and current issues, while the stress is on process and confrontations with the real environment. Students are observing and are creating instruments to refine their observations. They are collecting information, classifying it, and then generalizing from it. Thus they are laying a base for further learning, a cognitive structure that will permit the assimilation of new information. This kind of teaching and learning can be evaluated, but the supervisor will need to develop special criteria and instruments.[5]

The supervisor who questions, suggests, encourages, and reinforces teacher behavior is certainly evaluating teaching on a much higher plane than did his predecessor who filled out checklists. The resulting interactions between teacher and supervisor will occur in more professional context.

Rating Teachers

One district recently took to heart the idea of teacher evaluation. An elaborate check sheet was developed which got at a wide variety of minor as well as major items involved in the teaching act. Administrators were assigned the task of visiting each teacher several times during the year and completing the evaluative check sheet each time.

Discontent quickly arose on all sides. The administrators found the elaborate system too time-consuming, so they began to limit teacher contact to shorter and fewer visits. Teachers felt threatened by this new device to "get them" and resisted being rated in such detailed fashion by an administrator who often had had little or no professional work in their subject area.

This experiment quickly joined many others in the archives of "good ideas that didn't work." Had instructional supervisors been working with the teachers with a mutually accepted goal of professional improvement and without the threat, implied or otherwise, of punishment for unacceptable performance, the outcome might have been quite different.

But how can some satisfactory teacher evaluation occur?

---

[5] Association for Supervision and Curriculum Development, *Evaluation as Feedback and Guide* (Washington: The Association, 1967), p. 49.

Evaluating the Inservice Program

Several criteria may be used to evaluate the inservice program. Is the program adequate? Does it meet the needs of the personnel? Is it related to the number and kinds of changes brought about recently?[6] Is it useful? Does it really help teachers? Does it improve the curriculum? Does it improve instruction? Each of these criteria, and others the supervisor may propose to study, can be expanded and scaled for statistical treatment if desirable. An additional criterion to be kept in mind is diversity. Since teachers are different from each other, inservice programs must also be varied. An inservice program that ignores teacher differences does most of the teachers a great injustice.

To check out the hypothesis that there are few alternatives in the usual inservice program, a graduate class in supervision was asked to make several kinds of judgments about possible diversities in inservice programs. They were first to list the inservice activities that had been sponsored in their schools and then to prepare a master list.

The master list of activities included staff meetings, developing a school philosophy, group conferences, supervisor observations of classes, the use of teacher-rating scales, professional reading for teachers, teacher visits to classes, textbook selection, course of study construction, developing lesson plans, individual conferences, supervisory bulletins, engaging in or using research, demonstration teaching, and workshops. There was nothing unusual about this list and almost nothing in it to indicate what the substance might have been. Yet this is the usual format of inservice programs.

This class, made up of educators representing twenty-one school districts, was now asked to rank the items in order of their importance as a means of helping teachers to grow professionally under certain selected conditions. One condition was that the faculty was composed entirely of new college graduates working in a new suburban school. Another condition was that the faculty members were veterans with considerable teaching experience. The correlation of coefficient between these two orders was .536. The response of the class indicated that, on the basis of experience, there was

---

[6] Association for Supervision and Curriculum Development, *The Supervisor: Agent for Change in Teaching* (Washington: The Association, 1966), pp. 1, 96.

reason to develop different programs of inservice education for the two faculties. Yet, in actual practice, faculties were being exposed to much the same program.

Even more interesting and convincing was a study based on hypothetical levels of faculty professional preparation. Two levels were assumed: a faculty with almost no professional preparation and one with more than the average. Activities were ranked according to appropriateness for each level, and the coefficient of correlation was .058. One conclusion drawn by the study group was that supervision and inservice education projects must be chosen with extreme care to fit the needs of those they are meant to serve. The criterion of diversity is not well utilized at present in developing inservice programs in many school districts.

The study group compared a list of inservice activities proposed for an experienced faculty with one proposed for a faculty with considerable professional training, thus comparing experience to training. Here the coefficient of correlation was .729, indicating that similar activities were identified. When appropriate lists suggested for a faculty with little or no professional education and for one with no experience were compared, the coefficient of correlation was .888, conclusively indicating that similar activities were identified. This group of graduate students concurred with the concept that inservice education should be varied in terms of the faculty, its interests, and its needs.

The group prepared general criticisms each felt pertinent to his own school's inservice program. After duplications were eliminated, there remained eighteen criticisms, the first five of which applied to all of the twenty-one districts. The list is as follows:

1. There was no follow-up in the sense of finding out what happened to teachers, or what the effects of the program were.

2. There was no evaluation.

3. The program and the projects did not arise from a study of the needs or the problems of the teachers.

4. The program was not related to the school's philosophy of education.

5. The program lacked cooperative efforts by both teachers and supervisors in any or all of these processes: planning, initiating, executing, and evaluating.

6. Inservice education did not arise from the needs of the school.

7. The program was thrust upon the teacher.

8. There was little or no continuity in the program.

9. The program of inservice education was copied from the other school systems.

10. Teachers were improperly grouped in the activities.

11. There seemed to be no common problems or needs which gave rise to the program.

12. There was no publicity about the program, and it was difficult to get information about it in any detail.

13. There was little to stimulate growth and there was no opportunity to recognize progress. (This supports item 2, criticizing the programs for lack of evaluation.)

14. Most teachers put forth minimum effort, which probably hindered their growth.

15. The procedures were too authoritarian. Teachers attended, but many rebelled internally.

16. The time involved or alloted was too short, and very little was accomplished.

17. The lack of time and money plus too little effort doomed the program to failure.

18. The programs were weak in the exploration and study of new methods.

Such a study in his own school system could provide the supervisor with the basis for a sound and effective inservice program. Many such studies could be a means for improvement of the total services of supervision.

Evaluating Curriculum Development

The organization of and procedure for curriculum development must come in for rigorous evaluation. Who should be providing curriculum leadership? What process should be followed? How can the district determine the effectiveness of the present curriculum? Does the curriculum meet the needs of the student body? Who becomes involved in the various stages of curriculum development? Is there adequate articulation between segments of the total program? These and other related questions ought to be carefully posed and honestly answered. Supervision must play an important part in such activity if it is to have any sizable effect upon the entire instructional program.

How should curriculum evaluation occur in the face of changes resulting from negotiations? The establishment of a curriculum council by directive, with faculty members appointed by the administration, may no longer be a viable procedure. Other methods of recognizing the power, interest, and potential expertise of the new teacher-professional will be required.

Perhaps the new negotiations procedures will call for more involvement of teachers in all matters related to instructional needs and to decision making. Teachers are increasingly demanding access to the decision-making process and to the control of resources. They are also making known to administration, to boards of education, and to the public in general that they are no longer willing to always "make do" with inadequate equipment and supplies. They are saying in a loud voice that society can ill afford to provide this generation with a second-class education under the guise of economy. Mechanics in a garage demand new tools designed for working on new automobiles. They cannot continue to use antiquated implements which do not fit modern parts or which make working awkward and slow. Similarly, teachers cannot be expected to use new methods and curricula with old approaches. They are insisting on competent assistance, better, up-to-date equipment, and relevant materials.[7] If teachers are to be involved in curriculum making, they must also accept responsibility for involvement in evaluation or organization and procedures followed in curriculum development.

The Supervisor Evaluates Himself

The supervisor cannot adequately evaluate himself unless he has previously set up some objectives for himself and for his work. Basically, his whole professional life should be oriented toward people and his professional goal should be to help them. He might well ask himself, "Do I spend most of my time with people?" Then, of course, he must examine the results of his efforts to help people, his fundamental goal.

---

[7] Leslie J. Bishop, *Collective Negotiation in Curriculum and Instruction: Questions and Concerns* (Washington: Association for Supervision and Curriculum Development, 1967), pp. 1–22.

The components of a supervisory philosophy — all of which are important and all of which can help to ensure success — can be identified. As the supervisor engages in self-evaluation, he will do well to reflect upon each element. From the elements of his philosophy he derives his objectives.

One element in his philosophy is the use of reason for solving problems. Reason involves objectivity, accuracy, and valid alternatives. It calls for suspended judgment and critical analysis.

A second element is a belief in and a reliance on clear communication. Channels of communication in every direction must be kept free and open. Conversations between teachers from different grade levels and disciplines are to be encouraged. Information should flow freely between faculty and staff. Reasonable people, given the same information that the administrator or the supervisor possesses, will make very similar decisions. Withholding choice bits of information in order to increase another's dependence keeps a wholesome program from growing. Lack of communication is one reason for the present resentment of many teachers. How does the supervisor rate on this point?

A third element centers around participation. The supervisor should periodically examine his programs to see who is involved and how much. What role do the faculty leaders play in the planning and execution of inservice programs? How are the less aggressive drawn into the work? Participation takes place at several levels. Participation in informal meetings and social recreational committees is probably the lowest level. A higher level might be initiation and planning of a curriculum project, or writing a proposal for a Title III (ESEA) grant. A still higher level might consist in discussions leading to a district policy decision. The principle of participation requires that everyone on the faculty be involved at some level. Is this in fact the case? Does the supervisor feel that he should be the chairman of every meeting?

A fourth element in his philosophy of supervision requires that the supervisor ascertain whether there has been sufficient provision made for activities to meet the individual needs of teachers. Some, perhaps most, of the teachers will be working in groups. But for a few there must be individual, independent kinds of activities — opportunities, for example, to participate in the following:

Modifications of curriculum
New curriculum

A change of methods
Experimentation
New learning activities
Statements of objectives
Study groups (workshops in test construction, statistics, history, human growth and development, the disadvantaged child, the sociology of the inner city, etc.)[8]

As teachers assume a greater voice in school management, they must have an understanding of taxation and school finance, political processes, administrative decision making, community history and development, and public relations. The more knowledgeable they become, the more helpful to the district they can be. A faculty involved in several different activities can be a more satisfied faculty and a more productive one. The supervisor who can provide for and stimulate participation in professional activities which meet individual needs will be putting an element of his philosophy into practice.

Fifth, human relations within the profession as a whole is embraced in supervisory philosophy. Most people will agree at the verbal level that man is the most important value of all but will fail to support the concept at the operational level. Liberty, equality, and fraternity apply to all, and these values must constantly be demonstrated and practiced in the total program of supervision. Deceit, hidden agendas at meetings, favoritism, and pulling rank (variations of "I am the boss") are examples of behavior which the supervisor can neither practice himself nor condone in others. Nor should he simply "tolerate" people who are different. Since differences are what make each person unique and are the basis of his unique contribution to society, they should be cultivated, not discouraged. A person of an independent cast of mind can provide more innovative ideas and change than dozens of conformists. How has the supervisor managed the development of better human relations among the staff and faculty?

The sixth element of the supervisor's philosophy involves faith in the concept of freedom. It has been the cause of centuries of struggle. Freedom underlies growth and must prevail if learning is to progress at its best possible rate. Experimentation, exploration, and the raising of all types of questions cannot take place except

---

[8] National Education Association, *Profiles of Excellence* (Washington: The Association, 1966).

under conditions of freedom for all teachers and students. The supervisor, then, should foster freedom by cutting red tape, eliminating restrictions, reducing irritants, and clearing the way so that teachers may teach and students may learn. A pertinent question for the supervisor as he evaluates himself is: What provision have I made for freedom of the faculty?

The last element in supervisory philosophy deals with conversion of change into progress. Change is man's constant companion. Change is inevitable. But not all change is necessarily good. Change can be directed by the use of intelligence so that it results in progress. Change in teachers — in their methods, attitudes, and motivations — is converted into progress by supervision and through in-service education. Progress toward one's goals raises morale. Can the supervisor distinguish between change and progress? How does he measure progress?

These seven elements of the supervisor's philosophy can become his objectives. His success in using them must be carefully considered as he evaluates himself and his supervisory practices at regular intervals. As he performs this self-evaluation, he will also develop means for evaluating the growth of the faculty along the same lines.

A Working Philosophy

When Mr. French was in graduate school preparing to become a supervisor, he could not understand why so many of his professors kept relating course content to educational philosophy. He thought it somewhat ridiculous, in fact, that anyone would expect him to put his own educational philosophy on paper. After all, he had been a successful teacher of mathematics for six years and no one had asked him to do so before.

Now Mr. French is completing his first year as a new instructional supervisor. He reflects upon the varied, often crucial, and always pressured activities with which he has been engaged during the year. As he reviews his accomplishments and failures, it suddenly becomes plain why he needed a clear, well-thought-out educational philosophy. He remembers several times when under duress he made what at the time seemed snap judgments, required on the spot. He sees how his philosophy guided him in a consistent, steady pattern of operations which made some of his decisions rather easy and certainly very logical. They might have been extremely difficult without such a frame of reference. Indeed, his philosophy had stood him in good stead in the "daily battle."

Evaluation and Research

Research is a tool which can be used in the program of evaluation. Knowledge of research should be fed into the mainstream of instruction as often as possible to aid educators to evaluate.

Modern educational research is sophisticated. Multifactor analysis is producing, for example, more and better answers than were formerly possible. Such research has much to say about teaching, classroom interaction, teaching styles, motivation, and achievement.

One professional responsibility of the supervisor is to keep himself informed in the area of research.[9] His attitude and enthusiasm can gradually infect the faculty. Bit by bit, the concept of research is built until teachers accept research as useful. The professions and industry thrive on research. Can supervision do less?

Numerous publications are readily available to the supervisor who wants to enlarge his knowledge of research. For example, the section on "Research in Review" in current issues of the periodical *Educational Leadership* will be found useful. The January, 1968, issue of this publication contains Volume 1, Number 1 of the "Reseach Supplement." The American Educational Research Association publishes two periodicals, *American Educational Research Journal*, and *Review of Educational Research*, which should be in the teacher's professional library. *The Handbook of Research on Teaching*, edited by N. L. Gage, is practically indispensable to the supervisor; especially useful are the chapters dealing with research in the various subject matter areas.

The supervisor should engage in some research of his own. He might start with opinionnaires inquiring into what supervisory services are useful to teachers, what help is needed or neglected, or what types of services are least useful. He could employ opinionnaires to study other school systems and then compare the results with what he finds in his own system. Almost every school system has some teachers embarking upon graduate studies, who might undertake research into local problems for their major papers or dissertations. The conclusions reached in these studies could be fed back into the faculty discussions.

As new curricula and new methods are introduced into the district,

---

[9] Association for Supervision and Curriculum Development, "Research Supplement," Vol. 1, No. 1, *Educational Leadership*, 25:325–340 (Jan., 1968).

the supervisor might study their diffusion. The factors of resistance to change could provide valuable insights into the whole process of dissemination.

There is much ferment in the teaching profession today over participation in decision making. Some militant faculty members are insisting that they have a voice in matters relating to curriculum development and inservice programs. The supervisor may wish to investigate whether these teachers are better teachers. He will certainly want to know whether the existence of a negotiations agreement produces better instruction. A simple 2×2 design might reveal some interesting relationships. For example, this model might be used for a number of studies:

	High class performance	*Low class performance*
Militant teachers	% of class	% of class
Nonmilitant teachers	% of class	% of class

Such factors as teacher satisfaction, the amount of innovation in the school system, and pupil-centered instruction might be studied with reference to their relationship to class performance. Is there, for instance, any connection between militancy or lack of militancy and willingness to undertake experimentation in the classroom?

Even theoretical research into motivation and learning might be possible. Indeed, the school should be a laboratory where ideas are tried out. The profession cannot afford to wait on sporadic, piecemeal research by graduate students, or until results are turned out by regional educational laboratories. Action research is entirely feasible and highly desirable in any school system.

When the program of inservice education is evaluated, one of the criteria should be that of research. What use is made of it by the supervisor and the teachers? How much and what kind is going on? How are the results fed back into supervision and the instructional program?

Professional Associations Can Help

Supervisor Green likes to explain how his active participation in his professional organization made money for the district, as follows:

Mr. Green regularly attends the national meeting of his supervisors' organization. A few years back he became interested in research activities being conducted by some fellow members and he, too, became an active researcher. He worked with them and began to interact in person at the national meetings and by letter and phone at other times. He learned from them and found many new ideas to try from these contacts.

Now any one of a dozen projects carried out by the district recently could be cited as an example. Careful research design, followed by sophisticated evaluation, had not only saved the district money but resulted in much outside funding, otherwise unavailable locally. Both Supervisor Green and the district staff are very pleased with this example of "professional growth."

An Operational Approach

Challenging studies can be designed in such fields as teaching styles and their effects on pupils, how best to teach pupils to do critical thinking, and the effect of pupil attitudes toward courses and methods of instruction. The faculty improvement program should provide many studies of better ways to change teacher behavior.

The following list of possible areas for research and evaluation indicates the diversity of innovations being attempted by schools today.

    1.   New Curriculum Approaches[10]

        a.   Teacher-developed experimental courses
        b.   Independent study
        c.   Ungraded curriculum
        d.   Process curriculum
        e.   School-community materials
        f.   Use of human resources in the community
        g.   Linguistics
        h.   New reading methods
        i.   Inquiry method
        j.   Interdisciplinary planning and courses
        k.   Intercultural courses
        l.   Programming

---

[10] Staff, "Portfolio: How 10 Top Schools Innovate," *Nation's Schools,* 79:75–88 (Apr., 1967).

   m. Simulation
   n. TV instruction
   o. Teaching machines
   p. Developing teacher leaders in curriculum areas
   q. Seminars for better students with or without outside help
   r. Special study groups: new methods, child study, social studies, etc.

2. Physical Arrangements

   a. Resource center
   b. Library arrangements including special areas, communications center, study carrels, etc.
   c. Large and small rooms for large and small groups
   d. Rooms and equipment for multimedia methods
   e. Computer-assisted instruction
   f. Planetariums, and other similar facilities

3. Organizational Approaches[11]

   a. Flexible scheduling
   b. Team teaching
   c. Teacher aides
   d. Extending the school day and/or year
   e. Cooperative programs with some college
   f. Work-study programs

4. Use of the New Curricula[12]

   a. PSSC physics
   b. CHEM Study chemistry
   c. CBA chemistry
   d. SMSG mathematics
   e. UICSM mathematics
   f. ESCP physical science
   g. Humanities curriculum
   h. Social studies — one of the numerous curricula
   i. ESCP earth science
   j. BSCS biology
   k. English materials from one of the many centers (USOE, CEEB, etc.)

---

[11] Gordon Cawelti, "Innovative Practices in High Schools: Who Does What — and Why — and How," *Nation's Schools*, 79:56–74 (Apr., 1967).
[12] Nancy Faber, "America's Ten Top High Schools," *Ladies Home Journal*, 85:66–137 (May, 1968).

A grid helps the reader visualize the comprehensive of one possible inservice program. Element 1 (curriculum study) will be used with *d* (process curriculum), *e* (school-community materials), and *r* (special study groups). Element 2 (development of instructional materials) will be used with *b* (independent study) and with *e* (school-community materials). The reader may carry this illustration to its ultimate conclusion and prepare studies in a similar manner for "Physical Arrangements," "Organizational Approaches," "New Curricula," and others. There are eighteen ideas under "New Curriculum Approaches," six under "Physical Arrangements," six under "Organizational Approaches," and eleven under "New Curricula." The number of combinations, therefore, is very great. A few of these, coupled with a study-action program by teachers, would soon make a difference in the instructional program. Instructional materials, professional orientation materials, and inservice workshops on methods and materials would quickly bring about change. A program modeled after this system would directly affect the four characteristics of change described earlier: rate, direction, volume, and quality.

Inservice Grid

New Curriculum Approaches

	a	b	c	d	e	f	•	•	•	•	•	r
1				x	x							x
2		x			x							
3	x		x			x						
4	x	x	x									

(left axis label: Elements*)

* *Note:*   See list on pp. 294–295.

Summary

The chapter opened with a discussion of pressures from various groups which are growing in intensity and which affect the work of the supervisor. These include the militancy of teachers, industry-provided packaged curricula, the impact of the federal government, the use of computers, and the lengthening list of innovations. All must be evaluated as to their contributions to the improvement of both instruction and the curriculum.

Suggestions were given for evaluating the instructional program, teaching, the inservice program, curriculum development, and the supervisor himself. The importance of evaluation and research activities to the supervisor was emphasized. Suggestions were made, finally, for one approach to analytically examining the inservice program.

Problems for Group Discussion

Analyze the following situations. In each, identify supervisory principles representing sound theory, if any are included. What are the basic elements which made a difference? How would you have approached the situation?

1. District X is currently preparing a plan to evaluate its teachers. The superintendent and the board of education want a formal program established. The high school principal is adamant in his desire to receive written reports from the instructional supervisor. The supervisor stoutly resists such procedure. Which is right? How could this impasse be avoided?

2. The junior high principal has encouraged a team teaching experiment this year, utilizing both English and social studies teachers. Lately he has been receiving many questions from his patrons and he has not always been in a position to answer them. He turns to the supervisor and asks him to produce objective data giving a realistic evaluation of the experiment. How should the supervisor respond?

3. The supervisor has been receiving the results of the standardized testing program conducted in the district during the past five years. A careful analysis shows that mathematics scores have been consistently and significantly below all others. How should he use this information? What will the information do to the impending bond issue if it becomes public knowledge? How can information regarding poor achievement or poor test scores be used constructively with the community?

4. Considerable material has been coming to the attention of the supervisor regarding the increasing importance of the systems approach. He is vaguely aware of the level of refinement reached in the space industry, with its resulting success. The supervisor knows that he has a major task facing him in his district in the immediate future as a thorough revision of the curriculum is about to occur. Should he take the time and seek the assistance necessary to learn about and possibly establish a systems approach, or should he continue as he has in the past, relying upon the established procedures — "the tried and true"?

Selected Readings

American Association of School Administrators. *A Climate for Individuality.* Washington: The Association, 1965.

Association for Supervision and Curriculum Development. *Evaluation as Feedback and Guide.* Washington: The Association, 1967.

Association for Supervision and Curriculum Development. *The Supervisor: Agent for Change in Teaching.* Washington: The Association, 1966.

Association for Supervision and Curriculum Development. "Research Supplement," Vol. 1, No. 1, *Educational Leadership,* 25:325–340 (Jan., 1968).

Bellack, Arno A., ed. *Theory and Research in Teaching.* New York: Bureau of Publications, Teachers College, Columbia University, 1963.

Bellack, Arno A. "What Knowledge Is of Most Worth?" in William M. Alexander, ed., *The Changing Secondary School Curriculum, Readings.* New York: Holt, Rinehart & Winston, 1967.

Berman, Louise M., and Mary Lou Usery. *Personalized Supervision: Sources and Insights.* Washington: Association for Supervision and Curriculum Development, 1966.

Biddle, Bruce J., and William J. Ellena. *Contemporary Research on Teacher Effectiveness.* New York: Holt, Rinehart & Winston, 1964.

Bishop, Leslie J. *Collective Negotiation in Curriculum and Instruction: Questions and Concerns.* Washington: Association for Supervision and Curriculum Development, 1967.

Cawelti, Gordon. "Innovative Practices in High Schools: Who Does What — and Why — and How," *Nation's Schools,* 79:56–74 (Apr., 1967).

Faber, Nancy. "America's Ten Top High Schools," *Ladies Home Journal* 85:66, 68, 69, 137 (May, 1968).

Gage, N. L., ed. *Handbook of Research on Teaching.* Chicago: Rand McNally & Co., 1963.

Lindval, C. M. *Measuring Pupil Achievement and Aptitude.* New York: Harcourt, Brace & World, 1967.

National Education Association. *Profiles of Excellence.* Washington: The Association, 1966.

Staff. "Portfolio: How 10 Top Schools Innovate," *Nation's Schools,* 79:75–88 (Apr., 1967).

Tumin, Melvin M. "Teaching — A New Diagnosis," *The B.C. Teacher,* 47:93–99 (Dec., 1967). British Columbia Teachers' Federation.

twelve

•

The Emerging Supervisor and His Problems

The emerging supervisor encounters a variety of new problems as was demonstrated when reorganized district R-4 employed a supervisor for the first time last year. This was Garry Bixman. He reported to work late in August, obtained his key from Superintendent Crosley, and went to his new office.

Mr. Bixman had seven years of experience in teaching, three as an elementary school teacher and athletic coach and four as a science and mathematics teacher in high school. He found himself increasingly unhappy about the program and about the quality of teaching he observed. Returning to the university, he enrolled in a program for a specialist degree in curriculum and instruction. Included in his advanced work was an NDEA institute in science and mathematics. During the spring, as he was finishing his work on the specialist degree, he had accepted a position as supervisor in the R-4 schools. His full title was "director of instruction and professional studies."

Mr. Bixman stepped into his office and looked around. There was the essential furniture — desk, several chairs, a bookcase — and that was about all. Superintendent Crosley had warned him he would have to start from scratch. So it seemed! He opened the window, sat down at the desk, and began to think. What should he do first? His was a new position in an expanding school system. Not only that; the position was a new one for him. Would teachers and the community accept him as a professional person? Perhaps teachers would resent him and resist his ideas. Would they look upon him as another administrator who adds to the forms that must be filled out, and thinks up more rules to be observed?

How do teachers in the R-4 district perceive of instructional directors? Are they looked upon as in-line supervisors? And what *is* supervision really? Mr. Bixman viewed supervisors and directors of instruction as facilitators of change. And perhaps change had already come to the R-4 district in a superficial way but surrounded with rigid attitudes.

He left the office and began to walk through the building looking into all the classrooms for clues to the status of change in the district. He meant to visit all buildings and sample some rooms in each school this day. Perhaps he would find a teacher or two (an outside chance) who had returned early, whom he could engage in a conversation about professional concerns.

Professionalization

One of the questions Mr. Bixman thought about as he went down the corridor concerned his professional identity. Exactly who was he? What kinds of authority, if any, did he have? He knew there had been some serious disagreements between the teachers' association and the board of education. One compromise that had been negotiated was a delimitation of the authority of the principals and superintendents over what teachers did in the classroom and the substitution of a new position for the purpose of assisting teachers with problems in curriculum development and the improvement of instruction. That was now his position.

But there was no clear description of his responsibilities, his authority, his place, if any, in the professional family. He knew that in many institutions the board and the central administrators regarded supervision as a phase of administration, and the supervisor as a member of management. In some school systems the principals are the supervisors. Their qualifications for instructional supervision or direction of curriculum development have been seriously questioned in recent years. There are those who now say that any supervision by principals, and by administrators generally, is managerial supervision instituted and functioning largely as an efficiency and operations-control process.

Where did all this leave him? Would the principals constitute a problem for him? There could be overlap of authority, or influence, resulting in gray areas in which no one had any concern but trouble was developing. Since he would be able to operate very flexibly, he could, conceivably, align himself with the principals in the buildings in hope of assuring himself support for his position and his program. But what of the teachers? They might be very much opposed to this alignment and next year negotiate him out of his position!

The state department of education had certified him as a teacher several years ago, but not as a supervisor or a director of instruction. He did have the qualifications for certification as an assistant superintendent but had refrained from applying for this certificate because his studies of teacher-administrator relations caused him to view such certification as an impediment in working with teachers. Another problem that crossed Mr. Bixman's mind but was dismissed as a premature worry was the question of his tenure in the future. Supervisors as such, and administrators, had no tenure except as teachers. Since he had never taught in this system, presumably he could never achieve tenure. Tenure might be important a few years hence when his family had increased and his children were older — and the chasm between teachers and the administration widened. But for now there was an opportunity to be explored, and the matter of tenure could wait.

Later the problem came up again, however, displaying other ramifications. Not only could Mr. Bixman not achieve tenure; he could not be certified as a director of instruction, his professional position. There was no one to look after his welfare — his working conditions and salary. The principals had organized a bargaining unit; the teachers had one; he was, in a sense, a member of neither unit. His condition was shared by all the curriculum directors, directors of instruction (unless prior service in the school system and certification as an administrator gave them leverage), and supervisors in the state. Was forming a statewide organization to work for the professionalization of supervisors a project in which he should engage?[1]

One of the problems of which he was quite aware was professional negotiations. He wondered about this trend and where it might ultimately lead. By 1969–70 over half of all teachers in cities of 1,000 or more came under some form of negotiations agreement. It seemed to him that there were two large power groups in educa-

---

[1] William F. Young, "Influencing Professional Negotiations," in *The Supervisor: New Demands, New Dimensions* (Washington: Association for Supervision and Curriculum Development, 1969), pp. 29–45.

tion: the one composed of the board of education and the management, the other consisting of the teachers' organization. There was no question that both could exert great pressure. Both might, and sometimes do, use legal procedures to win their points. In an attempt to avoid the use of legal tactics and strikes, boards and teachers have developed guidelines for negotiations which in many instances have worked quite well.

But the problem for Mr. Bixman is that supervisors, principals, and the middle management group have been left out of many of these agreements. What will become of him in the future? Can he join forces with one group or another, or must he start negotiating for himself? If he must go it alone, is he in competition with the administration, *and* middle management, *and* the teachers' organization?[2] Will he ultimately have to move to another position in order to maintain his self-respect?

One consoling thought provided hope for the future. He was brought in to do a job that needed doing. He would make himself so useful in this position that any discussion of curriculum development, improved instruction, or inservice education could hardly ignore him. His work at the "grass roots," his rapport with teachers, his activities in the community in support of quality education would surely be recognized by an increase of his budget and appropriate increments in his salary. He knew what the processes and functions of supervisory positions were; he knew that he was needed by this school system.

The search for identity that Mr. Bixman was experiencing is not at all uncommon. Superintendents claim to be supervisors, and the literature plainly states that principals are; there is, indeed, documentation for the idea that many persons are, from time to time, supervisors. Thus, the definitions are fuzzy. Questions relating to the place of a director of instruction in the total scheme of education do come up.

It is relatively easy to see the community as a social and political entity containing a subsystem (the school) which has formally taken over much of the community's function of educating its young. Within this subsystem is a sub-subsystem organized for the purpose

[2] Association for Supervision and Curriculum Development, *Toward Professional Maturity of Supervisors and Curriculum Workers* (Washington: The Association, 1967).

of quality surveillance and for the improvement of instruction. This is where Mr. Bixman fits into the picture.

Mr. Bixman continued on his self-appointed rounds. Room after room showed no evidence of what was to happen in it since all equipment had been stored — if there was any — and all traces of activity had been removed from blackboards and bulletin boards. Were these rooms ever exciting places for learning? Or were they always utterly barren of any evidence of the inquiring mind, even as they were now?

A Frame of Reference

Most supervisors in their first responsible position find themselves thinking many of the same thoughts which coursed through Mr. Bixman's mind. Now the readings in graduate courses, the lectures of ivory-towered professors of theory are recalled. How did they analyze supervision, or the supervisory position? One kind of classification often recalled is: professional help for teachers. This includes helping teachers with student behavior, with studying individual behavior, with maximizing individual differences. Other types of assistance include pointing out the negative and punitive aspects of marking and grading, the instructional uses of tests and test results, and the applicability of a basic knowledge of statistics. Still others are related to curriculum development, group dynamics, the evolving of objectives, and the ever present professional brier bush — evaluation.

Learning occurs when students interact with their environment, when they respond to stimuli. The learning environment is, therefore, a most important consideration for the supervisor. Some learning environments are barren, the number and intensity of carefully chosen stimuli greatly reduced. But learning environments can be planned which are vibrant, interesting, attractive, provocative, and challenging. Supervision which attacks the teaching-learning process at this point has the best opportunity of influencing learning and hence its biggest challenge, for teachers have not demonstrated creativity and imagination here and schools have not developed optimum conditions for learning.[3]

---

[3] Alfred H. Gorman, *Teachers and Learners: The Interactive Process of Education* (Boston: Allyn & Bacon, 1969), pp. 40–41.

Most supervisors come back again and again to the consideration of power. What kind of authority should they have? It would be possible to move faster in certain directions if one could command conformity or action. Mr. Bixman decided that there were three sources of authority: (1) Some supervisors did indeed have authority from the superintendent and the board and could command the faculty to move upon specified programs. (2) A second source of authority was the faculty which had faith in the supervisor and therefore supported him. (3) A third source was the supervisor himself; if he could provide the help teachers required, the vision, and the direction, he would be perceived as the professional and personal resource a teacher needed to move ahead. This third kind of authority, in Mr. Bixman's view, was the best of all. It would generate faculty faith in him. It would lead to provision of authority from the board to start new activities or add professional assistance should he need such authority.

The New Hierarchy

No matter how he looked at his job, Garry Bixman was faced with some kind of bureaucracy. If he aligned himself with the management, he was in the administrative hierarchy. But suppose differentiated staffing caught on in a big way, through increasing recognition that teachers have different abilities, knowledge, and competence? Such teachers could be organized into teams to maximize their potential. If the district could afford to employ one special teacher in each discipline with the highest training possible, then, division by division, the following organization might prevail throughout the system:

Special teacher — Ph.D.
Master teacher — M.A. plus 15 to 30 credits or equivalent experience
Team teacher
Beginning teacher
Student teacher
Teacher aides
Clerical aides

Thus a new hierarchy would come into existence needing a different kind of instructional assistance.

Different roles would be demanded of the director of instruction calling for different kinds of abilities, competences, and knowledge. He would have to deal with subsystems within systems, within still other systems. If plans went awry, he would have to intervene at some level and he might have to choose among three or four possible courses of action. And now it would become very important for the supervisor to be included in the decision-making process at the right level — the highest level, it is to be hoped. Often he would know more about the real workings of the school system than anyone else. How could he be sure his voice would be heard where it counts?

Questions

This kind of analysis, Mr. Bixman concluded, raised still further questions. One of them related to evaluation. If he could assist teachers to evaluate their work (instruction) in such a way that some definitive conclusions could be made about the outcome (learning), he might establish himself as indispensable to teachers. In this way he and they could confront the community with concrete results, and if these were not acceptable, he and they would know beforehand what measures should be taken. His rapport with teachers would be excellent. Surely they would be willing to take coaching from him. His roles would be mainly those of helper and facilitator. Any imposition of merit rating by the administration would be on top of the base he had created and would not impair his relationships with teachers. Then came that nagging question: Should he help organize a merit evaluation scheme? And it seemed almost inescapable that his evaluations would be included in the decisions to grant or to withhold tenure. Can the supervisor avoid these kinds of involvement?

Tenure, merit ratings, and promotions bring the supervisor into confrontation with additional questions. Principals are usually involved in decisions about merit, tenure, and promotion.[4] Principals feel that the supervisor (director of instruction) has information that would be useful in making these decisions, and that they have

---

[4] National Education Association, "Evaluation of Teaching," *NEA Research Bulletin* 47:67–75 (Oct., 1969).

a right to such information. What does one do in this situation? But even more vexatious are the relationships created when the board and central office decide that supervision is a team affair of teacher, supervisor, and principal. If Mr. Bixman should find himself in this type of relationship, he really would be neither fish nor fowl. If the information he had were to be used by the management, he would be considered by teachers as management. He would eventually be of no value to anyone unless he could set the relationship straight before it had gone too far. If he worked with the faculty, he would undoubtedly be regarded by management as faculty.

A famous basketball coach was asked once to what he attributed his success. His reply was "Fundamentals." He spent some time each practice period on fundamentals. The five fundamentals in supervision are complicated but worthy of restudy: (1) the environmental condition for learning, including classroom, learning center, and other facilities; (2) student behavior, and the ability of the supervisor to assist teachers in analysis, understanding, and control; (3) the curriculum; (4) instructional materials and learning resources (How adequate are they? Are they relevant? Are they interesting? What is the range of difficulty and appeal?); and (5) instructional techniques and teacher behavior.

Many supervisors raise questions about the climate for learning. No one knows all the characteristics of this climate or which are of most importance. In 1965 the ASCD pamphlet *A Climate for Individuality* set forth the basic notion that the various student abilities must be cultivated in preference to conformity and adherence to the system. Even earlier, 1964, the ASCD was concerned with *Nurturing Individual Potential* — in contrast to nurturing the "system."

A climate for nurturing individual potential calls for rewards for individualism, for initiative, for unique ideas. Students are to be commended for raising questions, for whatever contributions they make. Negative reinforcement, pressure to conform in thought and action represses growth and individualism. Yet most teachers, supervisors, administrators, board members, and communities reward conformity with salary increases, promotions, tenure, and titles. All of these usually involve financial considerations, and money is a powerful persuader.

Few rewards are available for diversity or deviant behavior —
for innovators. But teachers who would make changes must be
accorded recognition and esteem. The question is, how? What
resources does the supervisor have which he can throw into the
cause for change and improvement? There *are* some. Thanks to
human nature, and our value system, they may not increase the income of teachers, but they do satisfy certain social and professional
needs.

The Reward System

Every supervisor must develop and invest his resources in support
of his program. He may have to work closely with the administrators,
or known power structures in the community, to achieve his goals,
but he must give attention to rewards because (as indicated above)
the system provides them for conforming behavior. If the supervisor cannot contravene these rewards with some just as important
of his own choosing, his projects may be doomed. Mr. Bixman was
informed by Superintendent Crosley when he applied for his position that there was about $200 reserved for emergency use but
otherwise he had no budget. Monetary benefits (merit?) seemed
to be undesirable and, in his situation, impossible.

Mr. Bixman was forced to develop a nonmonetary reward system.
It started with the basic need of all human beings — the need for
recognition. In cooperation with others in the hierarchy, and in the
community, he felt he could arrange for such rewards as:

Recognition
  Verbal: informal, formal; personal, public.
  Printed: informal (bulletins, letters, memos); public newspapers,
    TV announcements).
  Awards, gifts given publicly; tokens, faculty dinners, flowers.
  Certificates for outstanding service or significant contributions.
  Plaques — publicly displayed.
  Receptions for teachers, recognizing certain ones.
  Recognition in news articles and feature stories.
  Requests to serve on important committees — for selection of texts,
    materials, equipment, etc.
  Selection of individuals to help develop the budget.
  Selection of teachers to assist in developing policy at the board
    level.

Selection of teachers to contribute their knowledge in decision
making — whether policy or implementation.

Involvement in communication

Asking teachers for opinions and advice, for ideas.

Listening to criticism gracefully.

Listening to indirect, tangential sources for insights (students,
parents, colleagues, taxpayers, administrators).

Using group techniques to bring out the best in individuals.

Participation in decision making, curriculum activities.

Involvement in community affairs as the representative of one
school, or department, or project.

Inclusion on the mailing list of the central administration for newsletters and/or board minutes.

Improved working conditions

Improved and well-maintained facilities.

Ample supplies.

Clerical help.

Library facilities.

A large and accessible professional library.

A lunchroom for teachers — and a lounge.

Extra preparation time for certain teachers, new teachers, special
project teachers, etc.

Plenty of equipment. One movie projector per floor is worse than
none.

Protected teaching time. Don't interrupt. Outlaw the intercom!

Opportunities (extra period, time off, etc.) to try out ideas.

Time for planning, for developing ideas and projects.

Personnel management

Giving preference to some teachers when making teaching assignments.

Assignment to extracurricular activities on the basis of choice and
aptitude.

Assignment of certain teachers to key jobs: chairmanships on important committees.

Helping to find summer employment if it is not available in school.

Proper teaching assignments (in relation to majors and minors,
etc.).

Treating all teachers fairly, honestly, importantly.

Working for tenure when deserved, or promotions, or salary recognition.

Using, inventing job titles to give status.

Initiating leaves of absence for study.

Bringing in student teacher as assistant to a creative teacher.

Making opportunities for teacher to attend special workshops, conferences, institutes.

Insisting on controlling class size and class load.

Assisting in solving personal problems when appropriate.

Finding space for activities and projects.

Since each school system is unique, rewards may differ. Some of the basic elements in this reward system are space, facilities, daily and weekly schedules, equipment, materials for instruction, and recognition.

For the teacher who has come through the very best teacher preparation program one could devise, the classroom without equipment seems barren and sterile. Equipment must not only be available, accessible, and handy; it should preferably be in the room. Projectors, for example, are more heavily used when each room has one. There are and always will be cries of anguish over the cost of equipment, its nonuse by some teachers, rough usage and consequent increased maintenance. It costs a great deal to equip a machine shop, too! It would be no more expensive to supply a regular classroom with modern communications equipment. Communication, as shown earlier, is central to learning.

Obviously Mr. Bixman cannot obtain everything he might wish for all the classrooms, nor can he, then, expect the ultimate in teaching and learning. But at a convention he had recently attended he had looked at equipment which could bring teaching up to the mid-twentieth century. He hoped to develop television teaching — but television teaching will not prosper until the equipment is easily obtained and available in every room. Every room ought too to have a well-built copier. And teachers will not use computer-assisted instruction (CAI) unless computers are handy; this means one in each room — desk size, perhaps, but certainly a terminal. It is futile to study about computers and to learn computer language unless some use will be made of both. These items were the most costly he had seen but by no means exhausted the list, which went on to typewriters, adding machines, tape recorders, dictating apparatus, and a variety of audio-visual equipment. Perhaps, he thought, a room for large-group instruction might be so furnished in the near future.

Under such conditions, a new set of problems of instruction would be created, but so would a new set of rewards. To have the opportunity to be innovative, "to have been there first," to create new teaching materials, is very satisfying to the professional teacher. Yet in a few schools Mark Hopkins still does not have even a log, much less a television camera and monitor.

Conditions Constantly Change

Changes in society complicate the supervisor's life. Mr. Bixman had the opportunity of attending a national meeting of professionals of his kind where he learned of conditions in other parts of the country and of trends in both education and society which may sooner or later affect his work. After listening to several speeches and talking to a number of persons in supervisory positions, he divided his impressions into three categories. The first related to students, the second to the public, and the third to curriculum.

A majority of the speakers represented the large cities and frequently spoke of the rebellious students, the angry kids, the dropouts. Some students deliberately provoke the teacher, pretend in class, and gang up on the teacher. Student boycotts and underground newspapers keep students, and sometimes parents, stirred up and emotional.[5] High schools have been invaded by nonstudents who tried to create problems. Students who want to learn may come to school some morning to find it has been vandalized, or equipment has been sabotaged, or library books have been ruined. In some inner-city schools the enrollment may change completely as many as three times per term. And according to one colleague, 10 percent of school-age children are suffering from emotional disturbance.[6]

Many of the speakers, however, demonstrated empathy for students. They encouraged principals and teachers to "take time to listen to the kids." Young people seldom enjoy a blissful, easygoing, happy youth. Problems of adjustment to adult society and its customs and institutions are shared by all young people in all cultures. But our young people are more sophisticated about society's norms and conventions than any previous generation; indeed, they have much more knowledge of all kinds. Physiologically it has been

---

[5] National School Public Relations Association, "Anger in the Classroom," in *The Shape of Education for 1969–70* (Washington: The Association, 1969), pp. 34–38. Also "Students Do Their 'Thing' — Protest," pp. 5 ff.
[6] Betsy Bliss Strunk, "Helping the Disturbed Child," *School Management,* 13:53–54 (Sept., 1969).

estimated that young people mature from one to three years earlier than did the previous generations.

What does this mean for Mr. Bixman? He decided that he too must cultivate the art of listening and that one of his jobs is to open channels of communication between his office and the rest of the system. It was absolutely necessary that he obtain feedback from students, teachers, administrators, and the community. But also (and perhaps a more difficult task) he would have to convince teachers that they should do likewise. Old-line teachers often find it very difficult to listen to students. If he, Mr. Bixman, advocates that they do so, they will automatically align him with the radical student and raise suspicions about him, perhaps even hostility, among the faculty. He decided to take his time on that one, develop a sound basis of experience with students before moving to his primary target.

The fact remains that too often teachers and school personnel develop programs and courses for youth without seeking their advice. Thousands of young people have been forced into courses they did not want, disliked, and considered of no value. But there is some truth in the old cliché that "young people don't know what's good for them," so counseling has become important. Most theories of curriculum construction include the student as a source of knowledge for curriculum development. Ways must be found, or created, to allow students to express themselves about their experiences, and to develop more accurate information about their needs, interests, and abilities.[7]

Mr. Bixman decided that he would emphasize orientation for the first- and second-year teachers in the school system. He had not had any orientation to his position and its responsibilities, and he began to suspect that beginning teachers had none too. However, he would find out what had happened to every first-year teacher before he set up an orientation program for the next group. It occurred to him that he would be collecting reams of information and he would need help in processing it. Nevertheless, he would go after it because it would be needed to document requests for budgets, equipment, personnel, materials, etc. Now he began to worry over the fact that with so much preliminary work to do he might become

---

[7] Rudyard K. Bent and Adolph Unruh, *Secondary School Curriculum* (Boston: D. C. Heath & Company, 1969), pp. 300–306.

tied to his desk. He must get out into the schools, into classrooms, into departmental meetings, and develop some meetings for his own purposes. How was he going to accomplish all this?

Teachers and the Thirty-Six-to-One Ratio

As Mr. Bixman walked down the corridor on the third floor of the high school, he tried the doors to a number of classrooms but found them locked. Whether by accident or neglect, one door was unlocked, and he found himself inside a room. There wasn't much to see except the seats for the students, the teacher's desk and chair, and what must have been a storage cabinet in the right rear corner of the room. There was nothing unusual about this room; he had seen dozens like it before. But as he stood there, the empty room began to suggest ideas.

The first idea came from the arrangement of pupils' seats: six seats across the front exactly spaced, in a straight row; six rows, each chair positioned precisely like the one in front of it. Suddenly Mr. Bixman recalled a picture of an ancient Greek phalanx — soldiers in close order, their large shields before them forming an impenetrable protection. Arrows and spears launched by the enemy made no impression upon the phalanx. Thirty-six chairs, thirty-six youths, lined up in a phalanx awaiting the teacher. The teacher enters: here is a square room, six rows of audience facing her. This arrangement immediately arouses predetermined responses.

Mr. Bixman felt, rather than analyzed, that this situation was to blame for much undesirable teacher behavior. The teacher finds herself on a stage, and she is the only actor present. She starts talking. If she allowed students to raise questions, to begin a social discourse among themselves, they might well get out of hand. *She* asks questions, makes assignments, praises and scolds. She stays in control. The method works and she continues to use it because she has found security in it. Another potent weapon in her control of the phalanx is the grading system, which may be used to reward, punish, and motivate.

Mr. Bixman took a seat at the back of the room and imagined himself a student. He was closely hemmed in by students all around. It was almost suffocating! He saw only the backs of students, almost never their faces. The arrangement inhibited any interaction with students except three — one on his immediate right, one on his immediate left, and one in front. Students in the front row seemed so far away that he could not be much involved in what they were saying. And if they didn't speak up, as was so often the case, he would never know what they said. For the first time in his life Mr. Bixman felt he was a cog in a big machine; he had no control over what he was doing; there was not even a system that permitted him to say how he felt.

As he sat thinking about these things, the full impact of his new job became clear. How was he to break this lockstep, this phalanx, this centuries-old tradition? How was he to induce teachers to see what he saw, and when they did to be challenged to find a better way? Then he saw another phalanx: the teachers by departments, the teachers' organization, the administration and the administrative hierarchy, the board, and the community — all allied on the side of tradition. And for the first time Mr. Bixman's enthusiasm gave way to a bit of doubt. Could a change be made? Was he the right person to make it? He decided that this was the last time he would permit himself to entertain this doubt. From now on he was determined to do everything he could to improve education in the R-4 district.

Most teachers are much better prepared for the complicated task of teaching than they used to be. Teachers' meetings, state and national, have been upgraded considerably in recent years, as have inservice education programs. It is not at all unusual to find a Ph.D. among teachers in suburban and city schools, and many high school teachers have the master's degree. So the supervisor's problem is quite different from what it might be in a more rural school.

Supervision is a good word — contrary to popular opinion. It has a constructive meaning for some people, but for others it is a derogatory, debasing, demeaning kind of word. To some it means quality control — an insurance that every youngster will receive the same kind of educational opportunity. To others it means that rules of grammar, dates and names in history, theorems and formulas in mathematics, and specified content in science will be taught in prescribed ways so that all pupils may drink equally at these fonts of knowledge and wisdom. Today, however, every one of these assumptions has come under attack.

Community Expectations

In recent years communities have become greatly concerned with education. In many the school tax has been defeated numerous times; self-appointed committees discuss policy and influence policy decisions at the school board level. As an illustration of community involvement we can cite *Life,* September 19, 1969. In the article on sex education, *Life* lined up the right-wingers, the Christian Crusade and the John Birch Society, on the negative side, and the American Medical Association, the National Education Association, and the National Council of Churches on the positive side. SIECUS (Sex Information and Education Council of the United States) might be included on the side of sex education but is itself the subject of much controversy. Somewhere in the middle are the PTA, the clergy, and numerous civic leaders who want solid data on which to make decisions. In this area, as in others, there is little hard evidence but much emotion and thousands of opinions. Mr. Bixman, what is your next move?

Mr. Bixman knew that he had similar problems. While the protagonists are different, the principles of confrontation, communication, and education are the same. The problem may be vocational education, special education, a new testing program, a new inservice program, or plans to improve instruction. Perhaps his idea of more emphasis on inservice education will come under fire. Some board member might claim that the universities should prepare teachers to teach and it is not the function of the school district to train teachers. The same board member might try to scuttle every budgetary allotment for staff development and publicly justify his position by criticizing teacher training institutions and arguing for tax reductions. Many voters would flock to his side.

A Multi-Faceted Approach

Such thoughts brought many questions to Mr. Bixman's mind. Why were the rooms so bare of any evidence of recent activity? Was there no summer program of any kind? For students? For teachers? For administrative staff? For patrons? Where could he find answers to these questions — and the results of surveys of teacher and citizen opinions? Perhaps the authorities would only become defensive and even hostile if he asked them. Nevertheless, he thought that time spent in planning was time well invested. He considered many possibilities for projects, some of which began to fall into patterns in his thinking. Certain types of action seemed more important than others and these he placed at the top of his list of priorities.

For one thing, he would identify and study faculty leaders and teachers with leadership abilities. He would talk with as many teachers as possible, the central administration, and anyone who knew about the faculty from this point of view. These leaders would carry the ideas and the responsibilities for improving education in their school system. In both group and individual kinds of leadership action, Mr. Bixman's knowledge and expertise in group processes would be useful.[8]

A second approach would be to bring interest, relevance, and currency to the curriculum. For example, the science department might be induced to develop a unit around the pollution problems of the environment — water, air, land; pesticides and the results of their use; noise and its effect on living things; atomic fallout, etc. In the very near future it is conceivable that universities will grant degrees in environmental science or environmental control. The R-4 district could be a leader in this area of curriculum development.

Another way to make content relevant and current is illustrated in the increasing attention to and amount of printed material concerning the military-industrial complex in this country. Between eighty and eighty-five billion dollars is consumed annually by this economic giant, and most of the families in the United States are affected in some way by it. Millions of young people are serving in the armed forces, billions of dollars are invested in the securities related to the industrial sector, and many senators and representatives are engaged in obtaining industrial-military establishments for their areas. These are factors which influence policy decisions at the national level; they affect the cost of consumer goods, taxes, incomes, and living standards of all Americans. Social studies teachers should be able to obtain wholehearted support from their students in developing a unit on this topic because of its universal interest.

---

[8] Ben M. Harris and Wailand Bessent, *In-Service Education: A Guide to Better Practice* (Englewood Cliffs, N.J.: Prentice-Hall, 1969), pp. 253–260.

Still another way to change the curriculum would be to involve teachers in discussions of what the curriculum should be ten years hence. Over coffee in the lounge, at informal meetings after school, perhaps at luncheons and dinners which might include some of the central office staff and board members in order to keep them alert, talk may drift to different types of organizations for education. For example, some courses might be taught in the community — no classroom needed.[9] Several schools are experimenting along this line.

In ten years some completely new courses will be offered, and inservice workshops will be developed to support them. Even today biology teachers are talking about a course in oceanography; literature teachers are finding the mythology and superstitions surrounding the moon interesting enough to combine with science teachers in "moon studies." Better ways to look at politics and economics, and more relevant content, will revitalize these subjects. Ghetto experiments with different subjects now under way, projected to a point ten years hence, can spark worthwhile discussions among teachers.

A problem is sure to arise: If courses are to be added to the curriculum, what courses will be dropped? If none are to be dropped, how will the additions be incorporated? Discussion may shift to the twelve-month school, the eight-hour day, as one way to accommodate this change. Teachers may bring up the question of combining courses, as may be done in the humanities, and adding team teaching.

The important thing is that teachers will be involved in thinking and planning for the future. If Mr. Bixman can get them interested in this manner, he will have taken a step toward progress and change. So many of the problems in teaching are related to the present that there is little time or energy left to plan for ten years away.

Again on curriculum change, Mr. Bixman decided to talk with as many teachers as he could about summer workshops — what had been tried and how valuable teachers thought these sessions were. He would ask them to suggest changes, to dream up new offerings

---

[9] C. Edwin Linville, "New Directions in Secondary Education," *Bulletin of the National Association of Secondary School Principals,* 337:198–208 (May, 1969).

for next summer, to identify faculty leaders and outside consultants. A part of the workshop would be given to studies of relevance and to new curricula. Some departments would undoubtedly be farther along toward accepting and planning for change and might well be engaged in curriculum writing tasks. Activities and projects would be set up to meet diverse teacher needs. This plan would be consistent with the designs described in Chapter Five of this book relating to the scope of inservice programs.

Mr. Bixman thought on. He would initiate one or more pilot curricula or improved instruction projects. As this idea began to take shape, he visualized the following model based on the concept known as Program Evaluation and Review Technique (PERT). It is a method of planning which includes the functions of coordinating, reviewing, sequencing of events, evaluating, and predicting. Industry and the armed forces have utilized it for very large and complicated projects. Industry and big educational institutions use a similar technique which is called Planning, Programming, Budgeting System (PPBS).[10]

Mr. Bixman's plan for a social studies unit was a modification of PERT, and when he had the time, and had become more familiar with the entire school system, he hoped to PERT his total program for the next five years. The advantage in the model was that he could see, and show anyone else, a continuous flow of development toward the achievement of certain objectives. It was an organized and systematic approach to his work, with deadlines and feedback built in. This meant better communication, with all elements involved, and an opportunity to eliminate problems before they happened, as well as an opportunity to coordinate all the subsystems and integrate them with the mainstream of the project. The thought occurred to him that this technique is one all committee chairmen could use, particularly chairmen of his curriculum and instruction committees.

Garry Bixman — The Emerging Supervisor

Mr. Bixman finally arrived at the starting point of his inspection trip — his relatively empty office. He sat down at his desk to bring

---

[10] Harry J. Hartley, *Educational Planning-Programming-Budgeting, A Systems Approach* (Englewood Cliffs, N.J.: Prentice-Hall, 1968), pp. 253–257.

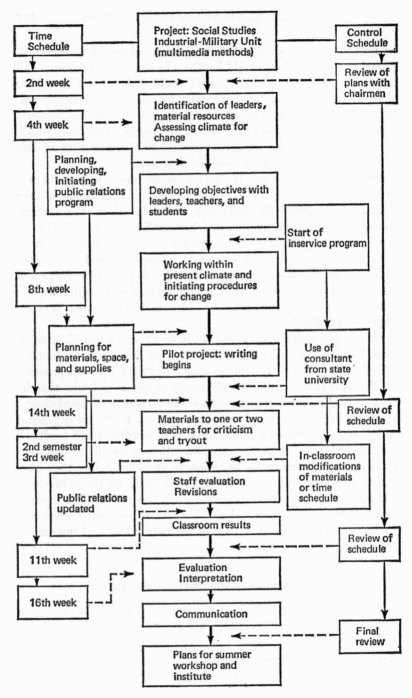

Fig. 8 *Mr. Bixman's Model*

his thoughts together. Not only was it necessary for him to look at his job, his position, and his work in the future. He had found that he had to look at the profession of supervision, by whatever title it came to be called, and where it would lead him. If he expected to have an impact upon the educational scene of tomorrow he would need to plan now to perform a vastly different role from the one his predecessors played.

He certainly cannot spend his time at a desk, nor will he be simply a technician. His will be a task fraught with risks, partly because he must work with a highly trained personnel and partly because one of his responsibilities is to monitor the crystal ball. This he must do if the curriculum is to remain relevant, appropriate to the times and trends.

Times and trends! This thought prompted the new supervisor to take a look at trends as he knew them, and to estimate whether the curriculum, as he knew it, had kept pace. He wrote down his ideas:

Phenomena and Trends	*Curriculum and Instruction*
Increasing mobility of our people	No
Revitalizing the inner city	No
Ghettos moving outward from the center	No
Increasing dehumanization and impersonalization of society	No
Increasing population and urban growth	No
Increased tax burden on the middle class but increased national wealth	No
Tensions all around the world — many fierce military clashes	No
Great military-industrial complex in America employing millions of people	No
Increasing knowledge	?
Medical progress	No
Chemically induced personality traits	No
Computerized daily living	No
Oceanography and new raw materials	No
Political realignment of countries into power blocks	?
Continued environmental pollution	?
Development of communication: theory and equipment	?

Mr. Bixman was disturbed with what he wrote. Either the curriculum had dropped far behind the developments in society or he didn't really know what was happening in the R-4 district. He resolved to make a study of trends, with the help of the faculty, and then relate curriculum developments in the R-4 schools to these trends. He might extend the study to the community — at least try it out on one PTA as a pilot project. And so his plans continued to develop.

Now he felt compelled to make some kind of evaluation of his first day at the office. What kinds of decisions had he made? Would they be solid enough to sustain him when pressures and problems began to descend upon his office and, in a few months, increase? Again he made some notes, partly to keep his thoughts from wandering but partly to examine what his summary might produce. The major points he wrote came out as follows: "As a new supervisor in a new position, I —"

1. Will have to give constant attention to communication and its improvement. Whether communication takes place between two persons, between persons and groups, or between persons and machines, the process must be more clearly understood and made more effective. Without communication there can be no teaching or learning.

2. Must pay more attention to ways of developing better morale and study the results of it. One of the new elements in this problem is the effect of teachers' organizations, negotiating agreements, and increasing fringe benefits.

3. Will try to develop better human relations as a basis for improving the educational program. The dominant-dependent relationships of the past must be replaced with more emphasis on peer relationships, less use of anxiety- and threat-producing situations, and more emphasis on the dignity of the individual. Perhaps a workshop in human relations for all faculty and staff could be planned for spring and summer.

4. Will take the broad view of supervision by setting up many and varied programs to help teachers at different levels of professional growth. The problems of the beginner will be sought out and the competence of the veteran will be respected and, it is hoped, utilized in the staff development program.

5. Will plan to learn about learning environments both within and without the traditional classroom. In terms of its possibilities the present learning environment is relatively barren. Too much of it is confined between four walls, which in some instances constitute a prison.

6. Must assist teachers to utilize whatever services are provided by the district. Most teachers would find helpful at one time or another speech therapy, psychological services, counseling services, health, library, and communications media.

7. Will involve the faculty, whether individually or by means of group processes, in decision making. Faculty groups, at times supplemented by talent from outside the school, will be used to assist teachers in their professional growth. The motivations generated by peer groups are very powerful, and ways must be found to build upon them.

8. Will find new ways to strengthen the inservice program. It will be tied to faculty needs, curriculum innovations, social-political trends. Workshops, institutes, clinics, and courses must all be developed with faculty needs in mind and hence at a variety of levels. Ways must be found of exposing teachers to new ideas and new practices. A program of teacher education at the local level seems to be imperative. There must be training in such fields as measurement and statistics, but also in leadership and human relations.

At this point Mr. Bixman ran out of ideas. This list would have to do for now. Tomorrow he would look at it again after he had seen the high school principal. Some points might have to be added — or subtracted. He would rest his case now, but he felt that he had a sound platform from which to launch a new service. He felt, too, that his platform would not change much in its basic statements for some years to come, but it was quite possible that methods of implementation would vary as new knowledge and improvements in technology became available to education.

Summary

This chapter was written for the purpose of delineating some of the problems in the field of supervision. An imaginary (but at the same time very real) person was confronted with these problems and his reactions were noted. First described was the need for a clear description of supervision and a consensus on what it is supposed to do. In many schools supervision just grows, and it may founder on the rocks of details and paper work. In other schools it makes a significant contribution to the improvement of education. Professional help is always desirable, but if supervision can be brought to bear at the point of planning, it is most advantageous. Tenure for supervisory staff, and a place at the negotiations table are other problems encountered by supervisors.

A discussion of authority located its origins in the superintendent and board of education, the faculty, and the supervisor himself. Authority usually is exercised within an organization or a bureaucracy. The supervisor is faced with at least three bureaucracies as he contemplates his future: the board-administration and staff, the teachers' organization, and the full-blown team teaching organization. He must find ways of penetrating all these bureaucracies if he is to be effective.

Some attention was given to the reward system, which is so important in developing desirable teacher behaviors. Sometimes nonmonetary rewards mean as much to teachers as the usual salary increments. Changing social conditions which impinge upon the supervisor's work were considered. Problems in the classroom, community expectations, and ways to organize curriculum projects were discussed. A brief look at trends and a review of the nature of supervision closed this chapter.

Problems for Group Discussion

1. Put yourself in Mr. Bixman's new position. How would you begin your work? What value do you think his inspection trip had in his effort to preassess his opportunities? Was his analysis of the classroom situation a fair one? Is the curriculum lag really as significant as he found it to be? (He did not go into this, but to what extent do you think there is a methodology lag?)

2. Supervision can be defined in terms of positions (superintendents, assistant superintendents, principals, assistant principals, consultants, etc.), or in terms of functions (planning, coordinating, decision making, curriculum development, etc.), or in terms of processes (psychological — thinking, learning, teaching, decision making; social — interaction, orientation, assimilation, etc.) or educational techniques (facilitating, organizing, communicating, etc.). Which of these definitions, or any other, means the most to you?

3. Another method of discovering what supervision means is to have faculty members of different school systems describe what passes for supervision in their schools. After numerous arrangements have been discussed, can the group recognize any common elements in all the programs described?

4. Perhaps the group would be interested in discussing the purposes and the relative merits of associations for supervision and curriculum development — local, state, and national. The group would need a set of criteria such as leadership, the development of curriculum materials, curriculum theory, research, etc. Since there are none, each group must develop its own. What criteria are needed?

Selected Readings

Association for Supervision and Curriculum Development. *A Climate for Individuality*. Washington: The Association, with the American Association of School Administrators, the National Association of Secondary School Principals, and the NEA Department of Rural Education, 1965.

Association for Supervision and Curriculum Development. *Nurturing Individual Potential*. Washington: The Association, 1964.

Association for Supervision and Curriculum Development. *Toward Professional Maturity of Supervisors and Curriculum Workers*. Washington: The Association, 1967.

Bent, Rudyard K., and Adolph Unruh. *Secondary School Curriculum*. Boston: D. C. Heath & Company, 1969.

Gorman, Alfred H. *Teachers and Learners: The Interactive Process of Education*. Boston: Allyn & Bacon, 1969.

Harris, Ben M., and Wailand Bessent. *In-Service Education: A Guide to Better Practice*. Englewood Cliffs, N.J.: Prentice-Hall, 1969.

Hartley, Harry J. *Educational Planning-Programming-Budgeting, A Systems Approach*. Englewood Cliffs, N.J.: Prentice-Hall, 1968.

Linville, C. Edwin. "New Directions in Secondary Education," *Bulletin of the National Association of Secondary School Principals*, 337:198–208 (May, 1969).

National Education Association. "Evaluation of Teaching," *NEA Research Bulletin*, 47:67–75 (Oct., 1969).

National School Public Relations Association. *The Shape of Education for 1969–70*. Washington: The Association, 1969.

Strunk, Betsy Bliss. "Helping the Disturbed Child," *School Management*, 13:53–54 (Sept., 1969).

Young, William F. "Influencing Professional Negotiations," in *The Supervisor: New Demands, New Dimensions*. Washington: Association for Supervision and Curriculum Development, 1969.

Index

•

Teaching:
  finding satisfaction in, 158–159, 172
  improvement of, 204
Team teaching:
  leader of, as supervisor, 11
  evaluation of, 278
Textbooks, selection of, 117
Travel, as agent of change, 185
Trump, Lloyd, 48

United States Office of Education, 244
University scholars, as agents of change, 186, 193, 250–251, 271
Usery, Mary Lou, 149

Vergason, A. L., 149

Wiles, Kimball, 20
Wynn, D. Richard, 56

Zander, Alvin, 207, 210